SACRIFICE

SACRIFICE

My Life in a Fascist Militia

ALESSANDRO ORSINI

Translated from the Italian by
SARAH JANE NODES

CORNELL UNIVERSITY PRESS
ITHACA AND LONDON

First published 2017 by Cornell University Press

Printed in the United States of America

Library of Congress Cataloging-in-Publication Data

Names: Orsini, Alessandro, 1975– author. | Nodes,
    Sarah Jane, translator.
Title: Sacrifice : my life in a fascist militia / Alessandro Orsini ;
    translated from the Italian by Sarah Jane Nodes.
Description: Ithaca : Cornell University Press, 2017. | Includes
    bibliographical references.
Identifiers: LCCN 2017006892 (print) | LCCN 2017008097 (ebook) |
    ISBN 9781501709838 (cloth : alk. paper) | ISBN 9781501712272
    (epub/mobi) | ISBN 9781501709630 (pdf)
Subjects: LCSH: Fascists—Italy—Social conditions—21st century. |
    Militia movements—Italy—History—21st century. | Fascism—
    Italy—1945– | Ethnology—Italy. | Orsini, Alessandro, 1975–
Classification: LCC HN490.R3 O57 2017 (print) | LCC HN490.R3
    (ebook) | DDC 320.53/30945—dc23
LC record available at https://lccn.loc.gov/2017006892

Cornell University Press strives to use environmentally responsible suppliers and materials to the fullest extent possible in the publishing of its books. Such materials include vegetable-based, low-VOC inks and acid-free papers that are recycled, totally chlorine-free, or partly composed of nonwood fibers. For further information, visit our website at cornellpress.cornell.edu.

To my father,
Arturo Orsini

CONTENTS

PREFACE

I was warned not to write this book.

I ask any reader who recognizes the facts and places I describe not to reveal their real identities. A kind of complicity is often created between a writer and his readers. I hope this also applies in my case.

Bloody noses, knifings, barroom brawls, murders, massacres, as well as ritual suicides like that of Dominique Venner, an intellectual and Fascist sympathizer who, on May 21, 2013, shot himself in the mouth before the altar of Notre-Dame de Paris to protest the presence of immigrants in Europe. This book talks about these things.

Contrary to the common belief that Fascist militants get caught up in violence because they are uneducated, I argue that they attack, kill, and commit suicide because they have studied, because they read certain books, and because they spend a lot of time debating the meaning of what they're reading. They study, they read, they reflect: the people I'm dealing with possess a political culture. Sacrifice is a Fascist organization that has been involved in numerous incidents of violence. (In this book I never use the expression "neofascist" because these people strongly reject the label.) In some cases it has been attacked by far-left organizations. In other cases Sacrifice members have been the attackers. Many of its militants are in prison for beating up political adversaries or for taking part in various kinds of clashes. But no Sacrifice militant has ever been arrested for larceny or robbery or drug pushing. Violence against people is always the reason for their arrest.

I managed to gain access to two cells in towns I call Mussolinia and Lenintown in order to understand the cultural significance that the Sacrifice comrades attribute to violence. The history of this research, recounted in the course of this book, is long and complicated and required me to move to more than one city. It lasted for five years and can be divided into three stages.

The first stage, the "approach stage," took roughly three and a half years. During that time I managed to become friendly with some important Sacrifice militants after taking out a membership in an excellent gym that they own. The gym is neither in Mussolinia nor in Lenintown.

The second stage, the "entry stage," lasted some four months, three of which I spent as a full-time militant. During those three months I played the part of a militant day in and day out, including weekends. This stage ended with my expulsion from the group and an explicit warning not to approach any comrade in the future.

The third stage, the "departure stage," lasted a year. Since I couldn't approach the group anymore, I continued to study it through the enormous quantity of documents the Sacrifice comrades publish on Facebook, and also thanks to a friendship I had developed over five years with a Sacrifice militant who doesn't live in Mussolinia or in Lenintown. This young man, though a highly respected militant, had begun a de-radicalization process after the birth of his son, but he had never spoken about this with his other comrades.

This is living ethnography.

SACRIFICE

1

THE ORGANIZATION OF EDUCATION

The Fight

It was one o'clock in the morning.

In Mussolinia a big party was in progress, organized by the mayor and town council. For the occasion, all the shops were staying open until six. Thousands of young people were drinking and dancing in the streets.

Caesar, a Sacrifice militant, was strolling downtown with fifteen buddies. For reasons that have never been made clear, not even during the trial that followed, he started insulting Joe, a man he had met by chance, and his friends. After a brief fight, the two groups separated without inflicting too much damage.

An hour later, Caesar, who had lost an eye in a brawl a few years earlier, went in search of his adversary, telling his pals that he wanted to humiliate the guy. When he saw Joe in the distance, Caesar broke a bottle and, holding it by the neck, took a run at Joe, jumped on him, and thrust the bottle into his eye. The victim fell to his knees, his face covered in blood, yelling for help. The two groups launched into a new fight, at the end of which Joe was taken to hospital.

My Arrival in Mussolinia

A week after the fight, I went to Mussolinia to collect information and interview people about what had happened. The doctors made it very clear: Joe had lost an eye.

Neither the mayor of Mussolinia, nor the political parties, nor the various cultural associations condemned Caesar's attack. After remaining at liberty for some months, he was arrested, tried, and sentenced to three and a half years in jail (and is still there as I write).

While the case against Caesar was under way, I tried to find out about the relations between Sacrifice and the political parties governing Mussolinia. I spoke with as many locals as I could, as well as politicians, journalists, and some police officers.

Although many Mussolinia residents condemned the brawl that Caesar had initiated, the political parties had decided not to organize any demonstrations against him and his political movement. As a Mussolinia shop owner said: "It's incredible what happened. It's incredible but also terrible. My son could have been there instead of Joe. How awful for the family of that poor boy, to have a son who's lost an eye!"

I managed to extract a more useful piece of information while eating with some friends in a pizzeria.

Jonathan, a forty-two-year-old engineer who owns a building company, told me that Caesar had lost an eye during a brawl at the Mussolinia stadium between "ultras," rabid fans of rival soccer teams. "Everyone knows about Caesar. He lost an eye during a fight at the stadium and now he's done the same thing to that poor kid. The Sacrifice militants are extremists and violent, but the mayor protects them."

Why?

Max, thirty-three, unemployed, and from a well-off family, explains to me that the mayor of Mussolinia, who today is the head of a liberal party, had been a far-right activist in his youth: "Mussolini loved Mussolinia and the people of Mussolinia loved Mussolini. The architecture of the town also tells you this. Haven't you noticed that there are Fascist symbols everywhere in Mussolinia? In the seventies we even had right-wing terrorists here." Max asserts that the mayor of Mussolinia is very friendly with the Sacrifice militants, who claim they oppose the bourgeoisie and capitalism but who go around secretly at night putting up electoral posters for the mayor, who has even given them a medal for bravery in peacetime. (*A medal for bravery?*)

"In the winter," Max continues, "there was a heavy snowfall. The Sacrifice militants shoveled the snow off the roads. That's all. I did the same thing with my friends, but nobody gave us a medal! The mayor wanted a pretext to show his loyalty to Sacrifice, and so he gave them a medal!"

Max raises his voice: "Do you think that's normal? What a shitty country we're living in! The mayor from a liberal party gave a medal for bravery in peacetime to an organization that praises Hitler and Mussolini!"

Max seems sincere, but he's a left-wing activist who hates Fascism.

To check his facts, I ask for an appointment with a Mussolinia councilman who belongs to the same party as the mayor. He answers my question courteously: "Yes, it's true, our mayor gave Sacrifice a medal. The Sacrifice militants are idealistic young people who are militant in politics in a very open manner." The councilman tells me that, when he was a boy in the eighties, he was active in the same Fascist party as the mayor. After various experiences, they both ended up in their present party. He remains friendly, however, with the Sacrifice leaders: "But I would ask you not to repeat what I'm telling you because I could have problems with the press. You know what journalists are like. I'm a member of a liberal party now, and I don't want to find myself labeled a Fascist."

The councilman knows that I'm a sociologist conducting ethnographic research, but from the way he talks to me, he seems convinced that I have far-right ideas. I have given him no reason for thinking so. The man talks to me as if we were longtime friends and explains that relations between his party and Sacrifice are good but have to remain hidden because many voters despise Fascism. "As you know," he says, "the Italian constitution forbids the reestablishment of the Fascist Party. We have to be very careful about what we say. We're on good terms with Sacrifice and Sacrifice is on good terms with us. But neither of us wants to advertise the fact."

I wasn't aware that the good relations between Sacrifice and the mayor of Mussolinia were so "unnoticeable."

I saw that the Sacrifice militants were permitted to organize public meetings in Mussolinia's most beautiful historic buildings. Great examples of elegant architecture, they are among the finest in Europe. The mayor has even asked for the building that dominates the town's main square to be designated a UNESCO World Heritage Site. Since it belongs to the municipality, the mayor has to authorize its use. And the mayor never asks the Sacrifice militants to pay, so they get to use its impressive conference room for free.

It is obvious that the Mussolinia militia has close ties with local political institutions and with the town's power centers.

Lenintown

Less than twenty miles from Mussolinia there's Lenintown, a city with the same number of residents as Mussolinia but located on the sea instead of in the hills. At the same time that extreme-right terrorism started to appear in Mussolinia in the 1970s, far-left terrorists in Lenintown—which has a strong left-wing tradition—were responsible for numerous homicides.

There is also a Sacrifice cell in Lenintown. Its leader is Leonidas, a twenty-eight-year-old professional boxer with a broken nose. He is covered with Fascist tattoos.

A year and a half after the Mussolinia brawl, Leonidas was in a downtown bar one Saturday evening with some comrades. Steering his way through a crowded room, he came face to face with Ashley, a pretty young woman wearing a short, tight skirt. Leonidas, as he himself admitted during his trial, bent over Ashley, whom he didn't know, and whispered some insults in her ear. The girl spun around and slapped his face. Leonidas was humiliated in front of his friends; he froze for a few seconds and then punched Ashley in the face. Witnesses asserted that he started kicking her after she fell to the ground. Leonidas declared that he never punched Ashley but only "slapped" her.

Ashley's friends intervened to defend her and a fight broke out. Leonidas managed to hit seven people before being immobilized by a youth who grabbed him from behind, putting his arm around Leonidas's neck.

The bartender called the police, and Ashley was taken to the hospital. The doctor found that Ashley's hearing had been permanently affected: "She won't hear well ever again. Her ear has been irreversibly damaged."

The mayor, with the backing of all the town's political parties, organized a public demonstration against Fascism and demanded that the Sacrifice headquarters in Lenintown be closed. These are the mayor's words, reported in a Lenintown newspaper: "The Sacrifice militants have nothing to do with politics. They're just a bunch of delinquents."

One month after the confrontation with Ashley, Leonidas was involved in another violent episode. One evening at a bar in town, he quarreled for no reason with a fifty-year-old man, threw him to the ground, and kicked him in the face. The man passed out and was taken to the hospital, where he underwent reconstructive surgery on his face. During the trial, Leonidas's lawyer asserted that his client was in another city at the time the man had been attacked.

Notwithstanding, the mayor stated that Leonidas's conduct was unacceptable, adding that the presence of Sacrifice in Lenintown represented a danger and a disgrace for the entire city.

The Chief of Police

After the episode involving Leonidas and the fifty-year-old man, I made an appointment with the chief of police in Lenintown, who received me in his office. He told me that he couldn't say anything about Leonidas since investigations were still under way. To prompt him to talk, I used a technique called "interviewing by comment," which is an attempt to elicit information by making a statement rather than by asking a direct question.[1]

From what I understand, Leonidas didn't do anything to this girl. The press exaggerated to sell more copies.

"You're wrong, Professor Orsini. There's a medical report. The girl has suffered permanent damage to her hearing. The doctors at the Lenintown hospital have stated that she no longer hears well in one ear." He added that the Sacrifice militants had been involved in numerous aggressive acts and that the violence against the girl was just one of many incidents.

At the end of a very cordial conversation lasting some thirty minutes, the chief of police advised me not to conduct research in Lenintown. All of a sudden his tone, until then friendly, became firm and decisive: "Professor Orsini, the people you want to study are dangerous and violent, and we might not be able to protect you. If you decide to go ahead with your research, you will have to assume complete responsibility for your choice. We have a special unit that deals with Sacrifice, and as I told you, we're conducting our investigation into the fights in which Leonidas is involved. I would also inform you that you could be charged if you break the law. Being a sociologist does not mean having special permission to commit crimes. Bear that in mind."

A few days after my meeting with the police chief, at the end of three and a half years of preparation, I was permitted to enter the Mussolinia and Lenintown cells. I joined at a significant moment, when the police, having already arrested Caesar, were finishing their investigations of Leonidas.

Mussolinia and Lenintown

Unlike his counterpart in Mussolinia, the mayor of Lenintown has come out against the militia there, who are seen as a "disgrace" by all the city's parties.

But there is more.

There have been various acts of sabotage against the Sacrifice headquarters in Lenintown. On the day Leonidas had appointed for the inauguration of the center, some unknown protesters dumped a great pile of shit at the front door, writing "Fascism = shit!" on the walls in red. Photos spread rapidly on social networks, but there was no negative reaction from the local people or the politicians. The political use of shit was praised on an extreme left-wing site managed by some Lenintown youths.

While the Mussolinia mayor does not condemn Sacrifice militants who carry out violent acts, the Lenintown mayor calls them "delinquents" and wants to close them down. Moreover, in Lenintown the mayor keeps quiet when the Sacrifice militants are provoked by extreme left-wing militants.

Karl, a Lenintown politician of the same party as the mayor, agreed to talk to me as long as I wouldn't reveal his name. "Sacrifice is a Fascist organization and shit is the essence of Fascism," he tells me, laughing and giving me a friendly slap on the back. "Perhaps it wasn't a nice gesture from a politically correct point of view, but it's good to know that the people of Lenintown think that Sacrifice is a political organization that deserves to be covered in shit. Lenintown is not Mussolinia. I'm proud of this."

Since the Sacrifice militants have been involved in violent acts both in Mussolinia, where they enjoy the favor of the mayor and the main political parties, and in Lenintown, where the mayor and the parties governing the city are against them, the relationship between Sacrifice cells and political authorities cannot be the deciding factor behind the involvement of these young Mussolini admirers in aggressive acts.

Fascism as Spiritual Dimension

On a splendid spring day, while I was handing out Fascist flyers in downtown Mussolinia, I was trying to question other comrades on what they thought about various subjects: sports, politics, sex, films, music, anything that might gain their trust.[2] Ethnographers have to grasp every opportunity to get social actors to speak about the significance they attribute to their actions while trying to put them at their ease.[3]

Julius, one of the most influential militants in Mussolinia, is twenty-eight and has a degree in philosophy, one of my own greatest passions. We start talking about the philosopher to whom he devoted his thesis, but then I manage to change the subject to the relationship between Mussolinia and Lenintown. I knew that there was a strong rivalry between the two soccer teams. Since almost all the comrades from Mussolinia and Lenintown are ultras—that is, rabid fans—have there ever been tensions between the two Sacrifice militias?

Julius tells me: "I'm a member of the Mussolinia ultras, but it makes no difference if a comrade lives in Mussolinia or in Lenintown. We all belong to the same spiritual race. We think, do, and say the same things. Sacrifice is more than a political organization; it's a way of being. Fascism is a set of immortal values. For many political movements, money comes before everything. None of us is in politics to get rich or to become famous. If you want to understand who we are, you have to understand that our battles are linked to our way of seeing the world."

Also distributing flyers is Varus, a sixteen-year-old, and I ask him about the brawls between partisans of the two teams. "I always go to the stadium," says Varus, "because I'm a member of the Mussolinia ultras. There's great rivalry between the Mussolinia and Lenintown ultras. There've even been clashes with knifings, but there's great respect among the comrades. What counts is we all have the same way of thinking; we're all Fascists and we all do the same things. Our motto is: we are what we do! This is the motto we learn when we enter Sacrifice. We're all brothers."

It's hot out. Cornelia is twenty-six, dresses heavy-metal style, and is the only female member of either town militia. She approaches me and Varus with a bottle of water and asks if we want a drink. I thank her, accept, and bring her into our conversation. Cornelia laughs and jokes, but when I ask her what Fascism is, she becomes serious: "Fascism is a way of being, it's a set of values that have been handed down for centuries. Mussolini said that Fascism is an idea. Do you know this saying of his? It's famous. During our demonstrations, you'll see this saying on many flags. Mussolini said that Fascism is an idea in the sense that . . . in the sense that it's a way of thinking. If you ask me to say what Fascism is for me, well, for me Fascism is something that made me see the world in another way. Fascism makes you see many things that this bourgeois society tries to hide."

The Mussolinia comrades define Fascism as a "set of immortal values." These "values" produce similar behaviors in different contexts, so we have to take them into serious consideration. And we have to study the socialization process through which Sacrifice educates young people to have a "new vision of the world."

Sacrifice asserts that its "ideology" can be found in books. "The values in which we believe," says Leonidas during a meeting, "have already been announced by some great men and have never changed. We have only to teach them and to keep them alive through example."

This is the reason why Sacrifice attaches great importance to the "study sessions," those weekly meetings in which books containing the essence of Fascism are read and discussed. "Beliefs matter," writes Nigel Fielding, "because they are capable of altering behaviour, and ideology affects action."[4]

In the chapters that follow, we will see how the Fascist mental universe develops, not only through reading books, but also through the ideological organization of sports, cinema, and music.

The Political Soldier

Lentulus is twenty-eight years old and is one of the founders of the Mussolinia militia. Two hours before our first appointment he texts me that he's coming to the meeting with his girlfriend. With the idea of limiting the influence of a third person in our conversation, I ask a woman friend of mine to come with me. My strategy works.

The two women get on well together and chat for the whole time without interrupting my dialogue with Lentulus, who doesn't fit the usual stereotypes of Fascist militants. He has no tattoos; he's courteous and deferential. He insists on paying the check: "You're my guest!" He wears his hair cut short like so many of his contemporaries, and he's dressed in the usual outfit of jeans, sneakers, and a shirt. He has an economics degree like his girlfriend, Livia, also a Fascist. Lentulus makes a point of telling us that Livia was a Sacrifice militant, or full member, before they got together but is now a supporter, or associate member.

To begin with, Lentulus asks me not to use the term "neofascist," saying: "We don't like being called neofascists. Neofascism is a label invented by journalists that doesn't mean anything. For us there is only Fascism as it was created by Mussolini. We don't need to invent a new type of Fascism. Our task is to reinstate the values on which Mussolini founded Fascism and to apply them to today's society. We're Fascists, not neofascists."

I ask Lentulus about his former life and that of his family, how he first approached Fascism, and the type of life he leads today. Then I ask him to tell me about the organization of the Mussolinia militia. Lentulus says that the militia is engaged in many activities, among them the distribution of food to poor Italians. They aid only ethnic Italians, not immigrants or minorities, and the organization of cultural events, including photographic exhibitions of the Fascist period as well as political debates open to the public and sporting events. This agenda involves relations between Sacrifice and the outside world, but in this first, long interview I'm particularly interested in learning about the inner life of the Mussolinia militia. Lentulus explains that it's mainly occupied with enrolling young boys to educate them in Fascism and turn them into "political soldiers."

What is a political soldier?

"The political soldier is the Fascist man."

What are the differences between the Fascist man and the common people?

"It's a spiritual difference. It's a difference in values. The political soldier's values are sacrifice, courage, honor, and obedience to the leader. I always tell all the comrades that, before discussing how we intend to take over the state, we have to talk about the spiritual education we want to give the young, because one day the state will be taken over by them— by the young.

"'Sacrifice,'" explains Lentulus, "is the first word the militant has to learn. Sacrifice for the group, sacrifice of free time to devote to the militia, sacrifice of personal interests for love of Fascism. But love of Fascism is not something abstract. Love of Fascism is shown by love toward the group. Entering Sacrifice means accepting a series of rules. This is what I always say: learn to sacrifice your egoism because the group comes first. The group's interests are more important than your interests."

Lentulus tells me that the Sacrifice comrades are continually subject to discrimination, especially at work: "Entering Sacrifice also requires this type of sacrifice. Many comrades lost their jobs for wearing tattoos of Fascist symbols. Others quarrel with their parents and relatives. Not to mention the teachers at school! Being a Fascist at fourteen is very difficult, but our group provides protection."

What is the group for you?

"The group is my family."

What would you be prepared to sacrifice for your group?

"I'd be prepared to die for my comrades. A true Fascist loves the militia more than his life."

I ask Lentulus what would happen to a comrade who has a rebellious nature and doesn't abide by the group's rules. He replies that the Sacrifice leadership has the power to expel militants. The procedure is very informal; there are no documents or written rules.

He sums up the matter very clearly: "We like strong personalities. You have to be strong to be a Fascist, but your personality must never come into conflict with the group's interests and rules."

What comes first, the group or the individual?

"I don't like the word 'individual.' It's a bourgeois word. Sacrifice hates individualism. Fascism is the enemy of individualism. It goes without saying that it's always the group that takes precedence over the comrade. It's not the group that has to adapt to the comrade's personality. It's the comrade who has to adapt to the group personality," says Lentulus, drawing air quotes around "group personality."

Before being expelled, comrades are reprimanded. If they still don't understand that they have to obey the group's rules, they're expelled on the basis of a decision made by a select committee that in the Mussolinia militia consists of four people. Lentulus explains that there are two types of expulsion, "normal" expulsion and "dishonorable" expulsion. In the first case, one of the leaders tells the militant to leave the group and it all ends peacefully. In the case of a dishonorable expulsion, the militant is humiliated before everyone and becomes an enemy of the group.

Lentulus has had to expel a comrade only once in three years, but he doesn't want to give me any details. I try to insist, in order to understand the dynamics and causes of the expulsion, but Lentulus says firmly: "It's something that created a lot of problems in my group. I don't want to talk about it."

As we'll see later, the expulsion that Lentulus didn't want to talk about was that of Caesar.

The Importance of Books

Besides having to accept a set of rules and a code of conduct imposed by the group, new recruits have to follow an educational pathway based on reading and group debates to understand how to live their lives according to the values of Fascism.

"Reading books written by Fascists," Lentulus explains, "serves to transmit their values, but this isn't enough. You have to live like Fascists."

After the members have read an assigned book, group debates are organized, but only among authentic militants, those possessing a membership card.

"The debates serve to discuss," says Lentulus, "to understand how we can apply the values of Fascism in our daily lives. Fascism is a lifestyle, it's a way of being with others, it's a way of living in and seeing the world."

Do you have an ideology?

"Of course I have an ideology!" he replies vehemently.

It's interesting that you say you have an ideology. Generally, people who have one deny they have any ideologies.

"This is because people think that an ideology is a negative thing. Instead it's something one has to be proud of. I'm proud of having an ideology. Ideology is fundamental. The fact of having an ideology makes me different from my peers. It helps me to understand the world."

What does "ideology" mean to you?

"Ideology is a set of precepts and values that acts as a guide. Ideology shows us how to move in the world and to understand the world.

"The greatest difficulty," Lentulus continues, "is that of freeing the minds of the young from the ideas of the bourgeois society to replace them with Fascist ideas. Bourgeois society has destroyed all the most important values on which the development of humanity is founded, such as love for the fatherland and the military culture. The young have to learn that the white race comes before all the other races, and they also have to learn that a nation that doesn't know how to make war, doesn't know how to kill, is a nation forced to capitulate. Sooner or later someone will always arrive who knows how to make war and will take everything that's yours: your home, your job, your woman. I dream that one day Italy will be populated only by Italians. No Chinese and no blacks. I would like to have only Italians in Italy. This is my dream."

The Lenintown militia is smaller and more recently organized than the one in Mussolinia. The first time I entered the Lenintown headquarters—an apartment consisting of two rooms and a bathroom plastered with Fascist flags and photos of Mussolini—I introduced myself and spoke for an hour and a half with all the militants.

The second time, I participated in a meeting to organize a trip by car to another town, where we were to celebrate the opening of a new Sacrifice office, and I paid five euros—about six dollars at the time—to become a member of the group.

The third time, I studied the collection of books in the meeting room. To be exact, there's only one shelf of books, but the Lenintown militants call it a "library."

What books do the Sacrifice militants claim are fundamental for their educational meetings? Cincinnatus, thirty years old, has the task of managing the Lenintown library. He explains that the comrades have very little money to buy books since they all come from relatively poor families, except for one whose parents own a shop: "As you heard in the meeting we held yesterday, there's very little money. Each comrade offers five euros a month to support the militia. Luckily we don't pay any rent since this apartment was given to us by a group of sympathizers. These are sixty-year-old men who, when they were young, were Fascists like us. They are no longer active militants but are still nostalgic for Fascism and they help us. They always tell us, it's up to you now! We just pay the light and water bills. Some comrades, the few comrades who have jobs, give us as much as twenty euros a month, but it's their choice. We ask for five euros a month as a commitment from everyone. If someone offers more, we're happy to receive it, but no one has to pay more than five euros a month."

The Lenintown militia is made up of twelve people. Eight are militants, and four are supporters, who don't pay the monthly dues. This means that the Lenintown militia can count on only forty euros a month.

"We organize all our initiatives on forty euros a month. Now that you've come on board, we have forty-five euros," says Cincinnatus, smiling. He explains that, because of the lack of money, books are bought only after careful discussion of each purchase:

"We can't buy the wrong book because we can't waste money. As you can see, we have very few books. Before we decide which ones to buy, we hold a meeting because we all have to be in agreement."

I gather these books are very important to you.

"Right. These books are important to us because they're about revolutionary Fascism. We only founded the Lenintown militia a year ago, and we need time to buy more books."

I count fifteen books on the shelf.

You've bought fifteen books?

Cincinnatus tells me that in fact they bought only five books; the others were already there: "These books belonged to the comrades who own this apartment. We found them here and we've kept them."

I want to know exactly what books the Sacrifice comrades bought, and Cincinnatus points them out, explaining that they're books that help them understand what revolutionary Fascism is.

When I ask Cincinnatus to explain revolutionary Fascism, he blushes in embarrassment and stutters. I remember that when he allowed me to record his voice during an interview about his life—a recording that I've listened to many times—he used the same words with the same embarrassment: "As I already mentioned when you interviewed me, I've always hated reading. This is one of my great limitations and I'm not proud of it. This is also why I agreed to manage this little library, because it might help me to read a book or two. Reading is something I've promised myself I'll do."

I insist. I want to understand how Cincinnatus interprets the phrase "revolutionary Fascism" that has become so important in his life. To help him get over his embarrassment, I express myself awkwardly, mixing up words and trying to appear as insecure as possible:

I don't know anything about any history of Fascism. Can you tell me what revolutionary Fascism is? What you understand it is?

Cincinnatus continues to be evasive. "I'd advise you to contact Marcus," the head of the Mussolinia militia. "He's much more expert than me. Or speak to Leonidas."

Thanks for the suggestion, I'll do it, but can you tell me something about revolutionary Fascism? If Marcus realizes that I don't know anything, I'll look stupid.

"Revolutionary Fascism is the purest Fascism, born from the people, and which fights against the church and against the rich. Revolutionary Fascism helps people fight against the bourgeoisie, the capitalists, and the banks. People are wrong when they say that Fascism is a friend of the bourgeoisie. Fascism is the enemy of the bourgeoisie. I think the bourgeoisie stinks."

Cincinnatus leaves me alone while he goes into the other room, where a small bar has been set up. From the noise I gather that he's arranging beer bottles in the fridge. I pull out my phone and take a photo of the books.

I say good-bye to Cincinnatus, go out into the street, and text Marcus to ask him to meet me in downtown Mussolinia.

Hi, Marcus! I'm in Lenintown, but I'm coming to Mussolinia. Do you have time to take a walk downtown? I'll buy you a drink.

"No prob. See you in an hour," he texts back, naming the bar where he will meet me.

Revolutionary Fascism

It's a splendid day for strolling around downtown Mussolinia.

Marcus is the head of the militia, whilst Lentulus is number two. Marcus spends many months a year studying at a university in another city. In his absence, Lentulus takes over as leader, but no decision can be made without the consent of Marcus, who is informed daily of everything that happens in Mussolinia. Marcus and Lentulus are close friends and loyal to each other.

Marcus has returned to Mussolinia for a few weeks. He's on vacation, has no commitments, and thus has a lot of free time. He's a sociable person and likes to have fun. I decide to go to the militia offices almost every day to spend as much time with him as I can.

Marcus is well known in Mussolinia. In recent years, his name has often appeared in the newspapers because he spent two days in jail, accused of having attacked a police officer who had tried to search him after a soccer game. Marcus is the leader of the Mussolinia ultras and is one of the few militants who agreed to let me record his voice while he recounted his life story in the militia headquarters during a sixty-five-minute interview.

Marcus explains to me that the Fascism that once ruled Italy had two great guiding spirits: the revolutionary spirit, dedicated to bringing down bourgeois society, and the conservative spirit, dedicated to defending the Italian bourgeoisie through an alliance with the monarchy and the Catholic Church.

In Marcus's story, revolutionary Fascism experienced two stages.

The first stage began on March 23, 1919, in Piazza San Sepolcro in Milan, when Mussolini announced the birth of the Fasci Italiani di Combattimento (Italian Fasci of Combat). As Marcus tells it, this stage ended with the March on Rome on October 28, 1922, which brought

Mussolini to power. Thus revolutionary Fascism came into being between 1919 and 1922.

"From 1925 up until 1943," Marcus continues, "Fascism held back its revolutionary impulse and made many compromises with the pope, the king, and the bourgeoisie." After almost twenty years, it once again took a leading role in the establishment of the Italian Social Republic, the state Mussolini founded on September 18, 1943. Hitler wanted this state to control the Italian territories that hadn't fallen into the hands of the Anglo-American army, following what Marcus called "the king's shameful betrayal." He believed that King Victor Emmanuel III should have saved Italy's honor by continuing to fight alongside Hitler instead of surrendering to the Americans.

When Marcus talks about the king's betrayal, he is referring to the armistice—in reality an unconditional surrender—signed in Cassibile, Sicily, on September 3, 1943, by the Italian and American generals Giuseppe Castellano and Walter Bedell Smith.

Marcus points out that revolutionary Fascism, which despised the bourgeoisie, the clergy, and the monarchy, remained active during Mussolini's regime, albeit with a marginal role. Sacrifice is a political organization that has revolutionary Fascism as its keystone. "In Italy and in Europe," Marcus tells me, "there are numerous Fascist organizations with different identities. We are revolutionary Fascists, and we have a particular strategy for gaining power and taking over society."

Are you a revolutionary Fascist?

"Yes."

Could you explain exactly what that means?

"I'm a *squadrista*," he says, a member of a Fascist action squad. "Lentulus would tell you the same. We consider ourselves *squadristi*."

Correct me if I'm wrong, but weren't the squadristi *those Fascists who organized themselves into squads and beat up Mussolini's opponents, who forced the socialists to drink castor oil . . .*

"Right. That's them."

They're also those who murdered Giacomo Matteotti . . . Matteotti was a socialist politician kidnapped and murdered in 1924 after publicly accusing the Fascists of electoral fraud.

"Hang on. I'm not saying that today you have to beat up your political adversaries. I don't tell my comrades to beat up left-wing youths.

I'm saying that they have to know how to defend themselves. If they're threatened or attacked, they mustn't go to the police. They have to defend themselves as a matter of honor. The actions you talked about, such as the murder of Matteotti, have to be placed in their historical context, and in that historical context they were right because the *squadristi* prevented Stalin from conquering Italy."

You told me that Fascism has many identities. How are you different from other Fascists?

"A first, important difference is that we don't belong to the church. Our organization doesn't listen to the pope. But for other Fascist movements, Catholicism is fundamentally important. For example, we reject everything the pope says about immigration. We're also in favor of the law permitting abortion. Our militants can have all the sex they want," he says, smiling.

"Through the manipulation of history books," Marcus explains, "the young have learned to fear Fascism. This is why Sacrifice has to enter the 'system' quietly, without frightening people with Fascist symbols; also because under Italian law, those who try to organize a new Fascist party can be arrested. The aim is to enter the political system to spread the values of Fascism in Italy. This strategy," Marcus continues, "also affects our way of dressing and saluting each other. The Sacrifice Fascists use a salute that consists of grasping each other's forearm."

Can you show me how you do it?

Marcus shows me how I should grasp his forearm. "You've got it!" He laughs. "We don't raise our right hand in a salute. We grasp each other's forearm, as the soldiers in the Roman militia used to do."

Why did the Roman legionnaires salute each other in this way? What is the meaning of this salute?

"The Roman legionnaires saluted each other in this way so they could see if someone was a traitor, hiding a knife to kill the general or emperor. For us Fascists, betrayal is the most despicable thing a person can do. To die defending your honor is the noblest thing."

What does this type of salute have to do with seizing power?

"There are two reasons why we prefer this salute. The first is that Italian law forbids the typical Fascist salute with your arm raised. Two of our militants are on trial because they made the Fascist salute during a gathering. The police saw them and reported them." The two militants, one of whom had previous convictions, were subsequently sentenced by the Italian supreme court.

"Our way of saluting is less obvious. Almost no one knows that it's a Fascist salute. The second reason is that people get alarmed when they see an arm held out. People immediately think of Hitler, of concentration camps, of World War II . . . Our task is to gain the trust of the young. We mustn't lose them. We have to find ways to bring them to us."

Marcus adds that there are some important differences between the way the Sacrifice comrades and the comrades of other organizations dress.

"The Fascists of the other organizations dress like the Fascists of a hundred years ago!" With his facial expressions, smirks, and body movements, Marcus delivers the message that he thinks they're ridiculous. "We dress like our contemporaries. Some of us have Fascist tattoos, but our militants are not required to tattoo themselves. Our hairstyles are the same as those of any other young person, and so are our clothes. No one could think we're Fascists on the basis of how we look. Do I look like a Fascist to you? We're slowly entering Italian society. We have more than fifty cells throughout Italy. We're present nationwide, we publish a magazine, and we own numerous sports centers, pubs, and even some restaurants, but none of these activities bear our name. You'll never see the name Sacrifice in our gyms."

Would you prefer to live in the democracy we have today in Italy or in a Fascist dictatorship?

"I'd like to live in a Fascist dictatorship."

Living in a Fascist dictatorship means living in a society in which there is no freedom of the press and in which there are no opposition parties. The Fascist regime sentenced people to life imprisonment or death if they opposed Il Duce . . .

"I know."

So you'd prefer to live in this type of society?

"Sure."

Why?

"Because a Fascist dictatorship is the best solution to all the Italians' problems, but this can't be achieved in the way Mussolini did it in 1922. The world we live in today is too different from then. The problem lies in building Fascism inside bourgeois democracy, which is what Hitler and Mussolini did. They didn't seize power like Lenin."

Hitler and Mussolini entered by the front door and—

"The door of parliament!" he interrupts, laughing.

And then they threw out everything that was inside.

"Exactly."

You're a nationalist, right?

"Right."

The Ardeatine massacre was a mass killing of 333 Italian political prisoners and Jewish civilians that the Nazis carried out in Rome on March 24, 1944, in reprisal for a partisan attack the previous day against the SS Police Regiment Bozen.

"I know."

When you think of that massacre, what side are you on? On Hitler's or on that of the Italians?

Marcus doesn't reply, and we both remain silent.

Which side are you on? Are you with Hitler or with the Italians?

Marcus seems to be struggling. He still doesn't answer. He moves his shoulders, waves his hands, and shakes his head to indicate that I'm asking a question he's not comfortable with. I sip some Coca-Cola to give him time to recover.

Marcus, are you with Hitler or the Italians?

"I'm with Hitler, obviously. I'm sorry that all those Italians died. Do you get that? I'm not saying that I'm happy all those people died, but the Nazis were right."

After this answer, I point out to Marcus that the Sacrifice national leaders, when they speak on the radio or on television, never say that their final goal is the creation of a Fascist dictatorship and they never admit to admiring Hitler.

Since courage is a fundamental value for Sacrifice, why don't its leaders say exactly what they think?

Marcus answers by explaining three points.

First of all, the Sacrifice leaders can't speak freely because the Italian constitution forbids the founding of a new Fascist party and the defense of Fascism. Sacrifice militants have to be careful about what they say to journalists because there is always the risk that the government will order that their organization be dismantled. This is why for years Sacrifice has been battling for the abolition of the so-called anti-Fascist articles of the constitution. Second, the Sacrifice leadership has always admitted, on radio and television, to being "Fascists" because Italian law cannot punish this. Third, the Italians are not yet culturally prepared to hear certain speeches about Hitler, so it's impossible to give them in public.

Marcus ends with these words: "It's got nothing to do with lacking courage. All the Sacrifice militants are courageous, but none of us would endanger the organization. The tactic is to gain power through the back door, without making too much noise. None of us today can think of seizing power by bursting in, because the bourgeoisie and the capitalists control everything. We need time; we have to build a new society from the bottom up."

In this first chapter, we've acquired some important information for starting our journey through the world of Sacrifice.

Mussolinia and Lenintown have the same number of inhabitants and are about twenty miles apart. The former is in the hills, the latter on the seacoast. The Mussolinia militia, in a town with a right-wing tradition, has excellent relations with the political authorities, while the militia of Lenintown, with a left-wing tradition, has very bad relations with the powers that be. And yet both the Mussolinia and Lenintown militias have been involved in violent incidents.

The Fascism that developed in Italy between 1919 and 1945 had two different guiding philosophies. Sacrifice supports revolutionary Fascism, an initial stage in which paramilitary groups known as action squads carried out violent acts.

Sacrifice, besides being a political movement, is also a cultural organization with the goal of teaching young people to love Fascism, demonstrated through absolute loyalty to the militia and submission to its leaders.

The first rule of Sacrifice is that the group is more important than the individual. The group has a "personality" to which individual comrades have to adapt. Those who do not respect this rule can be expelled on the basis of a decision reached by a specified number of leaders, four in the case of the Mussolinia militia.

Sacrifice asks its new recruits to read particular books. Its leaders organize a weekly meeting to see if the young people have understood what they're reading.

As Fascists they cannot freely express their ideals in public because they could be arrested: the Italian constitution forbids the establishment of a Fascist party. This limitation also affects the way militants dress and greet one another. The Sacrifice militants are planning to combat bourgeois democracy from the inside, as Hitler and Mussolini did.

Sociologists would say that, when young people enter a Sacrifice cell, they find an established world that exerts a coercive power over them. The content of this "world," made up of schemes for interpreting reality, is based on the principle of authority and transmitted from the top down. The leaders explain the significance of Fascism; the recruits accept and learn. Once they've entered the militia, new members are faced with a kind of interaction in which they have no say. The militia is a "reality," and no one can make it disappear simply by wishing it away.[5]

2

In Praise of Suicide

The Spiritual Guide

The books that are read by the Lenintown and Mussolinia militias can't be purchased in ordinary bookshops. You have to go in person to one of two shops in Rome specializing in "rare" books on Fascism, run by Fascist militants and sympathizers.

Since I was busy with my research, and fearing that the day of my expulsion would soon arrive, I was reluctant to leave my place in Lenintown so as not to waste even one day of participant observation. But I was wrong.

Talking to the comrades, I realized that my visit to the Fascist Mysticism bookshop wouldn't interrupt my research. On the contrary, meeting Romulus, the owner, was an extraordinary opportunity to enter one of the most importance places in Italy for disseminating Fascist culture.

I had a pleasant journey from Lenintown to Rome. I parked my car a few steps from St. Peter's Basilica and passed through the marvelous colonnade on foot. I reached the address, but I couldn't find the bookshop. I should explain that when I conduct my ethnographic research, I'm obsessively precise: I couldn't have gotten the address wrong. I asked some passersby for directions, but they all told me they'd never seen a bookshop on that street. How was that possible? I saw a man come out of a building and showed him the address I had written on a piece of paper. The man said: "It's inside here! It's inside this building. Go in and turn right." As I took my leave, he turned and said jokingly, "It's a secret bookshop!"

It didn't look like a bookshop. It had no sign, and it was impossible to recognize it from the outside. To enter I had to ring a doorbell. The door opened and I was confronted by a man of around seventy, Romulus, sitting behind a large, untidy desk. The bookshop, actually a storeroom, consisted of two book-filled rooms. I couldn't see a cashier's desk.

I had gathered a lot of information on the cultural significance of the place I was now standing in. I knew that Romulus had devoted his entire life to keeping alive the cultural universe of Hitler and Mussolini through incessant publishing. He didn't know me but I knew him. Romulus's main mission is to bring out books that no Italian publisher will touch, books on "Fascist spirituality," whose greatest representative is considered to be Niccolò Giani (1909–1941). Thanks to a long interview with Romulus that had appeared a few days earlier on a website, I had noted something in his personality that was useful during our first meeting. At times during the interview, Romulus becomes arrogant, as if convinced he's the only educated person in a world of fools.

At the outset, Romulus is unfriendly and makes it clear that I'm not welcome. I decide to use the technique that Jack D. Douglas calls "playing the boob,"[1] but Romulus seems annoyed by the questions of a stranger who apparently doesn't understand anything about Fascism and who hasn't called in advance:

"Why didn't you phone to arrange an appointment?"

I could answer that no bookshop in the world asks its customers to phone before arriving, but I want to gain his trust, and after a few minutes his attitude changes. Romulus seems flattered by my words:

Forgive me for asking these questions, but I don't understand anything about Fascism. I've been told you know everything about this subject and that you can help me. I've had a long journey to get here. I didn't have your telephone number, otherwise I'd have asked you for an appointment.

With my tone of voice and facial expression I nudge him into the role he loves best, that of spiritual guide engaged in helping young people find a moral reference point.

It works!

Romulus invites me to sit down and replies generously to my questions. Polite, helpful, understanding, he gives me all the information I need, besides selling me the books I'm looking for at 10 percent off. "We don't usually give discounts," he says, "but I'm making an exception for you."

Mission accomplished. In addition to acquiring the books the Lenintown and Mussolinia militants use for their training, I've gained a lot of invaluable information on the cultural universe of Sacrifice.

I purchase many books, including the four on the shelf in Lenintown: Niccolò Giani, *Mysticism of the Fascist Revolution*; Julius Evola, *Orientamenti*; Léon Degrelle, *Militia*; and Corneliu Z. Codreanu, *The Nest Leader's Manual*.

I look at Romulus like a child seeking a master.

"If you want to understand Fascism," he says, "you have to read many books. There are numerous books that teach you about Fascism. You also have to consider that there are different types of Fascism, and each type has its cult books. If you're a Catholic, you have to read particular authors. If you're an atheist, you have to read other authors. Do you see? In any case, you've chosen well. The books you've bought are fundamental for all Fascists, without distinction of age or religion. When a boy of fourteen comes to me and asks me to suggest a book about Fascism, I suggest the books you've got in your hands."

What's so important in these books? Can you tell me something about them?

"In these books there's the spiritual essence of Fascism. They'll help you to understand what the Fascist credo consists of and what a spiritual revolution is. They're not books on the organization of the state and on how to seize political power. These books make you understand that you can live a different life, based on different values."

I'm happy and satisfied. As I've already said, I'm not interested in studying the history of Fascism. I'm interested in understanding what Clifford Geertz would call the "webs of significance" of the Sacrifice militants—the cognitive categories through which they interpret the world to understand how these webs influence their social actions.[2]

Romulus says he knows Sacrifice very well. He explains that it's an organization that harks back to revolutionary Fascism. He repeats the ideas I had already heard during my meeting with Lentulus, but adds some important details. Romulus's lecture lasts some forty minutes. To summarize:

The term "neofascist" has to be rejected because "it's a stupid invention of the journalists." Neofascism does not exist. Only Fascism exists.

In Europe there are many Fascist and Nazi organizations, each of which has particular features. Sacrifice is based on revolutionary Fascism, the original Fascism (1919–1924) and the Fascism of the war's end (1943–1945), and it's an organization that despises the bourgeoisie, capitalism, and free enterprise.

Sacrifice is an organization that attributes enormous importance to the cultural education of the young because it maintains that the first revolution that must be carried out is a spiritual revolution. Before destroying the bourgeoisie, Sacrifice claims, it's necessary to destroy the bourgeois spirit that exists inside each of us.

Sacrifice's spiritual education is aimed at transmitting to young people the basic values of warrior societies: courage, sacrifice, and honor.

The Three Values of Revolutionary Fascism

Everyone agrees that the books of Niccolò Giani, Léon Degrelle, Julius Evola, and Corneliu Codreanu are fundamental for entering the mental universe of the Sacrifice militants. Fascist mysticism promotes a number of values, including love of family, loyalty to friends, fairness in sports competitions, solidarity with the poor, love for Italy, voluntary service, and physical exercise. These values, however, can be considered "secondary."

There are three fundamental, primary values that constitute the white-hot core of an education in revolutionary Fascism.

1. The first value is the courage you demonstrate by accepting or provoking fights with the enemy. As we shall see, education in courage is an

education in violence. When we look at the organization of sports, we'll see that sporting activity has the aim of developing the qualities of courage, sacrifice, and honor. Mixed martial arts (MMA) is the most violent combat sport in the world and is Sacrifice's "official" sport. Fighting inside an iron cage, combatants are allowed to use both striking and grappling techniques. With the exception of the head butt, anything goes: kicks in the face, punches, chokeholds, joint locks, arm bars, and knee bars.

The practical purpose of MMA is to teach the young how to be soldiers, which means learning to kill the enemy. The educational aim is to assemble thousands of comrades to celebrate collectively the values of revolutionary Fascism.

2. The second value is sacrifice: fighting even though you know you can't win. The mixed martial arts bouts I attended show how the value of sacrifice influences the way the athletes fight and how the public sees them.

3. The third value is honor, which Sacrifice comrades consider a consequence of courage and sacrifice. The greater the willingness of Sacrifice comrades to fight against a stronger enemy, the greater the honor.

The true Fascist is the person who fights knowing he will lose. One of the most popular films among the young Sacrifice militants is *300* (2006), directed by Zack Snyder, which recounts the Battle of Thermopylae in 480 BC, in which three hundred Spartans blocked the advance of the Persian king Xerxes I's army for three days. The Spartans are heroes for the Sacrifice militants because they decided to embrace death, demonstrating their courage and earning honor by sacrificing their lives.

Although they are indissolubly linked, these three principles have a hierarchical value. Courage and sacrifice are "instrumental" values in the sense that they represent the means to achieve the highest aim: honor.

In this chapter I describe the books that the Lenintown and Mussolinia militia members read. We are told that we have to study these works carefully because they will help us understand that the fights and attacks—those provoked and those suffered—are the "theater" in which the Sacrifice militants can prove they are "true Fascists," that they possess those values on which their self-respect and their prestige within the militia depend. But as Gary Allan Fine would say, ethnographers should avoid making culture the endpoint of analysis. Culture should be the data with which one begins.[3]

Fascist Mysticism

Leaving the bookshop, I nod to St. Peter's and go to the Colosseum, where I sit on a slab of rather uncomfortable marble next to the Arch of Constantine. The Colosseum, besides being the symbol of the Roman Empire's martial virtues that Mussolini lauded as opposing bourgeois pacifism, is also the favorite monument of the Sacrifice Fascists. With the Roman Forum behind me, I start reading *Mysticism of the Fascist Revolution*, the collection of writings published by Niccolò Giani between 1932 and 1941.

An Italian journalist and philosopher, Giani was the head of the Sandro Italico Mussolini School of Fascist Mysticism, which he founded in Milan in 1930 to train National Fascist Party leaders. Although he was a university professor, he decided to enroll as a soldier in the 1936 war in Ethiopia.

In 1939 he joined the Fascist campaign against Jews, declaring himself a supporter of "spiritual racism." On October 28, 1940, Mussolini attacked Greece in order to claim his right to sit at the winners' table alongside Hitler—a table that he never saw. Giani again enlisted. Arriving on the battlefield, he volunteered for a dangerous mission involving an assault on a well-fortified Greek position. At first the assault was successful, but then the Greeks counterattacked and Giani was killed in the fighting on March 14, 1941.

After his death he was awarded the gold medal of military valor for being one of the most courageous Fascists of his time. During his lifetime he had received bronze and silver medals for his bravery under fire. Sacrifice militants consider the life of Niccolò Giani to be filled with courage, sacrifice, and honor.

The publishing house that brought out his book is run by Fascist militants, and the description on the back cover helps us understand their admiration. Besides celebrating the values of courage, sacrifice, and honor, the jacket copy praises Giani's contempt for bourgeois society, distinguishing the revolutionary Fascist who chose to die in war for love of Fascism from the bourgeois Fascists, who were cowards.

Giani is presented as a hero:

This anthology represents the first systematic collection of Niccolò Giani's most significant writings from the period 1932 to 1941. We consider it the best way to illustrate directly his person, his thinking, and his action. It's an homage to someone who witnessed universal and intransigent Fascism, who never made compromises with the "comfortable life," who was the spiritual and political revivalist of an entire generation. An example of heroism who, over and beyond historical contingency, was consistent with his principles, living the ideal up to the supreme sacrifice; almost raising Fascism to a universal category of being, as an inexhaustible font of spirituality from which to carry out the revolution of humanity and of the world. Niccolò Giani, born in Muggia on June 20, 1909, fell at the Greek front on March 14, 1941, in the thick of the battle, and is now transfigured into mute heroism. He demonstrated with his life and beyond the harmony between thought and faith, the continuity between doctrine and action, and he remains the pure representative of the authentic revolution of new youth. For this reason, his example will be the beacon for the difficult journey of tomorrow. He knew how to point the way with action, and with intransigence he taught his example. "Card-carrying members" were his adversaries. He fought against them, against the deceitful, the presumptuous, the exhibitionists, the rhetoricians, the social climbers—against all those who considered the Revolution an act of ordinary administration, to be exploited for personal ends.

Niccolò Giani considered original Fascism, centered on action squads that were ordered to assault political opponents, the purest form of Fascism. He praised the San Sepolcro program, also called the "Manifesto dei fasci di combattimento," published on March 24, 1919, in *Il Popolo d'Italia*, the newspaper founded by Mussolini. The action squads consisted of disgruntled former soldiers who, after fighting in World War I, had returned to civilian life without work and without any recognition from the state. Initially these men were organized into squads to respond to the violence of the socialists during the so-called Red Biennium of 1919–20, but they later used violence indiscriminately against all opponents of Fascism.

In brief, there are three reasons why Niccolò Giani is so beloved by the young militants of Sacrifice.

First, Giani claimed that Fascism is a form of spiritual education, an inner challenge you set yourself to reject bourgeois values. To understand the ability of Sacrifice to instill Fascist values in its young militants, it may be helpful to listen to the words of Arminius, an eighteen-year-old comrade who tells me he comes from a "poor" family." His father lost his job and his mother, formerly a housewife, is now forced to take menial and poorly paid jobs.

It's lunchtime and we're strolling around Lenintown's main square. "Girls think that we Sacrifice militants are losers," he tells me. "That's how it is in bourgeois society. Girls only look at you if you've got money, if you drive an expensive car. Lenintown is one of the most bourgeois towns in the world. The truth is that money isn't important. What counts is the spirit. Values count. Young people today have sick souls. You can see it with your own eyes. You just have to look at today's youth to understand that they're sick."

Sick souls! I'm struck by this expression and ask Arminius to explain it better.

"Having a sick soul means . . ." Arminius pauses, then continues: "Young people today think only of money, of success, of appearing on TV, of buying designer clothes. You just have to look around you. All the young people use drugs. The Lenintown girls think we're losers. I don't care, because it means we're different from the others. It means that our spirit is different from the other guys' in this town. We have values, they have nothing. Did you ever read the letter that Niccolò Giani wrote to his son? That letter is very important for me."

Arminius gives me the name of the website from which Sacrifice militants can download Giani's letter. In it, he urges his young son to sacrifice his life for love of Italy and explains how good it is to die in war. The letter also celebrates the values of loyalty and friendship:

Dear Romolo Vittorio,

. . . You won't experience factions or parties. You won't see enemies inside the sacred borders of the Fatherland. You'll know only one name: "Italia"; you'll love only one thing: "Italia"; and only for her must you be capable of leaving everything, of losing everything, of forgetting everything. Of being hated and vilified, humiliated and tormented; only, only for this Italia you must know how to die with your body and with your soul; and never, ever must you forget that for this sacred name mothers have smiled as they said farewell to their sons who went to their death, husbands have with noble joy left their young brides, fathers have proudly kissed their children for the last time. That for this Italia the rivers have run with blood, the mountains have trembled, the dead have risen from the earth. And that for her I today don't know you and perhaps never will: but if this were to be so, you must love her also for me, sacrifice yourself also for me, die again also for me.

And remember that when you see your dearest friend, he who is your spiritual brother, and have time only to bend over and kiss him, not a single word of anger will come out of your mouth and there will be no thought of imprecation in your mind, but you will want only to advance to know Victory, and in doing this you will be certain to avenge your fallen friend, then, then as soon as you're certain you've learned to know her, you will be certain you love her!

The second reason why Giani is so admired is that, although he could have gone on living a comfortable life as the director of a cultural institution, he preferred to die in war. As Arminius says: "Niccolò Giani could have lived like all the bourgeoisie, but he sacrificed his life for the Fascist ideal, dying in war as a volunteer soldier. This is the noblest and most glorious way to die."

The Sacrifice militants continually repeat that the noblest action a man can perform is to die in war. I heard an interesting conversation between two Sacrifice militants in the locker room of a gym after a boxing training session. It helps us understand the value of sacrifice in the group's culture.

For years, Sacrifice has been fighting to stop immigrants from arriving in Italy. While I was under the shower with two Sacrifice militants, Spartacus and Tiberius, I provoked a debate between them by commenting on the Lampedusa tragedy, in which 366 refugees fleeing Libya burned to death when fire broke out on a sinking ship near the Mediterranean island of Lampedusa on October 3, 2013. Some thirty minutes after this brief debate, since I couldn't transcribe the discussion in my notebook, I locked myself in the gym bathroom and recorded it by speaking into my phone.

Spartacus, age forty-three, is an unemployed nurse covered in Fascist tattoos. He's muscular, but also overweight, and is about five foot eleven. Tiberius, age thirty, is a personal trainer with a degree in sports science. He has a small Fascist tattoo. Thin and not very muscular, he's as tall as Spartacus.

Spartacus responds first: "Europe is being invaded by blacks from Africa. Very soon Italy won't exist anymore. There'll be a huge mosque in place of the Vatican. Italians have become spineless. Know what I'm saying? I can't wait for the Africans to start a war in our country so we can get rid of them all; that way at least I'll be able to have a glorious death, fighting in war. At least I'll be able to sacrifice myself for an ideal. Better to die fighting than live this shitty life in this bourgeois society. This is how we'll end up thanks to our politicians. We're being invaded by blacks and by Muslims and nobody's doing anything to stop them. Anders Breivik was right."

"What are you talking about?" says Tiberius. "Anders Breivik was a lunatic who killed a lot of innocent people!"

Spartacus seems to be taken aback by Tiberius's answer and pauses while he puts his things in his gym bag. "I'm not talking about what Breivik did, but what he wrote in his manifesto. His ideas were right. Don't you agree?"

Tiberius tells him: "If I had to give an example, I wouldn't use Breivik. I'd quote Niccolò Giani, a hero who sacrificed himself for an ideal. Giani was a brave man because he tackled soldiers like himself, knowing that they could shoot and kill him. A person like Breivik is a madman." Spartacus doesn't reply and the conversation ends.

Although they disagree about Breivik—the Norwegian terrorist who on July 22, 2011, killed seventy-seven people, most of them young summer campers, to protest the Muslim presence in Europe—Spartacus and Tiberius both concur that the values of honor, courage, and sacrifice, as understood by Fascism, are the most important values to transmit to the young.

The Sick Soul

During our first meeting, Lentulus had told me that the most important books for his training as a militant were *Militia* by Léon Degrelle and *The Nest Leader's Manual* by Corneliu Codreanu. "When young people first enter the Mussolinia branch," Lentulus explains, "they have to read these books and show they've understood their content. This is why we organize weekly study sessions. I point out the book to read and, after seven days, we meet around seven in the evening to discuss it together. Since we're talking about young people who are still in school, I assign only one chapter. They don't have to read an entire book in seven days! I also prefer that they read one chapter at a time because they have homework to do. With my method, the reading of the book takes longer, it's discussed for weeks, and you learn the concepts better."

Like all the books I'd purchased from Romulus, Degrelle's work consists of a few densely packed pages. Degrelle, who wrote *Militia* while he was fighting alongside the Nazis, uses very evocative metaphors. After asserting that the world we're living in has sunk into moral corruption, he constructs his discourse around the words "soul" and "spirit."

Remember when Arminius said that his contemporaries had "sick souls?"

Here is what Degrelle writes:

> The disease of the century isn't in our bodies. The body is sick because the soul is sick.
> This is what was needed, what will be needed—whatever it takes—to recover and to revitalize.
> This is the true, great revolution to accomplish.
>   Spiritual revolution
>   Or the failure of the century.
> The salvation of the world depends on the will of the souls who believe.[4]

Degrelle continually uses the word "sacrifice." The world is sunk in immorality and desperation. Only those with a higher spirituality can save it by sacrificing themselves. Degrelle writes that the first moral duty is to "kill self-love" and make the final sacrifice for humanity. Once again, the author sings the praises of death as the triumph of life: "It doesn't matter if you die twenty years before or twenty years after. What is important is to die well. Only then does life begin."

Two pages later, Degrelle recounts seeing a pig about to be slaughtered, writhing and grunting in the desperate attempt to cling to life. Men, says Degrelle, have to learn to act differently from pigs when they face death because the greatest good is honor. To free themselves from the fear of death, men have to impose a strict inner discipline. The real man is the man who dies heroically. You have to teach young people the values of suffering, sacrifice, and discipline.

The reader should pay careful attention to these words of Degrelle:

> Easiness puts the ideal to sleep. Nothing awakens it better than the whips and lashes of a harsh life: it enables us to grasp the profundity of the duties to be accomplished, the mission of which we must be worthy.
> The rest doesn't matter. Health is of no importance.

There is no systematic thinking in Degrelle's book. It's a collection of existential thoughts and reflections, full of evocative metaphors. In the end, its message boils down to this: sacrifice your life for an ideal, submit to your leader, and live in a heroic manner.

The Spiritual Nobility of Suicide

To pass along Degrelle's Fascist mysticism, based on the idea of sacrifice as a form of self-destruction, to the next generation, Sacrifice organizes cultural events that are run like religious ceremonies.

One of the most suggestive and important events in which I participated in all the years I devoted to studying Sacrifice was the commemoration of Dominique Venner, an intellectual and Fascist sympathizer who, on May 21, 2013, placed a pistol in his mouth and shot himself dead in front of the altar at Notre-Dame de Paris. This event enabled me to gather an extraordinary quantity of information on Sacrifice's cultural universe thanks to the presence of a "guest of honor," a man I'll call François, the disciple who followed Venner up to the altar with the task of ensuring that the suicide was performed according to a highly symbolic ritual.

Dominique Venner had served as a paratrooper in the war that France fought to prevent Algeria from gaining its independence (1954–1962), and throughout his adult life had been one of the leading figures of the French far-right scene. He killed himself just as the French parliament was approving a law permitting same-sex marriage. Venner opposed the law, but this wasn't the primary reason for his gesture. Same-sex marriage, he believed, was a symptom of a deeper problem—the loss of identity of European peoples caused by what the Sacrifice militants called the "the cursed process of the Islamization of Europe."

A few days before the commemoration, Sacrifice had sent all its militants an extract from a letter that Venner had written in 1995 to protest the opening in Rome of one of the largest mosques in Europe. In that letter, which I read while in the Mussolinia militia offices, Venner invited the young to "go for the throats" of Muslims trying to build places of worship in Europe: "I don't have anything against Islam, which is the business of Muslims, but I am scientifically sure that a people that doesn't go for the throats of those who, in its house, come to challenge its gods faces certain death, if it isn't already dead."

I asked the local comrades if they were interested in taking a trip in order to participate in Venner's commemoration. In the hope of being able to spend some time with them, I offered to drive them there: "We could go together. I've got room for four in my car!" They all said they'd like to attend, but each militia ought to celebrate the memory of Venner in its own town. "Thanks," said Lentulus, "but we need to celebrate Venner in Mussolinia and Lenintown. But if you want to go . . ."

So I went. I arrived twenty minutes early, when the sun had only just set.

The apartment where the event took place was plastered with Fascist manifestos, and there was a festive air. Some comrades were buying books laid out on a wooden table; others were talking and laughing. There were some one hundred Sacrifice militants in the room, who fell into a profound silence when Augustus, one of the organization's national leaders, took the floor. A university graduate and an author, Augustus is considered the most cultured person in Sacrifice. With a skillful use of body language, facial expression, and tone of voice, in a few seconds he managed to communicate great emotional tension.

"Comrades," he said, "this is the most important event that Sacrifice has ever organized. It's not a political event. It's a spiritual event. We're meeting to celebrate the memory of one of the greatest men of this century. A man who deserves the greatest respect and the greatest admiration. A year after his death, we remember and pay homage to Dominique Venner and to his courage. Dominique Venner wasn't crazy. He was someone who gave proof of spiritual completeness and who transformed his life into an example. Thanks to Venner's gesture, our lives have acquired meaning. Venner wanted to reawaken us. He wanted to tell us that nothing is decided by fate. The world can be different from what it is today. None of us have to resign ourselves to immigration. Immigration and capitalism are not historical necessities. Immigration can be stopped."

Next to me, a man of around thirty with a Fascist symbol tattooed on his neck bent over, resting his elbows on his knees, and clasped his head between his hands with a pained expression. Then he turned to look at Augustus again. Augustus had started to talk about the philosopher Heidegger: "As Heidegger wrote in a text of 1936, this people will only be able to forge a destiny if it creates in itself a resonance!"

Augustus's rhetorical skill made his listeners gasp when he asserted that he had felt "joy" as soon as he read the news of Venner's death. But after shocking everyone, he explained what he meant: "When I heard that Venner had taken his life, I felt joy. Yes, I was joyful! I realized we were experiencing a historic moment. I realized that I had had the luck to be present during a gesture of great spiritual nobility. I had the fortune to live in an epoch in which there is still the power to give us spiritual examples. We're lucky to be contemporaries of Venner. We're lucky to have witnessed this gesture. All our branches throughout Italy are celebrating his memory. Venner was a prestigious intellectual, author of important books. As I speak, there are hundreds of Sacrifice comrades who are remembering him in all our branches. Venner was one of the few free men of our time."

Augustus accused the Italian newspapers of having described Venner as a lunatic, a fanatic, and a homophobe. Instead, he claimed, Venner was a hero who performed the noblest and most heroic gesture that a man can carry out: the sacrifice of his life to defend the purity of the Western race.

A letter written by Venner to explain his gesture was read at all the Sacrifice branches. His suicide, said Venner, was based on soul, spirit, race, blood, courage, honor, sacrifice, moral purity, altruism, assertion of will, and the desire to give one's life for the future of the world. When I read the letter, it was as if I had a page from Degrelle's book in front of me.

The Freikorps

When Augustus ended his speech, everyone turned to look at François, who started to read a text written in French as a young woman translated simultaneously into Italian. François, who had accompanied Venner to Notre-Dame, provided me with a great deal of information that has never been made public before. The faithful disciple, who first met Venner in 1995, spoke slowly and solemnly. Giving each word rhythm and melody, he presented a detailed description of what Venner did before kneeling in front of the altar: gestures, movements, phrases, and appearance.

According to François, Venner had organized his suicide in every detail without talking to anyone about it, not even to François, to whom he first revealed his intentions just before they entered the cathedral. He was also concerned about protecting the lives of the people who were in the church.

"Venner, my great master, was a weapons expert," François recounted. "Before shooting himself in the mouth, he had calculated exactly where the bullet would end up." The bullet, François continued, lodged in a marble statue depicting a symbol of ancient Rome, which, in Venner's mental universe, had particular significance.

François recalled that Venner had great admiration for the Sacrifice militants, whom he considered the "survivors of a chosen people." These are François's precise words, which I recorded in my notebook: "Venner wrote that you Sacrifice comrades are the Freikorps; you are the members of a superior race. He wrote that you're a dying species. I wanted to come to you to celebrate the first anniversary of Venner's death because, like Venner, I respect and admire you greatly."

The name Freikorps refers to the paramilitary units that arose in Germany in 1918, consisting of those Germans who, on returning from the war, found it difficult to reenter civilian life. These men gathered together to create a social group with an internal organization like that of the army: a militia. The Freikorps did not accept the Treaty of Versailles, which ended the war, considered humiliating for Germany, and wanted to make their opposition heard, as well as their opposition to the communist movements that had become more aggressive after Lenin's revolution.

Some Nazi leaders had enrolled in the Freikorps. They included Ernst Röhm, who held high office in Hitler's first government but who was killed on the Führer's orders on July 1, 1934, after the so-called Night of the Long Knives.

There was also the SS general Leonardo Conti, who, during World War II, was ordered to kill Jews who were unable to carry out forced labor. On May 5, 1945, Conti was arrested by the Americans, who brought him to trial at Nuremberg. Certain that he would be condemned to death, he hanged himself in his cell on October 6, 1945. Conti was a physician and played an important part in the "Aktion T4" euthanasia program against the disabled.

Another member of the Freikorps was Rudolf Höss, an SS officer who was also the first commander of Auschwitz. Höss ordered the use of Zyklon B gas to speed up the killing of Jews in the gas chambers. Found guilty of crimes against humanity by the Supreme National Tribunal in Warsaw, he was hanged on April 16, 1947.

Martin Bormann, Hitler's private secretary from April 12, 1943, onward, was also a Freikorps member.

A Ritual Suicide

François, after explaining that Venner had planned his suicide some months in advance, dramatically described the moment when he took his master's hand for the last time among hundreds of tourists. Venner looked him in the eye, said farewell, and walked away. Arriving at the altar, he knelt on one knee and put the pistol in his mouth.

A tourist saw the pistol and shouted. The gun went off, and tourists started to flee in panic as Venner's blood flowed from his head onto the floor.

François addressed his listeners: "Sacrifice comrades, you will help to make the sun return! Venner was convinced of this." (In Sacrifice terms, the return of the sun indicates the return of Nazism.)

Venner had instructed François to accompany him in order to confirm that he was dead and to inform his wife and children immediately. But François was convinced that Venner had asked him to follow him to the altar for another reason, one linked to the culture of the samurai, whom Venner admired. That is, the moment Venner told François of his intention to kill himself, he could no longer turn back, since a witness could reveal that the "Fascist samurai" hadn't had the courage to go through with it.

Here are François's actual words, which I carefully transcribed in my notebook, aided by the slow pace at which the Italian interpreter was translating:

"I think I can say that I had both an explicit and an implicit role [in Venner's suicide]. Let me explain. My first role, the mission that Venner gave me openly that day, was that of telling his wife and children as soon as I had confirmed that his suicide was successful. He didn't want his family to learn about it from the media. But knowing his interest, I would even say his fascination, with Japan and the world of the samurai,

I think I can say that the presence of a faithful friend 'obliges' the person who has decided to end his life to carry out his intention. Thus he couldn't turn back because he would have lost honor in the eyes of the community. As we approached Notre-Dame, Venner talked to me about the need to be loyal and trustworthy to the end. I hope I've been worthy of his trust because, up to his last breath, his acts were consistent with his thinking."

When François finished speaking, Augustus thanked him and asked those listening not to applaud and not to say anything: "This is a spiritual call to arms. It's not an intellectual debate. Comrades, let's go home and think about what we've heard!" The audience rose in silence and left the room.

The premises where the event was held remained full of comrades staying on to talk among themselves. I took the opportunity to approach them. I decided to speak to a twenty-seven-year-old man, Crassus, who was also one of Sacrifice's leaders:

Crassus, what François said was extremely interesting. Thank you for inviting me. I've learned a lot of things.

"François honored us. Since it's the first anniversary of Venner's death, he had received invitations from many European cities, but in the end he chose to come here because, as you heard, Venner had a lot of respect for us.

Yes, I read the letter Venner dedicated to the Sacrifice comrades. Tell me, what do you admire most about Venner?

"Venner has only been dead a year, but he's already become a spiritual symbol for all of us. As Augustus said, we're fortunate in being his contemporaries. Venner defended all the values in which we believe: honor, courage, sacrifice, and the fight against a multicultural society that is contaminating our identity."

Augustus said that you need a lot of courage to kill yourself as Venner did . . .

"That's right. Venner wasn't afraid of death. We live in a society that teaches us to fear death and to love life above all. Venner taught us that life isn't the most valuable good. The most valuable good is the spiritual purity demonstrated by the courage to defend an idea. So we've decided to call Venner 'the samurai of the West' because his gesture is as noble as those of [Yukio] Mishima and [Jan] Palach."

This comparison had already been proposed by Augustus in a letter sent to all the Sacrifice comrades. To continue our research into the cultural universe of Sacrifice, it is important to understand who Mishima and Palach were.

Crassus informed me that Mishima was an internationally famous Japanese author, poet, and playwright. On November 25, 1970, at the age of forty-five, he killed himself on live television by stabbing himself in the abdomen with a sword, in the ritual of the Japanese samurai called *seppuku*. Like Dominique Venner, Yukio Mishima had also carefully planned his suicide, which was carried out during a symbolic occupation of the Ministry of Defense. Crassus told me that, before leaving home, Mishima had left a note. I looked it up on the Internet as soon as I returned to Lenintown. This is what it says: "Human life is limited but I would like to live forever."

Mishima was a nationalist who had founded a paramilitary organization called the Shield Society with the symbolic function of enrolling only a select number of "pure men" (around one hundred) to keep alive the warrior spirit that Japan had lost after its defeat in World War II. More specifically, Mishima despised the Treaty of San Francisco, signed on September 8, 1951, in which Japan, besides giving up its own army, submitted to the United States and entrusted its defense to America.

Jan Palach was the Czech philosophy student who, on January 16, 1969, set himself on fire in the center of Prague, in front of the National Museum, to protest the Soviet occupation of Czechoslovakia, which had put an end to Alexander Dubček's liberal reforms. In the letter he wrote before his self-immolation, Palach stated he belonged to an organization that had sworn to fight the communist dictatorship by committing suicide and that he was the first to be chosen by lot.

As soon as I went back to the Mussolinia offices, I looked for Palach's letter on the only computer the militia possessed. Late at night, after a table soccer game, a comrade named Fritigernus helped me find it. Palach had written the letter to his parents just before killing himself. Fritigernus had never seen it before and was very impressed. It reads:

Mother, Father, brother, little sister! When you read this letter, I will already be dead or close to death. I know what a severe blow my act will be to you, but don't be angry at me. Unfortunately, we are not alone in this world.

I am not doing this because I am tired of life but on the contrary, because I cherish it too much. Hopefully my act will make life better. I know the value of life and I know it is the most precious thing. But I want a lot for you, for everyone, so I have to pay a lot. Do not lose heart after my sacrifice, tell Jacek to study harder and Marta too. You must never accept injustice, be it in any form; my death will bind you. I am sorry that I will never again see you or that which I loved so much. Please forgive me that I fought with you so much. Do not let them make me out to be a madman. Say hi to the boys, the river, and the forest.

This was my dialogue with Fritigernus, who felt that Palach was a very brave man who had chosen to give his life for a cause:

But Jan Palach wasn't a Fascist.

"That doesn't matter. What matters is that he had the courage to sacrifice his life to defend his ideal."

There are lots of people who died to defend their ideals. You admire them all? All these people? For example, do you admire the socialist Giacomo Matteotti, who was killed by the Fascists?

"Wait, there's a difference between admiring and respecting. I respect all those who have the courage to die to defend their ideals. That's the difference between a Fascist and a communist. A communist would reply that the life of a Fascist is worthless. A Fascist would tell you that all those who choose to die to defend their ideas are people to be respected. What counts are honor and courage. Men stand out for what they do."

So for you, Dominique Venner, Jan Palach, and Giacomo Matteotti are equals?

"Absolutely not. I've just told you that. I'm not saying they're all the same. It's clear that Dominique Venner's suicide is worth more because the society for which he fought is a spiritually higher society; it's the society for which we fight as well. And then Giacomo Matteotti didn't kill himself. We're talking about different things. Giacomo Matteotti was a socialist. He's not a hero to me! But I recognize his bravery and I respect it. I would never say that he was a pig as the communists do when they speak of Mussolini or Hitler!"

Léon Degrelle and Dominique Venner, Yukio Mishima and Jan Palach based their existence on principles of courage, sacrifice, and honor. These men lived different lives, but their stories have a shared characteristic.

Whether they were killed in war, or killed themselves while involved in spiritual war, the common feature is the eradication of life to achieve honor.

Honor is achieved through courage and sacrifice. Honor is the highest cause.

Submission to the Leader

There's another very important book on the Lenintown shelf. It's *The Nest Leader's Manual* by Corneliu Zela Codreanu, the political leader, and admirer of Hitler and Mussolini, who founded the Legionary Movement in interwar Romania.

His book is a cult object for the Sacrifice militants. Anti-Semitic, anti-Bolshevik, anti-capitalist, anti-bourgeois, but also Christian fundamentalist, Codreanu had made the archangel Gabriel the pivot of his political life and was profoundly influenced by mysticism.

He was arrested several times for his subversive activities. On May 8, 1924, the police chief of Iaşi, Constantin Manciu, gave orders to attack his movement. Codreanu assassinated him on October 25, 1924, but he pleaded self-defense and was acquitted thanks to public support. In 1927 he founded the Legion of the Archangel Michael with the intention of achieving the moral regeneration of Romania. He used Fascist symbols, even though he didn't agree with the idea of the cooperative state. In 1930 the Legion created a youth movement called the Iron Guard, which committed numerous acts of terrorism against Jews and left-wing political leaders. The Romanian government dissolved the Legion in 1933, but it continued to be active. In the parliamentary elections of December 1937, Codreanu's movement gained many seats, making it the third-largest political force in Romania, with 17 percent of the vote.[5] On February 12, 1938, King Carol II carried out a coup d'état, suspended the constitution, disbanded political parties, and installed a police state. Immediately a violent repression was initiated against Codreanu, who was arrested and executed by the royal guards on November 30, 1938.

Right up to the end, Codreanu reiterated his desire to join forces with Hitler and Mussolini, as he stated on November, 28, 1937, in *Buna Vestire,* his movement's newspaper.[6]

The Sacrifice militants hail him as a martyr, an example of high morality. Remember Legrelle's speech about the "sick soul" echoed by Arminius, the young Lenintown militant? We find the same idea, the same phrases, in this passage from Codreanu, one that is particularly beloved by Sacrifice militants: "Our Legionary Movement has more the character of a great spiritual school. It tends to kindle unsuspected beliefs, it tends to transform and revolutionize the Romanian soul. Shout out loud in every direction that evil, misery, and ruin come from the soul. The soul is the cardinal point around which we must act at the present moment—the soul of the individual and the soul of the multitude."[7]

The Nest Leader's Manual has one characteristic not found in Degrelle's *Militia*. Besides extolling Fascist mysticism, the book contains a series of very precise rules for militia behavior that perfectly describe daily life in the Lenintown and Mussolinia militias. There are many of these rules, and they aim to train the young to be courageous and to sacrifice their lives in the name of honor. The first page of the book explains that the *cuib* (nest) members must love one another like "brothers" and show total obedience to their leader.

Immediately thereafter, Codreanu lists the six fundamental laws that all comrades have to observe:

The law of discipline: A comrade must always follow the leader, whatever he does. The comrade must follow his leader through thick and thin.

The law of honor: All of a comrade's actions must follow the path of honor.

The law of education: When he enters the nest, a comrade must become another person. He must become a hero. He must educate himself to see life as a means in the service of an ideal that can be achieved only through heroism.

The law of reciprocal help: A comrade must never abandon his nest brothers when they fall into disgrace. A comrade must always take the part of his brothers, whatever happens. The nest is like a family that requires absolute love.

The law of work: A comrade must always work, not for his personal satisfaction but to gain honor through the nest's undertakings.

The law of silence: A comrade must speak little and act for love of his nest.

Sacrifice militants learn that their "nest" is a holy place, a "temple."

I asked seventeen Mussolinia and Lenintown militants the following question, interviewing them separately so their answers wouldn't be influenced by those of the others:

What would you be willing to sacrifice for your militia?

They all replied in the same identical words: "I would be willing to sacrifice my life for my comrades!"

What happens if a comrade commits a crime and is arrested? Does Codreanu's law of reciprocal help require them to lie and give false testimony in court? As we shall see, I tried to get an answer to this question through participant observation, but it's too soon to tackle this subject here. In the meantime, I find it useful to listen to Caligula, who doesn't belong to either the Mussolinia or the Lenintown militia. Caligula, thirty-two years of age, a university graduate and married, has a son a few months old. Although he remains a Sacrifice militant, he has started to become critical of the group's ideas and laws. He embraced Fascism as a child because his father and grandfather were militant Fascists. "My family," he said, "has a long Fascist tradition. I was one of the first Sacrifice militants. I was a friend of the Sacrifice leaders even before they founded the organization."

Caligula and I have been friends for five years. He has often said to me: "I respect you a lot because you're a cultured person without prejudices. I like talking about politics with you." I feel that I can speak freely to Caligula.

This conversation, taking place in a weight room, lasted for almost an hour.

I've read that some Sacrifice militants are in prison. Is that true?

Quite a few, unfortunately. The number of our militants in jail has grown in recent years.

Why are they in prison?

Our militants are usually arrested because they've committed violence. Some are in jail because they've been in fights in the stadium during a soccer game. Some have been sentenced because they've beaten up left-wingers. Others have been in brawls in pubs or in the street.

Sacrifice constantly supports these young people. I've heard that Sacrifice pays for their lawyers and organizes demonstrations on their behalf. Why do the Sacrifice leaders defend these comrades if they know they're guilty?

Caligula's expression seems to communicate his disagreement with the way Sacrifice acts in these cases. "Well, this is a problem that's always existed in Sacrifice and that damages our public image. There are very strict rules in our organization, and one of these rules is to show solidarity with other comrades. Whatever a comrade does, he must always be defended."

I seem to have read this somewhere.

"What do you mean?"

What you just said, that comrades must always defend each other, whatever they might do.

"Codreanu."

Exactly, Codreanu! What does Codreanu say? I don't remember.

"There is the so-called blood pact between comrades, and blood comes before anything else, even before the law. The law is to defend yourself always and at whatever cost."

What law?

"The law, the law. The law of the state."

Where Is *Mein Kampf*?

Of the authors I found on the Lenintown library shelf, Julius Evola is doubtless the most erudite and challenging. Besides devoting his life to history and philosophy, he was also a Fascist militant and a prolific writer.

In the 1970s, his book *Ride the Tiger* was used for training both Italian Fascist militants and far-right terrorists. Sacrifice militants read *Orientamenti*, such a small book that it can easily fit in a coat pocket. *Orientamenti* summarizes all Evola's moral convictions and contains some principles to guide the young in their daily lives.

I've searched many times, but Hitler's autobiography is nowhere to be found on those shelves, neither in the Mussolinia nor in the Lenintown offices. And yet Hitler is considered a hero by the Sacrifice militants, even though his name is never spoken in public. Why isn't *Mein Kampf* there? I'd like to ask, but I receive the answer accidentally.

It comes from Leonidas, leader of the Lenintown militia, who is talking to his comrade Cincinnatus:

"Cincinnatus, did you take the flyers to Mussolinia?"

"No, at the last moment I couldn't go to Mussolinia."

"Why not? The Mussolinia comrades called me! They're waiting for the flyers."

"When I got into the car to drive to Mussolinia, I remembered that I hadn't taken Hitler's books out of the trunk, and I was afraid I might be stopped by the police."

A few hours later, finding myself alone with Cincinnatus, I asked him why he was frightened of going around with Hitler's books in his car. Cincinnatus told me he was convinced that the police were following him after the brawl in the Lenintown bar, at which he had been present. He had decided to testify on behalf of Leonidas.

He said: "This is a difficult period for me. The police are collecting evidence against Leonidas, and I'm a witness. We've removed Hitler's *Mein Kampf* from our library as well as other books by Mussolini and we've put them in my car. It's going to create a lot of problems if the police find these books."

3

THE CONSTRUCTION OF THE
PARALLEL WORLD

In the political culture of Sacrifice, the physical contest, which finds its ultimate expression in war, is the best way to show you're courageous and ready for sacrifice.

It's clear that for Sacrifice, the ideal man is the soldier. But there's a problem. Italy is one of the most peaceful countries in the world.

Not only are Italians not very violent, but also the nation's constitution rejects war as an instrument for solving international conflicts. It must also be remembered that Italy, having lost World War II, was not allowed to arm itself, which means it has such a weak army that it wouldn't be able to fight any real war. In 2005 the Italian state abolished national service, introduced in 1861. At least once in their life, young Italian men had been obliged to live like soldiers for twelve consecutive months. Today this is no longer the case.

The Sacrifice Fascists, who exalt the figure of the soldier, are condemned to live in a peaceful society that rejects war and has no well-equipped armed forces. The Italian army can participate only in humanitarian missions, or in missions that aim to bring peace to countries at war.

Niccolò Giani had had the opportunity of fighting in Ethiopia and Greece. But the Sacrifice militants? What can they do to follow the example of Giani, of Degrelle, of Codreanu and Mussolini? Many of them would like to put into practice the spiritual education they've received, but they are forced to make do in this "shitty" bourgeois society that makes them live in peace with everyone. How can they demonstrate their courage and their ability to sacrifice themselves for an ideal and for their militia?

The Sacrifice militants often speak of their desire to die in war. I've noted that when they say this, they're thinking of a very specific war—a war against Muslim immigrants, and in particular against those from Africa.

I've never heard Sacrifice militants worry about the presence of Jews in Italy or anywhere else in the world, and I've never heard them say anything against Jews in general. The only anti-Semitic expressions I've heard are those directed against other comrades. When a Sacrifice militant wants to insult another comrade, he says, "Fucking Jew!" or "Look at this fucking Jew!" Sometimes they say "Jew!" without any adjectives.

Let's listen to the words of Macrinus, a forty-three-year-old boxing trainer with a lean, muscular body. Our conversation takes place in the same gym as the dialogue between Spartacus and Tiberius described in chapter 2.

Macrinus is one of the most aggressive militants I ever came across. In the presence of his older brother and another man who goes to the gym, he told me that, when he was younger, he had tried to get into the Italian police force. He passed all the exams but was rejected after an interview with the psychologist, who said that Macrinus was naturally violent and warned that this could be dangerous. Macrinus, furious at the rejection, yelled at the psychologist: "You think I'm crazy? You're right, I'm mad! I'm mad! I'm mad!" As he relates this, his face takes on an aggressive expression and he raises his voice, as if reliving that tense moment.

Since I've never observed Macrinus outside the gym, I don't know if his aggression has ever turned into violence. According to Randall Collins, many aggressive people never hit anyone because they can't overcome the emotional barrier of the fear of inflicting harm.[1] Yet when Macrinus speaks of politics, he is always full of contempt for black people.

Here is what he tells me one summer day on the deck of the gym swimming pool, both of us wearing trunks.

This account is useful for three reasons. First of all, Macrinus expresses the desire to die in war and echoes Sacrifice's admiration for the figure of the soldier. Second, he makes it very obvious that he despises the culture of peace, a trait typical of Sacrifice militants and sympathizers. Third, he helps us understand that the social group today's Fascists hate most isn't Jews, as it was in the past, but Muslims.

"I'm not a racist. Racism doesn't exist. Only history exists. What does history say? History says that niggers are shit. Pure shit. When I say that niggers are shit, I mean that they have shit inside, they have shit in their hearts, souls, and minds. Niggers are the most obscene race in the world because they kill each other ruthlessly. If you know the history of Africa you know this. The niggers slaughter each other, they massacre each other. Hitler knew this, and this is why he didn't want the German race to be contaminated by them, because the problem isn't their skin but their souls."

Some days later, while a big soccer match was in progress, I decided to sit next to Macrinus in a comfortable leather armchair in front of the gym television set. The first half was over and we were watching an ad for Tiziano Ferro, one of Italy's most famous pop singers, who has openly declared his homosexuality.

As soon as Macrinus sees Ferro's face, he becomes angry and says: "Fucking faggot. That disgusting piece of shit. I'd burn that faggot alive. He's ruined my day."

After letting Macrinus finish expressing his thoughts, I start a conversation by pretending I didn't know that Ferro was gay.

Tiziano Ferro is a faggot? Really? I didn't know.

"You bet your ass he's a fucking faggot! He said so in an interview on TV."

The world is changing . . .

"You can bet on it. The world is becoming a shithole because of these people."

The faggots?

"The faggots, the faggots."

What do you hate most about faggots? What is it that pisses you off most?

"What I hate most is that the world was once dominated by soldiers. Now it's dominated by faggots. Once men lived and died as heroes, in war. Today we're condemned to live like maggots, without honor. Television fucks us up every day. What do we teach our young people? To fuck around! When war breaks out, we'll be crushed. We teach our young the culture of peace while the Muslims learn to make war, and they'll come to take everything we have. But it's better this way. It's better if a war breaks out with the immigrants so I can die with honor. Better to die fighting with a gun in your hand than to die slowly in this society ruled by faggots!"

Like Spartacus, the Breivik admirer we met in the previous chapter, Macrinus also hopes for a war to break out in Italy against the immigrants so he can die like a soldier. It's obvious that Macrinus has taken to heart the military values promoted in the books by Codreanu and Legrelle, but it's important to stress that the typical Sacrifice militant doesn't express himself like this because, as we'll see later on, he has been taught what he can say in public and how he must say it.

I met very few Fascists who expressed themselves like Macrinus. Generally, those who do are Sacrifice sympathizers rather than militants. Macrinus is an exception, and he seems aware of this when he says: "I was a Sacrifice militant but now I've distanced myself from the group because it's become too moderate. Once I was a militant, now I'm a sympathizer. If I had to choose between Nazism and Fascism, I'd take Nazism. We Italians have a tendency to moderate everything, even Fascism."

Nonetheless, Macrinus helps us to understand that one of the aspects of bourgeois society that Sacrifice militants hate most is the peace culture.

The Construction of the Parallel World

To escape from bourgeois society, the Sacrifice comrades are trying to build a social reality in which they can demonstrate that they are courageous and that they merit honor through sacrifice, loyalty to the group, and obedience to the leaders' orders.

This symbolic and cultural mission—what I call construction of the parallel world—is achieved in three ways.

The first is through sport. One way to build the parallel world is to organize a "war." This is the purpose of the mixed martial arts contests organized by Sacrifice, in which athletes from all over Europe participate. Enclosed in an iron cage surrounded by hundreds of yelling spectators, the contestants fight each other without foot protection and with minimal protection for their hands, as the gladiators did in the Colosseum when Rome ruled the world. Mixed martial arts is the most violent sport in the world. You're allowed to use elbow and knee strikes. The combatants are naked except for shorts, because when your face is hit, the blood running down your body must be clearly visible. Clothes would absorb the blood and make it hard for the spectators to see.

The second way of building the parallel world consists of creating a climate of continual tension with far-left groups. While thousands stroll light-heartedly past the glittering shop windows in Lenintown and Mussolinia, dozens of other people are engaged in a constant effort to re-create the same symbolic and emotional climate that existed between 1919 and 1925, when Italy was a battlefield on which Fascists and communists fought each other.

The third way is through brawling. Although many people believe that barroom brawls are caused by irrational behavior and have nothing to do with Fascist culture, it's precisely the brawls that reveal a more complicated interaction. They are steeped in symbolism. Street violence enables those involved to apply Codreanu's rules very effectively. To understand the cultural significance of street brawls, we can observe what happens after the fighting has ended. Brawls manage to create a parallel world that can last months or years. After clashes, the comrades enter a daily reality based on values of honor, courage, sacrifice, group loyalty, and submission to the leader.

In the remainder of this chapter I investigate each of these three pillars that support the parallel world.

Let's begin with the ideological use of sport.

Building the Parallel World through Sports

Thanks to Sacrifice, I was able to attend a mixed martial arts event for the first time in my life. When the Sacrifice national leaders announced it, I was in the Mussolinia branch, where I was putting milk, pasta, and canned food into bags to distribute to the needy.

Marcus told me that the Mussolinia and Lenintown comrades were organizing a trip to another town to attend the tournament. I immediately said I would go too. Unfortunately, when the day arrived, because of an engagement connected with my teaching job, I was already in the town where the contest would take place, so I missed the opportunity to travel with the comrades. I always did everything I could to travel with them. Being enclosed in a car with a group of people for many hours enables you to learn a great deal about how they interact.

I arrived punctually at the arena, but the fights didn't start until two hours after the time indicated on the flyers.

This was a great opportunity for me. In the hours before the fighting began, I was able to observe hundreds of details. It was a unique chance to immerse myself in the environment. I listened to the conversation of dozens of comrades and took note of how they interacted. I observed tattoos, counted the number of women present, studied the physical characteristics of the arena, the flags, the Mussolini slogans on the walls, and many other details. I was also able to chat with dozens of Sacrifice militants whom I had never met before.

The event had attracted comrades from all over Italy. There were even some Nazi militants from France, Britain, Poland, Russia, the Czech Republic, Belgium, Romania, and Greece.

You could immediately tell the difference between the Italians and the foreigners by their tattoos. The Italians were covered in Fascist symbols, while the others had Nazi and Hitler tattoos. Hitler is much more popular than Mussolini outside Italy. I did not see a single foreign militant with a Fascist symbol in the arena that day.

I can't give a detailed description of the arena because that would make the place recognizable, but I can describe its symbols and the cultural universe.

What first attracted my attention were the words written on a large banner. It was a quotation from Mussolini saying that Fascism is an "idea," a phrase that Cornelia, Sacrifice's only female militant, had brought to my attention. While I was at the arena, I never took out my notebook. To tell the truth, I hadn't even brought it with me for fear of being noticed, or even perhaps losing it in a place where only Fascist and Nazi militants were present. Pretending to speak on the phone, I recorded my comments and descriptions of what I observed.

I noticed that the Mussolini quotation was longer than the phrase Cornelia had mentioned, although she had conveyed the essence of its message. It's true that Mussolini had described Fascism as an idea.

These are the words that were written on the great banner at the entrance to the arena: "The boldest, most original, and most Mediterranean and European of ideas."

In fact, the original phrase is even longer, but if the Sacrifice militants had quoted it in its entirety, they would have risked arrest as apologists for Fascism.

This is the complete quotation: "The world, even after my death, will still need the idea that it [Fascism] has been and will again be the boldest, the most original, and the most Mediterranean and European of ideas. History will prove me right."

I leave the courtyard behind me and enter the building, where I see the cage inside which the fights will take place. From a distance it's impossible to tell if the net is rubber or metal. I go over to touch it and discover it's iron. I imagine that if I were thrown against such a net, I'd hurt myself. I take a photo of the cage and inspect the banners on the walls in the hope of understanding more about the relationship between this combat sport and the world of Sacrifice.

I take a seat as near as possible to the cage. The bleachers consist of wooden benches with seating for some 150 spectators. There are already at least two hundred comrades chatting and drinking beer while others are still arriving. I decide to sit in the second row. According to Bronislaw Malinowski, ethnography is first of all description,[2] and this location seems to be the best for carrying out my work. In the first row I would be able to observe the combatants but not the spectators; in the second I can observe both. I need to understand how the spectators will settle around the cage, what they will chant, and what they will say about the contestants.

Two young men aged around twenty sit beside me, and I immediately engage them in conversation. Priam and Patroclus, two Sacrifice sympathizers, tell me that they love mixed martial arts. They've been buying tickets for years to attend this Sacrifice event.

I introduce myself as Alessandro Orsini, professor of sociology from Rome University writing a book on Sacrifice. Priam, the young man sitting beside me, smiles at me and tells me he's a student at my university. From this moment on he's very polite and respectful to me, and I decide to ask for his help in deciphering the symbolic universe I see before me, and to tell me about his personal perceptions.

First of all, I ask him to explain the combat rules. "The regulations," he says, "allow you to hit your adversary on any part of the body. The only illegal blows are eye gouging, head butting, groin strikes, and biting." It is also forbidden to hold on to the metal cage for any reason.

The matches take place in a cage around six feet in height, open at the top, with only one entrance. The professional tournaments consist of three five-minute rounds. The nonprofessional ones consist of three three-minute rounds. There is a one-minute break between one round and the next.

When the gate closes, the two fighters are alone with the referee. Priam explains to me that the amateurs fight first, wearing foot protection to reduce the impact of the blows, and then the professionals, whose only protection is a pair of small gloves. The MMA fighters' gloves are different from boxing gloves. Instead of covering the whole hand, they protect only the knuckles, leaving the fingers free for joint locks and chokes. "The amateurs serve to warm up the spectators. The professionals kill each other. The best come from Russia."

It's now 8:30 in the evening, and the match should have started long ago. Marcianus, one of the organizers, enters the iron cage, apologizes for the delay, and welcomes the crowd, while a woman beside him translates into English. Marcianus explains that the sporting event has an interesting political dimension: "The fighters are all European. We're all Europeans! With this event I want to remind you that we all belong to the same family." He repeats this concept more than once.

I ask Priam to explain why Sacrifice decided to allow only European fighters to take part in the tournament:

What does he mean when he says that the fighters are all European?

"They're all European in the sense that they're all white."

In what way are they all white?

"It means that there are no blacks." Patroclus, sitting beside Priam, laughs.

So it's a racial issue?

"Racial?" Priam seems embarrassed by my question.

Yes, racial. Is it a racial issue?

"No, I don't think it's a racial issue . . ."

Priam is visibly embarrassed and doesn't want to answer my question. This often happens when someone fears he or she is going to be judged. I call this phenomenon the "professor effect." Priam is talking to a professor from his university and is probably worried I'll judge him.

Patroclus, Priam's friend, takes over: "The Sacrifice leaders don't want blacks in Italy, so as you can imagine, they want them even less in the sports events they organize so carefully!"

I know that black fighters are very strong . . . I leave the rest of the sentence in the air.

"This event isn't just a sports competition. It's a way to remember that the European race has always been a warrior race. For thousands of years, Europe was a land of warriors who fought to defend their territory. These are European warriors, and Europeans are white."

Patroclus continues his explanation, repeating the Islamic invasion theory we have already seen in the letter that Dominique Venner wrote opposing the construction of a mosque in Rome. He says he's scared that Muslim immigrants could corrupt the Western race.

I understand, but aren't you describing a kind of racism? In the end, the fighters are admitted to the tournament according to the color of their skin. No?

"The issue isn't the color of the skin. The issue is the soul. Those who come from Africa have a different history, a different culture, a different soul. If you mix up all these traditions, the European with the African and the Chinese, the result is a different tradition that isn't either African or European or Chinese."

I respect your ideas, but many people think that your way of reasoning is a form of racism.

"I'm not bothered about what people think. Anyway, I don't have any problems with the word 'racism.' I just want to make it clear that mine is a spiritual racism, not a biological racism."

It's still a form of racism.

"Yes, but spiritual racism."

What is spiritual racism?

"It's what I've already explained. Every race has a different culture, a different spirit. The spirit is a way of feeling. It's not a way of thinking."

It's not just a group of athletes who are entering the cage. It's an entire political culture.

Sitting in the front row, a few inches from the cage, there's a woman with two children, a girl of around five and a boy of three.

I turn to Priam in amazement.

Do you see that! There, two young children! What on earth?

"Yes, I saw them too." Priam smiles.

It's incredible! If someone were to report them to the police, that woman would have serious problems!

"Perhaps the children's father is fighting. That must be why they're here."

If you think about it, in Sparta children were taught to fight from an early age.

"Exactly, and not only in Sparta, but also in Rome and in all the warrior civilizations. The best way to learn to do something is to watch others do it."

The gate opens, and the first match starts under the eyes of the two children. The amateurs hit each other ferociously, but the protection they wear means that no blood can be seen.

The amateur contests end and the professionals make their entrance.

The formidable Russian fighters are standing in front of me.

Some of them are thin; others have muscular physiques. All of them are covered in swastika tattoos.

A German fighter, who looks like a pleasant guy with his neatly combed hair and no bulging muscles on display, enters the cage first. I look at him, thinking he won't survive for more than twenty seconds. Priam is more explicit: "That German guy's crazy! What does he think he's doing with that body? The Russian will kill him in no time."

The Russian is a little shorter than the German, but he has enormous muscles and a furious expression on his face. What impresses most are his neck muscles. Priam comments: "Did you see that neck? He's like a bull!"

The spectators are all rooting for the Russian, while the German seems to have no fans. I feel sorry for the guy. My stomach tightens as I imagine the painful end awaiting him. I want to open the gate and let him out.

I ask myself, *Why is he doing it?*

Then I remember what I read in Degrelle about how courage produces honor. Competing against a stronger opponent knowing that you'll lose is the greatest honor for a fighter.

The referee starts the match, and the Russian rushes at the German, raining blows on his face and head. After four seconds I realize that none of the Russian's blows are actually hitting the German, who, driven by his opponent's momentum, steps back against the iron net. The Russian continues to rain down blows with great ferocity, but the German dodges and avoids them all with rapid movements of his torso and hips.

The German thinks, reflects, controls his breathing. All his movements are perfectly executed and he doesn't waste energy.

Then an amazing thing happens.

With the elegance of a ballet dancer, the German leaps into the air and, while in flight, stretches his arms and legs toward his adversary, wrapping them around him like a gigantic octopus engulfing his victim with a thousand tentacles. The Russian is on the floor, paralyzed, his drawn face expressing immense anger. I get to my feet, climb over the people in front of me, and press my face up to the net. The Russian's eyes are a few inches from mine.

He looks bewildered.

It must be psychologically devastating to launch yourself against someone to destroy him and then after a few seconds find yourself facedown on the mat, your body immobilized and your ass in the air. The German is completely calm, his breathing normal. He grasps the Russian's right arm and, while he clasps the Russian's neck between his legs, slightly arches his back on the mat and tenses his lumbar muscles. Then with a thrust of his back he springs up, bringing his adversary's arm under his leg.

And he starts to break it.

The spectators are all dumbfounded at what is happening. Nobody speaks.

They are all astonished because none of them ever imagined that the German, with his physique, was such an extraordinary athlete from the point of view of technique.

Priam: "The Russian is fucked. The German is breaking his arm. He's got to surrender."

But the Russian doesn't surrender.

With all his strength and a world of desperation, he starts slowly slithering and freeing his arm from that terrible grip.

The German's hand is sweaty and he loses his grasp.

The fighters separate, get back on their feet, and, as they look each other in the eye, recover energy and focus.

The spectators clap loudly.

The Russian uses the same technique, rushing at the German with the momentum of a cavalry charge: kicks, punches, elbow strikes.

The German dodges the blows, twists his hip, and launches himself at the Russian, who crashes down on the mat again with the German's feet around his neck.

The German has to win the match very soon because he doesn't have the same stamina as the Russian. As the minutes pass, his strength diminishes.

I started practicing karate when I was nine. I took part in many competitions and was a black belt in two styles of karate, Shotokan and Shito-Ryu. I then took up full contact and boxing at the amateur level but without ever participating in any kind of competition. I'm able to judge a fight from the point of view of technique, and I realize that the German must be an expert in jujitsu, the martial art practiced by the Japanese samurai from which both judo and karate are derived.

When the second round begins, the German is clearly tired while the Russian is still full of energy. The same pattern is repeated. The Russian throws himself against the German, who tries to immobilize his adversary's arms, but this time a punch from the Russian hits the mark and the German loses his balance and falls. The Russian sits on the German's back, puts his arm around his neck, and starts to strangle him. After a few seconds of desperate struggle, the German bangs his hand on the ground as a sign of surrender. The referee stops the fight.

The German has lost.

His technique was no match for the Russian's strength.

When the winner is proclaimed, I turn to Priam.

He lost, but the German was astonishing.

"I agree. The German showed great courage in entering the cage. The Russian is famous because he's massacred many adversaries in the past. The German has lost, but the honor is his."

The honor? The Russian beat the German into submission. Isn't it a humiliation to lose like this? The referee said that the German lost by submission. He used these exact words: victory by submission.

"Hang on, I'll explain. To lose by submission is the technical expression that is always used in mixed martial arts when someone wins by strangling. Submission means strangling. Many mixed martial arts fights end like this. The losers beat their hands on the mat twice when they're in a submission hold, which is a mortal technique. The German fought to the death, even though he didn't die. He lost with honor because he fought against a much stronger opponent."

After two very violent matches, both ending with a knockout, two new competitors enter the cage: a Russian and a twenty-seven-year-old Sacrifice militant, Leopoldus.

This was the match that helped me understand the relationship between the political culture of revolutionary Fascism and the pedagogical use of the mixed martial arts events that Sacrifice organizes.

Let's follow it.

The referee starts the match, and the spectators, at least three hundred of them, are all rooting for the Sacrifice comrade. The Russian uses the same technique as his compatriot who beat the German. He hurls himself at the Italian, who takes one, two, three, four blows to the face. (I counted them later when viewing the video at home.) Punch after punch, the Italian is forced backward until his shoulders hit the iron net. The Russian kicks him in the knee; the Italian bends his left leg, grabs his opponent, and throws him onto the mat. For about a minute, Leopoldus succeeds in controlling the Russian's fury, but the Russian manages to put his elbow in Leopoldus's eye, and blood starts flowing from a large cut on his forehead. The Italian is now almost defenseless, with blood streaming into his eyes. The Russian sits on his opponent's chest, blocks both his arms with his knees, and starts smashing his face with both hands. The referee realizes that the Italian is no longer able to protect himself and stops the fight.

Leopoldus wasn't a well-trained fighter. He had no combat discipline to fall back on. He didn't know how to dodge or parry a blow, he didn't know how to strike. Leopoldus's face is covered with blood, and I ask myself how such a poor athlete could possibly challenge an opponent who is so much stronger.

The Russians are excited. They jump up and down, chanting.

Priam says: "Fuck me! Did you see how often Leopoldus was hit? What an asshole! Leopoldus is our comrade, he's a Sacrifice militant. This humiliates our whole movement."

There are two nurses and a doctor outside the cage, ready to go in if something serious occurs.

They enter the cage and bend over Leopoldus, who is still lying on the mat in pain.

Utter defeat.

At this point, the event presenter enters the cage, takes the microphone, and speaks with emotion in his voice: "Comrades, silence, please! Could I have a minute of silence? I think that we have watched an event that deserves all our respect. Leopoldus only started practicing this sport six months ago. We all told him not to take part in the tournament, but he wouldn't listen to us. I'm asking you to applaud Leopoldus for the courage he's shown and for the example he gave us. Honor to Leopoldus!"

The spectators listen in silence and then explode into long applause.

Leopoldus, who in the meantime has gotten up with the aid of a young nurse, salutes with his right hand and bends over slightly to thank the spectators, while the nurse holds a white towel to his face.

As two other fighters enter the cage, I see Leonidas standing among the crowd on the opposite side across from me. I get up and go over to him. Leonidas has a large glass of beer in his hand and gives me a friendly welcome: "Hi!" Then he turns to a comrade I've never met before and tells him proudly, "This is a professor of sociology who is writing a book about me!"

I ask Leonidas what he thinks about this sport. Leonidas, who is a professional boxer, gives me an interesting answer that can be summarized as: the sport is disgusting, but it transmits the right values.

Leonidas, many of these fighters are useless at punching. I think that if one of them ever came up against a professional boxer, he'd lose in a matter of minutes.

"You're wrong. The mixed martial arts fighters aren't good at boxing, that's true, but they have many more opportunities for striking than a boxer does. They can use kicks, elbows, knees, joint locks, chokes. While I was fighting in the Lenintown bar, a guy managed to get his arm around my neck and he was trying to strangle me."

Really? I didn't know. He was going to strangle you?

"Yes, yes. They stopped him in time. I couldn't breathe; I was about to pass out."

Do you like mixed martial arts?

"It makes me sick."

In what way?

"It makes me sick. I hate the sport. They're like animals. They get locked up in this cage . . . Like animals. But it's not the sport that matters. What matters is the way in which you fight and the values you show you possess as a man."

What are these values?

"They're the values of warriors."

While Leonidas talks, I look at the posters advertising the competition. Above the heads of some aggressive-looking mixed martial arts fighters is written "Warrior stock!"

It doesn't say "warrior race"; it says "stock."

I provoke Leonidas, using the "interviewing by comment" technique to learn more about his reasoning.

I figure the warrior ethos of the West will never die. It'll always exist. No one will be able to eradicate it.

"The warrior ethos has been dead for a long time. Multiculturalism is destroying our values. It's destroying our civilization. Our task is to keep a small flame alive. What is important is to keep a flame lit, even if it's only a small one. You need a flame to start a fire. In the cage, we're fighting against a way of being. We're fighting against a certain type of society that is afraid to fight to defend itself."

Leonidas and I remain together for the rest of the event.

The next day, as I was eating lunch, I decided to text him using WhatsApp. I find that people pay more attention to what they say when they're asked to describe their values in writing.

Not long before my expulsion from the militia, I asked Marcus to write down what aspects of the Fascist society he liked the most. This was his answer: "You want something in writing? No way. We can talk as much as you want, but I'm not writing anything down. We're always very careful about what we write and we always will be as long as the law forbidding the reestablishment of the Fascist Party exists. One of our militants was taken to court because a policeman saw him making a Fascist salute with his arm held out during a march. Can you imagine what would happen if we wrote down what we think of Hitler and Mussolini? They'd arrest me immediately!"

The comrades don't want to leave documents because they're frightened of being arrested, but there's also another reason why anything in writing by the comrades is particularly interesting. When writing something for a professor who is studying his movement, the Sacrifice militant tries to imagine his reader's reaction, and this forces him to pay more attention to what he's writing. When a militant agrees to communicate his values in writing, he becomes more aware of the difference between the dominant values of society and those of his group. George Herbert Mead has helped us understand the function that writing has in the perception of the self.[3]

When they act in public, individuals work out a series of strategies for influencing spectators' judgment.[4] The Sacrifice militants are no different from the vacationing Englishman mentioned by Erving Goffman in his book *The Presentation of Self in Everyday Life*, who wanders around the beach with a Spanish translation of Homer hoping to project a positive image of himself.[5]

I wanted Leonidas to write something about what Sacrifice thinks of the pedagogical aspect of mixed martial arts tournaments, so I sent him this text:

I heard that Sacrifice has recorded all the fights we saw yesterday. Do you think they'll send you the video when it's done?

"I hope not!"

Why do you hope not?

"I told you. I hate that sport. They're like animals. They lock them in an iron cage and they kill each other like beasts."

I want to write a chapter of the book on these fights. You can help me clear up a lot of things. Can I ask you a question?

"Sure"

Can you explain better what you told me yesterday?

"What?"

You told me that those fights were against the bourgeoisie. I didn't really get what you meant.

"Those fights are not against the bourgeoisie. They are against the bourgeois man, against a type of man who's afraid of everything, who doesn't know how to fight anymore, who is frightened of risking his life to defend our civilization."

Can I say that the fights serve to teach young people violence?

"We're not saying that the young have to be violent. We're saying that they have to get used to seeing violence because they always need to be ready to go to war. There's always someone who wants to attack us, and sooner or later, even Italy will be attacked. Our comrades must know how to defend themselves. If someone hits me, I hit back. Never turn the other cheek. Never! This applies as much to the entire nation as it does to every single comrade. Italy must never turn the other cheek."

I noticed something.

"What?"

There were no black fighters. They were all white.

"It's obvious. We don't want immigrants in Italy. Immigrants have the right to exist, but they must remain in their own place. None of us would want a black at one of our events. It wouldn't make sense. We only want Italians in Italy."

But yours is a sporting event, not a political event. Am I right?

"No, you've got it wrong. I'll explain everything on Saturday in Lenintown. Come a little before the political meeting so we can have a chat. We have to collect money to buy food for poor Italians. I'm with my lawyer now because of the problems I told you about. I'll see you in Lenintown."

The Problem of the Communists

I arrive in the Lenintown HQ a half hour early, as I always do.

Leonidas arrives on time, and the meeting starts. He doesn't mention what he was doing with his lawyer and I don't ask him about it. We arrange the chairs in a circle in the meeting room and sit down.

Leonidas says that he has been caught up in some personal issues lately that have prevented him from taking an active part in the militia and that now it's time to plan some initiatives.

Leonidas attributes great importance to the preparation of large banners to put up at night in protest against the Lenintown mayor and town council. He assigns us the task of preparing a banner to protest spending cuts for the Lenintown hospital. Leonidas says that the Fascist state always helped Italians with financial problems and that we should fight for hospitals to receive more funds from the state.

I take a can of black spray paint and offer to write on the white banner that Leonidas has unrolled on the floor. He wants it to say "Shame on you, Mayor. More money for hospitals!" The banner is signed "Sacrifice, Lenintown militia."

Leonidas tells me that Mithridates is the expert in making banners: "It seems easy to write on them, but it isn't. I often get it wrong." I immediately pass the spray can to Mithridates, who does a great job. Then Leonidas tells me that, once we finish, I can take photos of the banner, but he points out that I will need a camera with flash. The banner will be put up in front of the hospital at night so the cops won't see them doing it. You have to climb over a large gate and scale a high wall. The photos will be published the next day on the militia's Facebook page.

Once the job is finished, with the room now smelling of paint, Leonidas explains that we have to try to raise the level of confrontation with the Lenintown far-left movements. During political meetings, I never allowed myself to interrupt with questions. I realized that the first rule was to show respect toward the leader. Leonidas was Leonidas and I was a guest. When the meeting ended, we moved to the room where there was a cooler with beer. As soon as the discussion turned from politics to women, I told Leonidas that I would be happy to help in hanging the banner at the hospital entrance. Leonidas put a hand on my shoulder to express his approval, and I asked him:

Are we going into action at night because we don't want the police to see us or to avoid encounters with the communists?

"The police are the problem, especially right now. The Lenintown police chief has set up a special team just to keep an eye on us. I have good relations with these cops. They've told me that they have nothing personal against me, but that we mustn't create problems or otherwise their chief will start harassing them and they'll be forced to harass us in turn. If they see us climbing over the hospital wall, it's obvious they'll arrest us."

And the communists? I want to know if I have to worry about the communists.

"The communists are dickheads. You don't have to worry about them. They're cowards, they're scum. They're scared to fight. The only problem is, if they see us, they could call the cops. They're losers, that's how they fight us."

But the communists also put up banners at night. Why don't you call the cops? You could do as they do.

"Impossible. Calling the cops is against our code of honor."

What does your code of honor say?

"For us it's dishonorable to let other people defend us. We have the moral duty to defend ourselves alone. Always. We never ask the police for help, not even if a communist arrives with a gun. If a communist threatens us, we threaten him. If a communist provokes us, we react. If he tries to strike us, we'll destroy him. We never turn the other cheek. When I inaugurated the Lenintown HQ, the communists threw shit against our door to welcome us, but none of us went to the cops."

During the meeting you said that the confrontation with the communists will soon become more bitter. What do you mean?

"I've got nothing against the communists. For me the communists don't exist; they're just scum. They exist to give us bullshit, but we couldn't give a fuck about them. Over the coming weeks we're organizing a series of initiatives, and these will certainly lead the communists to attack us. That's how they think. If they try something, we leave them alone and don't react. But they don't think we have a right to exist. Whatever we do, the communists are a pain in the ass, with public complaints and everything else. Their problem is that we exist. We annoy them just by breathing."

Mithridates interrupts, saying that he likes the idea of fighting the communists. According to Mithridates, it's true that the communists exist to give Sacrifice a hard time, but he wants to make it clear that he likes the idea of being able to beat them up: "I agree when you say that the communists have fuck all to do and they exist to be a pain in the ass for us, but it's always great to give a communist a couple of kicks in the butt!"

Leonidas continues the speech he had started during the political meeting, but it's difficult to summarize because he touched on a lot of different subjects, often losing the thread.

In short, he told the comrades to be careful because the communists are part of social reality and this has to be accepted because you can't change the world with just your thoughts: "The communists have been here for many years and they're fighting to hold on to their territory. When we inaugurated our branch, they welcomed us with shit, and you all remember the event they organized in the Lenintown center to stop us from opening. Even though they're just a bunch of losers, the communists are dangerous because they're looking for an excuse to ask the mayor to close our branch down."

When the night arrived on which we were to put up our banner, I wasn't called and I didn't take part. As I explain in the preface, in both the Lenintown and the Mussolinia militias there were some comrades who were friendly toward me. But other militants were against having me in the group because they thought I might reveal information that should remain secret.

In Mussolinia, the comrade who was most against my presence was Lentulus. In Lenintown, it was Camillus.

Marcus told me more than once that Lentulus liked me and insisted that his concern was only of a "political" nature. One afternoon, while we were taking one of our long walks in downtown Mussolinia, I asked Marcus if he could get me included in the trip to the mountains that the Sacrifice national leaders were organizing, as they do every year, for comrades from all the Italian militias.

I was extremely interested in taking part. I thought it would be a great chance to learn more about Sacrifice's cultural universe. Walking in the mountains for a week; sharing food with the comrades; participating in their "spiritual retreat"; listening to their conversations; observing their way of interacting. It would have been an extraordinary opportunity.

Marcus told me he would do all he could, but he was very doubtful that I would be allowed to come. According to him, Lentulus wouldn't agree to it.

This is what he said: "Lentulus says that you're an honest and respectful guy. He doesn't have anything against you personally. Lentulus and I are close friends, but we have a rather different vision of the militia. I think that we should open up to the outside world, and as I've always told you, I figure that a book written by a specialist like you would be a unique opportunity to show that we've got nothing to hide. But Lentulus has a more restricted vision."

As I've already explained, Marcus was in Mussolinia on vacation and was very happy to pass his time walking and chatting. His life as a university student wasn't easy. He was away from Mussolinia for many months of the year, and besides studying in one of the top Italian universities, he was specializing in a very demanding subject. We strolled around for hours, and I could ask him anything I liked.

Marcus respected me.

In the end, the banner was put up in front of the hospital, and the young communists reacted by publishing a series of comments on their group's Facebook page.

Without naming Sacrifice, one of the far-left groups most vocally opposed to Sacrifice wrote: "The Lenintown citizens who pass in front of the hospital will ask themselves, why doesn't the mayor intervene? Because he's pretending he can't see it? How long do we have to put up with the presence of this ignominy in our town?"

4

THE WAR AGAINST
THE FAR-LEFT EXTREMISTS

At the end of the last chapter, I started to describe the way in which young communists and young Fascists interact, creating a small social universe based on confrontation. This conflict gives the Sacrifice comrades the impression that they are living in a world at war, as in Italy in 1919–1922, the period when revolutionary Fascism came into being.

This parallel world can be successfully constructed only if four basic conditions, which I call "pillars," exist. First of all, you have to have an ideology that teaches you to interpret reality according to the cognitive schemata mapped out by the Fascists during the time of Hitler and Mussolini. Fascism—as the Sacrifice militants tell us—is primarily a way of looking at the world. Referring to Max Weber, I would say that Fascism is an "interpretative procedure."[1]

Second, there have to be two collective movements prepared to fight each other, each labeling the other as absolute evil.

Third, there has to be an ongoing conflict between these groups and the police, with the result that the Fascist militia becomes the only physical and psychological bulwark against the external world, which is seen as a battlefield filled with dangers.

Finally, there has to be a network of Fascist and communist movements which feeds the conviction that the battle is being fought throughout Italy and not only locally.

Like society as a whole, the parallel world "consists in the interaction of individual human beings. The actions of its members are shaped largely by the actual and anticipated responses of others."[2] In the end, the parallel world is what Georg Simmel calls a "system of interactions."[3]

So far, we have observed only the Mussolinia and Lenintown militias. The time has come to study the role of the far-left movements.

In the Communist Parallel World

When Leonidas announced that Sacrifice would be opening a new branch in Lenintown, the far-left movements organized a demonstration in the town center at which I was present as an observer. The most active participants in the march were a group of anarchists and some young people from W La Rivoluzione, a Marxist-Leninist political party that, in the past, had had representatives in both the Italian Chamber of Deputies and the Senate. They were distributing leaflets denouncing Sacrifice, playing drums, and blowing whistles. A man with a W La Rivoluzione T-shirt and a bullhorn was yelling: "Get the Fascists out of Lenintown! Get the Fascists out of Lenintown!"

While I was watching the march, a woman of around twenty stopped to hand me one of the leaflets she was carrying, and I grasped the chance to ask her something, hoping to start a conversation.

Hi, I'm just visiting. I don't really understand what you're demonstrating for. Can you enlighten me?

"We're demonstrating against the opening of a Sacrifice branch in Lenintown. Have you heard of this movement?"

What is it?

"It's a Fascist movement. Their militants are criminals. They beat up people, use violence everywhere. A lot of them are in prison. They've got a group in Mussolinia, where one of their militants shoved a broken bottle into a guy's face during a local celebration. It happened in downtown Mussolinia. The victim lost an eye, and the Sacrifice militant has been arrested."

A Fascist movement in Lenintown? I look amazed.

"Yeah. They've arrived here too."

Are they to be taken seriously? Is there a danger that Fascism could return?

"A danger? These Fascists are already active all over Italy. Once they've opened their branch in Lenintown, they'll do the same things they've already done in Mussolinia and in many other towns. We've asked the mayor to stop them. We want to make the citizens aware. If you're interested, come and see us. We've prepared a dossier on Sacrifice violence. I can give you a copy. This is our website. You can also find a lot of information on Sacrifice violence online. You just have to Google 'Sacrifice violence in Mussolinia.'"

The woman leaves to follow the march. I go over to a guy and a girl. They're also wearing W La Rivoluzione T-shirts and handing out leaflets. I address the boy, who can't be much older than eighteen:

Hi, can you tell me what's happening?

"We're protesting against the opening of a Sacrifice branch in Lenintown."

What's Sacrifice?

"It's a Fascist movement. Of all the Fascists, they're the worst, the most violent. They call themselves *squadristi*. They're brutal thugs."

Have they beaten up anyone?

"Anyone? They've beaten up lots of people! In Mussolinia they attacked a guy for no reason at all. One of them took a bottle and smashed it into his face as he was walking with a group of friends. He lost an eye."

Who lost an eye?

"The guy whose face was smashed up. It was a Sacrifice Fascist who did it, or rather Fascists, because these wimps only look for fights in a group. You can find it on the Internet. There's lots of articles about it online. It happened in Mussolinia."

Do you know the Sacrifice people who are opening the branch in Lenintown?

"I know their leader, who's a professional boxer. But I only know him by sight. I don't know him personally."

The fact that he's a professional boxer doesn't automatically mean that he'll attack people in the street.

After I say this, a man of around sixty who has been listening to our conversation joins in. He's wearing a T-shirt with the symbol of the Italian Communist Party, which was dissolved in 1991, and has a W La Rivoluzione flag in his hand.

"It's a broader issue. The issue isn't only the opening of a Sacrifice branch in Lenintown, which in itself is a serious matter. The problem is that Fascism is returning in a big way. They've arrived in Mussolinia, and now they want to open a branch in Lenintown, but they're also present in other towns close to Lenintown."

In what way is Fascism returning? I don't see a lot of Fascists around.

"Are you joking? Italy is full of Fascists. There's been a notable growth in Fascist movements in recent years. It's more necessary than ever now to go to schools and tell the children about Mussolini's crimes; we have to take to the streets and protest to inform the young, who have no collective memory. We have to explain to our children that the partisans' work is not over and will never be over because Fascism can always return."

The expression "the partisans' work is not over"—alluding to the anti-Fascist resistance during the Mussolini era—interests me greatly because it's one of those slogans that contribute to the construction of the parallel world.

I persist with the interviewing by comment technique:

I understand your reasons, I understand that you're here to defend the values of freedom, but the war between Fascists and partisans is over. The partisans won. Fascism won't come back. Fascism was defeated seventy years ago!

After I say this, a woman of around twenty-three interrupts: "No! No, you're wrong! Fascism isn't dead! That's the danger! The danger is people like you, who think like you do!"

With my tone of voice and facial expression I convey irritation at being accused, and I use this to provoke an emotional reaction from the woman.

People like me? Excuse me, what have I said that's wrong!?

"What's wrong? You're saying what the Fascists want to make us believe! They want us to believe that the danger is over so they can stab us in the back!

What did I say that was wrong? You said that I'm mistaken? So tell me why.

"You've got it wrong! Get real! Don't you read the papers? Have you ever read anything about Sacrifice? A friend of mine who goes to school in Mussolinia was attacked by the Sacrifice Fascists during a demonstration against racism!"

I understand, but these are isolated cases. Fascism was defeated seventy years ago.

"No! Fascism is spreading throughout Italy!" The woman raises her voice, shakes her fists, and frowns. "The Sacrifice militants will also beat up the Lenintown kids! They're Fascists; they stop people from talking. They say they're *squadristi*. You get that? That's what they call themselves! It's not us who say it, it's them who are proud to say they're Fascist action squads!

Who are the squadristi?

The sixty-year-old man with the Italian Communist Party T-shirt joins in again:

"They're the Fascists who killed Giacomo Matteotti and who helped Mussolini gain power by attacking the Socialists. How do you think Mussolini came to power? By killing people!"

He walks off without a backward glance.

I move on and continue to question other young people participating in the march. By the end of the demonstration, I must have spoken to fourteen participants, who all repeat the same ideas. They're convinced that Fascism is returning in Italy and that the opening of a militia branch in Lenintown must be stopped.

These demonstrators use military language: "It'll be war"; "we have to resist as the partisans did"; "we have to control the territory"; "we have to fight against Fascism"; "they're Fascist scum and we mustn't let them out of the sewers."

The "Big World" and the "Little World"

During the event, I talked to some militants of W La Rivoluzione, a Marxist-Leninist party. I didn't manage to talk to the anarchists, however. I was particularly interested in them since they carry out most of the acts of sabotage against the Fascists, as I had learned from talking to some police officers occupied with youth movements.

In the construction of the parallel world, the young anarchists and the young W La Rivoluzione members play different roles. The W La Rivoluzione militants avoid any type of behavior that could create problems with the police. They want everyone to see that they oppose Sacrifice in the hope of attracting political support. Since W La Rivoluzione puts up candidates for election, young communists want to publicize their initiatives. Their reasoning is simple and can be summarized as "more visibility, more votes."

In addition, the young people of W La Rivoluzione have a strong sense of hierarchies within the party. Everything they do has first to be approved by the older people who are their leaders. The young W La Rivoluzione members have an office downtown, with heating in the winter and air-conditioning in the summer. They have a desk, a computer with Internet connection, a photocopier, a telephone, and some financing. All this is paid for by the party leaders, who also decide who is to head up the youth movements in Lenintown and Mussolinia. These people are privileged in comparison to their contemporaries who aren't organized and so have to finance themselves if they want to enter politics. But they pay a price for their privileges. They're young, they're full of enthusiasm and original ideas, but they can't act without the permission of older communists, who don't want problems with the police so as not to damage their image and lose votes.

They're privileged but they have little freedom.

The young anarchists are in a different position. They don't belong to any organization and have to finance themselves, but they reject any type of hierarchy and do whatever they want. They don't have money, they don't have offices, they don't have a computer, and they don't have leaders—the anarchists don't have "constituents" who are providing resources.[4] In some cases they act in groups; in others they act individually, without any organization.

A few days after the demonstration, I went looking for young anarchists. It's usually quite easy to speak to an anarchist. The communist anarchists (there are various types) have a political culture based on common ownership, free trade, and propaganda that requires them to be willing to speak to others. I have studied the anarchist world for over twenty years, and I am familiar with their cultural universe.

Once I had found the place where the younger anarchists met, I took to walking up and down the block at times when they were most likely to be on the streets. When I got closer, in order to observe their faces and their way of interacting, I pretended I was talking on my cell phone. I stopped a few yards from them and continued to talk, trying not to be noticed. On the day when I was ready to establish direct contact, I wore a blue tracksuit, sneakers, and a white T-shirt. No writing, no designer brands, no watch, and no chain around my neck. When adopting "approach strategies," the sociologist has to wear clothes that provide as little information as possible about his or her identity.

The first encounter occurred in a public park where Lenintown citizens take their dogs for a run. After asking my good friend Neo if I could take his little dog for a walk, I approached Freedom, a boy of around eighteen. We were dressed the same. He was wearing a tracksuit and sneakers and had a dog larger than mine.

Without looking at him, I said: "What a great dog! What's he called?" While I stroked his dog, I made friends with Freedom. I told him I was a sociology professor at the University of Rome, specializing in the study of political youth movements, and immediately after pointed to the anarchist symbol on his T-shirt, smiling to express my approval. I told him that, when I was sixteen, I had been impressed by something written by Errico Malatesta, a famous Italian anarchist who died in 1932. He had refused to explain his ideas for the organization of an anarchist society out of fear that he would condition future generations, restricting their freedom of choice.

Freedom asked me for the title of the book I had mentioned, and I explained that it could be bought only from La Fiaccola, the small publishing house of an anarchist cultural association in Sicily. I gave him the Internet address, www.sicilialibertaria.it. Then I took from my pocket a small book by Malatesta. I told him that I was sorry I couldn't lend it to him because it was a rare book. Freedom recognized it and said: "This book isn't rare. I know it! You can download it online!" He was right.[5] We laughed, and I realized that my embarrassment was useful in creating a closer relationship. Freedom told me that Lenintown was a bourgeois and conservative town and he was bored there. The only thing that excited him was fighting the Fascists. Then he said something I found very interesting:

"People don't realize it because they're always thinking about worthless things such as money, cars, designer clothes . . . But there's a war going on in Lenintown. The problem is that only we anti-Fascists are fighting this war. People only care about their own fucking interests. My contemporaries are all minding their own fucking business; they're not worried about Fascism. The Fascists are gaining ground thanks to the indifference of people who care only about their own crap. This is exactly what happened in Italy when Mussolini came to power."

Until then, I had heard no political militant so clearly explain the meaning of the parallel world.

Freedom helped me to understand that a "small world" existed in Lenintown made up of a few dozen anti-Fascist youths, completely unknown to the "big world" in which thousands of people were going about their daily business without realizing that a "civil war" was being waged between young Fascists and young anti-Fascists.

The World within the World

Thanks to Freedom, I gained information that enabled me to contact other young members of the anarchist "network."

Sarah, with whom I had seven encounters, is the most interesting political militant I have ever met in my career as a sociologist. She is also the person who has best described the awareness of living in a parallel world, what she calls "the world within the world." After our interviews, she offered to write a short autobiography for me to ensure that no aspect of her life had been misinterpreted.

Sarah allowed me to record three interviews for a total of three hours, and also gave me permission to publish her name and surname, but I chose not to do so because the personal information she gave could have negative effects for her both now and in the future. Many far-left and far-right young people asked me to reveal their identity without realizing that it could backfire on them when they got older. In my career as a sociologist, I've seen many young people profoundly modify their ideas in the space of a few years, often feeling very embarrassed about their earlier beliefs.

Sarah is a philosophy student who is very well educated for her age. She has achieved very high grades at one of the best Italian universities. She was twenty-three when I met her and comes from a very wealthy family. She has been arrested by the Italian police for having taken part in illegal actions, and after her release from jail—where she spent just one night—her apartment was searched twice. About a year before our meeting, she had started a de-radicalization process. Today she asserts she is no longer engaged in anarchist movements.

Recently she asked me to supervise her thesis; I had to decline because she was enrolled at a different university. When I talked with Sarah, I was always struck by her critical reasoning and her sophisticated language. Sarah has published several articles on a website, including one on the relationship between Islam and the West, and has written a long manuscript on anarchist violence.

Sarah's story is so complex and so interesting that it merits a book of its own. When she was eight, her father fell in love with a younger woman and left home. In revenge, her mother forced Sarah and her younger brother to report their father for incest and sexual violence. At the age of thirteen, Sarah experienced a great trauma, the death of her beloved parrot, which brought her to the brink of suicide.

"I wanted to kill myself," she told me, "because I was a very lonely child. I lived through the novels I read. My parrot was the only thing I loved. My life had been devastated by the fact that my brother and I had accused my father of incest. I was a girl with an immense burden of pain and I was confused. My father had always respected us, but at a certain point, I started to think that he had really sexually abused me because my mother repeated it to me constantly and told me that I had repressed the fact. When I was around fourteen, my mother started to have serious psychological problems and became violent with me. I was very unhappy, and one day I cut my wrists because I wanted to die . . . I had nothing. I had no ideals, I had no family, and I had no points of reference. I didn't believe in God; the only thing I had was the music of the band Green Day."

While her father was facing the trial that would destroy his reputation, Sarah started to perform a series of actions for which she was judged mentally ill and shut up in a psychiatric hospital between the ages of fifteen and sixteen. As soon as she arrived at the hospital, she tried to hang herself in her room and went into a coma. When she came out of the coma, she underwent therapy that she defined as "very severe." She recalled: "The doctors said that my mind had separated itself from my body. To make me return to my body, they tied my hands and feet and covered me with ice. It was extremely painful. The doctors kept me under constant control, and this made me even more desperate because I realized I couldn't try to kill myself anymore."

After she left the mental hospital, Sarah was adopted by a family she had never met before and of whom she speaks with great affection and gratitude: "Finally I had found a father and a mother who gave me the love I was looking for. They saved my life with their love."

After finding a new family, Sarah decided that her mission in life was to help the poor. She became an anarchist militant, dressed in punk style, and wanted to destroy capitalism and the bourgeoisie, which she considered the cause of all the evils in the world.

Once we had created a relationship of mutual trust, Sarah gave me the password to access the Facebook page of a group of anarchists, some of whom, Sarah said, "are those who cover their faces and fight the police during demonstrations."

Sarah sent an email to Jack, the anarchist who managed the Facebook page, and told him I would be contacting him: "He's called Alessandro Orsini, he's a sociology professor. I've given him my password for accessing our group. Alessandro will contact you using my Facebook profile to ask for a personal interview. You can trust him. He's a good guy."

Sarah told me that Jack had agreed, commenting on Sarah's email with a joke: "Cool. Let's just hope your friend isn't a cop!"

Thanks to Sarah and to the Facebook page Jack managed, I could read daily hundreds of messages that are available only to members of this group. I saw that the anarchists write on many subjects, but their basic credo is that the world is dominated by Fascists. In the cultural universe of these young people, Fascism is a very broad category. The capitalists are Fascists, the bourgeoisie is Fascist, those who eat meat are Fascists, the police are Fascists, the prime minister is a Fascist, all the members of the Italian government are Fascists.

During an interview conducted via Skype, in which we could see each other on the webcam, Sarah asserted that, after having left the anarchist group, she realized that she had been living in a "different world." This is what she told me:

"I come from a very wealthy family, but I hated the bourgeoisie and I was convinced I was fighting a war to save the world from Fascism. Everything was Fascist because I was surrounded by people who saw Fascism everywhere. My comrades convinced me that a war was in progress against the Fascists, but I also convinced others that we were at war with the Fascists. It's a chain reaction. I felt I was living under siege."

Under siege by whom?

"By the Fascists. It's not easy to explain what I experienced. Maybe this doesn't interest you . . ."

I'm very interested in what you say. Please go on.

"Thanks," she said with a smile. "When I was still part of the anarchist world, I started to realize that this world was different, a kind of world within a world. It's like living on a parallel track. On one side, there I was with my anarchist comrades, and on the other, there was a whole world going in another direction entirely. The bourgeois world, as we called it, didn't know we existed. Perhaps that's also why so many of these anarchists shatter windows and destroy cars during demonstrations. I think that we act in this way to make people notice us, because we're reacting to the frustration of living in a different world."

Have you ever smashed up a car or destroyed a shop window?

"Do you think a cop's listening in?" Sarah smiled again.

Let's hope not! Have you ever smashed up a car?

"No, no, I never did those things. Others did them . . ."

Don't worry if you don't want to answer these questions.

"Let's change the subject. My place has been searched twice, I have a court case in progress, and I'm sure I'm being watched. However, I've never smashed up cars."

The Flag in the John

The anarchists and communists are obsessed with the Sacrifice Fascists.

And the Lenintown and Mussolinia comrades?

During the time I was part of the Lenintown and Mussolinia militias, I realized that the "communist" problem was always present in the comrades' conversations. The construction of the parallel world is a symbolic undertaking that has to be kept alive daily.

Saturday was the day of the political meeting, when the most important group matters were discussed, as well as the main events in national and local politics. We had just finished organizing a trip to another town, where we were to meet up with some Sacrifice comrades who needed our help in organizing a demonstration. While I was on the balcony of the apartment with a view of a shop-filled street, Leonidas turned to three comrades and said: "Let's go. I've got something I want to do." I waited for him to return with the other comrades.

After about an hour, Leonidas came back with a large red flag. The comrades who had gone with him were smiling with looks of pride and satisfaction on their faces.

Annoyed, one of the comrades who had been waiting with me asked: "What the fuck have you been doing? Where the fuck have you been?"

With a big grin, Leonidas went into the washroom, taking a chair with him. He stood on it holding the flag.

I said:

Leonidas, do you need help?

"Yeah. Get the duct tape and give it to me."

Here you are!

When Leonidas had finished, the entire wall of the small washroom was covered by the large red flag. The comrade who had been waiting became even more annoyed: "Holy shit, guys! Look at it! Why didn't you take me with you?"

I was the only one who didn't understand, and I asked Leonidas to explain exactly what he had done. I didn't have to press him because he was proud of his feat. He took out his cell phone and showed everyone the photos documenting his achievement. For someone like me who suffers from vertigo, they were very impressive. They showed Leonidas climbing up a fifty-foot tower using only his hands and feet. Arriving at the top, he had replaced the red flag, put up there some days earlier by the militia's left-wing enemies, with the Italian flag. The tower, the property of the municipality, was on a hill, and its summit was visible from the sea and the expressway.

The left-wing militants would soon realize that the tricolor was waving in place of the communist flag.

Stepping down from the chair, Leonidas turned to look at the red flag and said: "This flag is in its rightful place in the can."

The comrades gazed at him in admiration. Then Leonidas warned that the communists would certainly retaliate and that we would have to be careful: "Comrades, watch your backs. The communists will be pissed off."

Besides contributing to the construction of the parallel world, Leonidas had also shown his courage by performing a risky undertaking for love of the militia.

He turned to a comrade and told him to publish the photos on the Lenintown militia's Facebook page "so the communists will see the tower and can see for themselves who stole their flag," but taking care not to include any photo with him in it.

Unlike the Mussolinia militia, the Lenintown cell doesn't have a computer, and the photos didn't appear until the next morning.

Danger in the Night

How would the communists react? The chance for a new confrontation came when Leonidas organized two groups of comrades to put up posters at night for Harmatus, a politician engaged in a difficult election campaign for the European Parliament.

Harmatus had asked Sacrifice to help him win votes and to put up his posters in exchange for a small contribution to the fund for financing the Lenintown militia's activities. The problem was that, although he had declared his admiration for Mussolini, Harmatus belonged to the Visigoths, a bourgeois party that had always declared it was "anti-Fascist."

The Visigoths and Sacrifice both opposed immigration and the European single currency. Otherwise their ideologies were very different.

Harmatus had made a secret agreement with the national leaders of Sacrifice, who had ordered all the Italian comrades not to take sides openly because support for the candidate of a bourgeois anti-Fascist party was not compatible with the ideology of the revolutionary Fascists. Harmatus had promised the Sacrifice leaders that, if he were elected, he would defend their militants should the police ever try to dismantle the organization.

All this information was given to us by Camillus during a meeting in the ancient streets of Carthage, a city full of history, about an hour by car from Lenintown, where we had gone one Saturday afternoon to listen to Hercules, the Sacrifice leader in that splendid town.

Hercules told us that it's important to admit that you're "Fascist" and that you mustn't be afraid of saying, "I'm a Fascist." He spoke against the Italian government and bourgeois society, against capitalism, against the organization of schools, against the massacre of Italians by Yugoslav partisans in 1945, against communism, and against history books written by left-wing authors. When he had finished his speech, the Lenintown comrades and I approached a table where sandwiches were being offered to the attendees. Leonidas, who had not been able to come with us, had appointed Camillus as his deputy.

Camillus, who was twenty and had embarked on a very demanding course of studies, said to us: "Before you eat, I have to talk to you. Come with me."

It was hot out and it was raining; we walked fast.

A comrade who had put a cap on his head was immediately told off by another comrade: "Fucking Jew! What the fuck are you doing with that hat! And you're a Fascist? Scared of two drops of water! Go and fight a war, dickhead! What a fucking Jewish asshole!"

After a minute or so, Camillus stopped under a magnificent arch dating back to the Roman era and, sheltered from the rain, said: "Guys, Leonidas asked me to tell you something. I realize that you won't like what I'm about to tell you. I don't like it either, but we're political soldiers and we've received clear orders from the national leaders."

Camillus put his hands in his pocket, lowered his head, and paused. Then he looked us in the eye and, with a gloomy expression on his face, said: "We have to support Harmatus, who's running in the upcoming election. We have to vote for him. We have to put up posters for his election campaign. Leonidas phoned to tell me all this. He told me to tell you and say that we'll discuss it together when we hold the next meeting."

The comrades were dumbfounded.

One of them said: "Fuck! Harmatus? I don't believe it! Harmatus is a dickhead. Everyone knows that he's a scumbag. What's he got to do with Sacrifice?"

Despite his youth, Camillus adopted a paternal tone: "Guys, you know that we're a family, and I completely understand your reaction. I've always thought that Harmatus is an asshole too, but we're political soldiers and the leaders' orders have to be obeyed. But no one can know that we support Harmatus, is that clear?"

Another comrade said: "You bet that no one can ever know! Sacrifice supports Harmatus? How the fuck is that possible? People would never get their heads around this."

Camillus said that the national leaders must have a strategy in mind, even though he couldn't imagine what it would be.

A few days later Leonidas returned to Lenintown, and the election posters arrived to be put up surreptitiously at night. I noticed that Harmatus had made an important political concession, proving that the Sacrifice leaders had played their cards well. The slogan appearing under Harmatus's picture was one that Sacrifice had been using for years against immigrants. I don't know who had delivered the posters because, when I arrived in the Lenintown offices, they were already on the meeting room table. The comrades looked miserable, and I didn't ask any questions. One of them picked up a poster and said: "What the fuck! I became a Sacrifice militant to start a revolution, and here I am putting up posters for this dickhead Harmatus!"

Leonidas took the floor: "Guys, I asked Camillus to tell you about this. I've already spoken to some of you on the phone, but now I want to talk to you while we're all together. I think that Harmatus is a dickhead too, but these are the orders arriving from the national leaders. We're a militia. We have to do what our leaders tell us. If Harmatus is elected to the European Parliament, we'll have someone who will defend us. Shit, that's really something! We don't ask anyone for favors, you know that. And we never asked Harmatus for them. He came to us."

Leonidas then said that we had to form two groups and arrange for two cars to carry the glue and the posters: "Wear tracksuits, because this shit job ruins your clothes. I've posted lots of signs, and this fucking glue sticks to everything." I asked Leonidas if I could join in the postering, and he answered me with these exact words: "Listen to me. I respect you because you're someone who's ready for anything, but I have to give the comrades preference. Don't feel bad. I'll tell you what I'm going to do. I'll organize two cars without counting you in. If there's an extra place I'll call you. Get it? I want you to come, but the others have to take precedence." I told Leonidas that I understood his reasoning perfectly.

The next day, around lunchtime, a text arrived from Leonidas via WhatsApp: "Hi, there's a place in the car because a comrade hasn't been able to make it. We're meeting in our offices this evening around 10 p.m. You coming?"

I thanked Leonidas and promised I'd arrive on time to join in the postering expedition.

Two hours later, my mother phoned and said she needed me urgently. In January the doctors had found a tumor in my father's lung. He seemed fine, but he was actually already dying. The cancer had started to spread in March, and now it was already May. It would kill him in October. My father, who was a professor of psychology at the Sapienza University of Rome, was the only scholar I had talked to about my ethnographic research with the Sacrifice Fascists. I decided to sleep at my parents' home, as my mother asked, so I could accompany my father to the hospital the next day and have a chance to discuss with him what I had observed in Lenintown and Mussolinia.

I texted Leonidas: "I'm really sorry. My father has cancer and my mother has asked me to return to Rome immediately."

Leonidas replied: "I didn't know. I'm really sorry. See you in Lenintown."

Once again my father refused to undergo chemotherapy. He told me that my grandfather had had the same tumor and that the doctors had "ripped him apart" by subjecting him to a series of operations that hadn't resolved anything. He added that he wasn't frightened of dying and that he would try alternative medicine.

While we were driving home, I explained my research and my father suggested that Leonidas was a person who tried to make himself the center of attention because he needed to feel appreciated by others. Then he gave me a paper, "Attention Is Energy," that he had written for a conference in Paris, in which he analyzed the struggle all people go through to make others pay attention to them. The chat with my father and the paper he gave me, now available online, were of great help when I transcribed my interviews with Leonidas because they led me to concentrate on an important trait in his personality.[6]

Since I will be using this paper in a later chapter to explain my understanding of Leonidas's actions, it may perhaps be helpful to quote some parts of it here:

Attention is the most valuable asset in our world. As Luis Ansa says, "In the universe in which we live, everything becomes a ruthless struggle of energies around human attention."

The experience of our daily lives tells us that people always want others to notice them. To be at the center of other people's attention, to attract their attention, to have their attention: our affective life revolves around this game.

To obtain this, one is willing to do anything.

This game requires immense energy, and the dynamics are subtle and often perverse (guilt complex, psychological blackmail, etc.).

It has to be understood that it can involve both positive and negative energies, but in both cases the dialectic of attention always creates a state of dependence, whether I want to attract the attention of others or whether I give them my entire attention.

When I returned to Lenintown, I arrived at the militia offices half an hour early and waited at the front door. Camillus was the first to arrive, and he let me in.

Camillus, how did posting the signs go the other night?

"Not too well."

What do you mean? What happened?

"What happened was that, while we were putting up the posters at night, some communists arrived. One of them had a hammer in his hand."

No way! Were you there?

"No, I was with the other group. We had divided up into two teams."

Were they the W La Rivoluzione communists?

"No, they belonged to another far-left movement."

Who was there when the communists arrived?

"Mithridates with another three comrades."

What did Mithridates tell you? Did they fight?

"The communists had a hammer. They said: 'You can't put up your posters here. This area is ours!'"

What did Leonidas do?

"Leonidas?" Camillus laughed. "Leonidas wasn't there. If the communists had said these things to Leonidas . . . they would all be in the hospital. The communists run away when they see Leonidas."

Was Leonidas told?

"Sure."

Where is he?

"He's in Gaugamela."

Leonidas had gone to Gaugamela, a city a hundred and fifty miles away, for a reason I can't reveal because it would make it easier to discover his real identity. I phoned him and said I would be passing through Gaugamela for work reasons, and that I would like to meet up with him.

Leonidas agreed, and I set off.

The journey from Lenintown to Gaugamela took four and a half hours. When I arrived, Leonidas was in a building with a large courtyard illegally occupied by a group of Sacrifice militants. In Gaugamela, the comrades had done a good job of organizing themselves. They had transformed a basement into a makeshift gym for poor Italians and had opened a small restaurant with eight tables.

I found a militant at the entrance and asked for Leonidas, but I was told he was resting. After around twenty minutes, Leonidas arrived wearing a bloodstained white T-shirt.

Leonidas, your nose is bleeding! What's the matter?

"Fuck, this nosebleed has lasted for hours. What fucking luck! Come with me. I can offer you a drink at the bar."

The young woman and the man working in the bar treated Leonidas with respect.

While we ordered our drinks, Leonidas, still losing blood from his nose, starting reading a text message on his cellphone. "Wait a minute," he said. "I have to reply to this asshole."

Who's this asshole?

"He's a fucking communist. Did the guys tell you what happened?"

Do you mean the story of the hammer during the postering?

"Yeah."

The guys didn't tell me much. I still don't know exactly what happened. What do you know?

"Wait. I have to reply to this shitface. Look at these messages that have been arriving on my Facebook page since this morning."

As Leonidas showed me the display on his smartphone, which he kept in his hand, I asked him what the communist militant he was texting was called. He told me his name was Fidel, the leader of a Lenintown communist movement.

Since I couldn't transcribe the messages right there, I'm basing my account of them on notes I made a couple of hours later.

The message that had started the conversation was from Leonidas himself, who said: "I've been told that your militants threatened my comrades with a hammer while they were putting up posters. You were very lucky I wasn't there. I never turn the other cheek. Watch out. If you want war, you'll get war."

Fidel replied in very correct and elegant Italian. He denied that his militants had been carrying a hammer and turned things around by saying that the responsibility lay with Leonidas's comrades.

Leonidas replied with a threat: "It happened the way I said it did. I'm not saying any more. We have to meet."

The communist leader remained calm in his reply: "You keep using threatening language. Threats are not part of our culture."

Fidel's writing demonstrated a higher level of education than Leonidas's. I suspected that Fidel, knowing the other man was being investigated by the police, had written the messages with the possibility in mind that they might be intercepted by the police. Some months later, I learned that I'd been right: Leonidas's phone was being tapped.

To be honest, I felt sorry for Leonidas. I realized the extent to which a guy who had soaked up Codreanu's and Legrelle's writings and, what's more, who didn't have much education, could be his own worst enemy. Convinced he was baring his teeth, Leonidas was in fact baring his neck like a defenseless lamb.

It wouldn't take long for Leonidas to end up in jail.

This is what I wrote in my ethnographic notebook, drawing on my father's paper "Attention Is Energy": "I can't help but feel sorry for Leonidas, who doesn't know how to handle the dangers around him. Leonidas is eager for some part of the world to recognize his importance, but his behavior makes it difficult for people to value and respect him. He wants others to notice him. It's very likely that Fidel thought that the police were tapping Leonidas's phone. His messages were written to be filed in a lawyer's brief."

The confrontation between Leonidas and Fidel had no follow-up, but the comrades swore that they would take their revenge at the first opportunity.

It's a War!

Another important ritual for keeping the parallel world alive is represented by clashes between the Sacrifice militants and the young communists during the commemoration of the *foibe* massacres during World War II, in which communists from Yugoslavia killed thousands of Italians in the borderlands between Italy and Yugoslavia. The term *foibe* refers to the sinkholes that dot the local terrain, although it has taken on a symbolic meaning.

The Mussolinia comrades had succeeded in getting the mayor to name a town square after these martyrs. In fact, it's not really a square but a park so tiny that I found it hard to imagine I was looking at a public square.

Thanks to sabotage by far-left activists, who periodically deface the plaque commemorating the killings, the Mussolinia comrades feel themselves to be under attack and organize protection for what they consider a sacred place.

After the Berlin Wall fell, the Italian Social Movement (MSI), which was inspired by Fascism, became an important political party thanks to an alliance with Silvio Berlusconi, who won the elections of March 27, 1994. At that time its leader was Gianfranco Fini, who strove to gain official commemoration for the victims of communist violence.

The day of remembrance for the *foibe* martyrs, celebrated nationwide on February 10 each year, was established by a law of the Italian Parliament of March 30, 2004, ten years after the Italian Social Movement had changed its name to the National Alliance (Alleanza Nazionale). At the time the bill was approved, Berlusconi was prime minister and Fini was deputy prime minister.

My conversation with Ephialtes, a young Mussolinia comrade, will help us understand how the far-left and far-right militants keep their parallel world alive by interacting with each other:

"The night before February 10, I went with some other comrades to the square dedicated to the *foibe* victims, the square that we had won with our battles. I stayed there all night to make sure the communists didn't do anything to the plaque."

Wasn't it dangerous?

"Wasn't what dangerous?"

Wasn't there a risk that a fight could break out between you and the communists?

"But that's what I was hoping for!"

What were you hoping for?

"That those crappy communists would arrive at night so we could get out of our cars and jump on them. Those bastards work at night, under cover. The communists are afraid of fighting in the open."

I understand that, but if you clash with the communists, isn't there the risk of a feud?

"What feud?"

I mean, you clash, and then the communists start going after you, and you'll never stop fighting each other.

"That's a risk, but it's not a problem. We're strong, we're united, and we can count on the help of the Lenintown comrades and those from other towns close to Mussolinia. In Lenintown, you know, there's Leonidas, who's a professional boxer. The Mussolinia leaders don't hold back either. Everyone respects Marcus. If you get his fist in your face, you really feel it."

I know. But what happens if all the communists start coming after you?

"You know what will happen if the communists come after us? All our comrades will show up in Mussolinia and we'll have a war!"

Do you really think it's a war?

"It's a war, it's a war! We don't want to attack the communists. They're the ones who attack us. We want to be free to exist with our ideas, while the communists say they want to crush us. They say they want to shut us up. Do you want to destroy my plaque? Do you want to offend the Italians who died in the *foibe*? Right! You just try it!" His voice fills with emotional tension. He raises his right fist and waves it around.

I sit down on a bench with Ephialtes and obtain some information on his life as a student in Mussolinia. He says that at his school there was a confrontation between some Sacrifice comrades and a group of far-left students. He tells me his version of the facts and asserts that the communists are liars who always distort the truth.

In Mussolinia an assembly of student representatives had been elected by their peers according to the formal procedures established by the Ministry of Education. A meeting took place inside a building in the town. The left-wing militants, in a statement issued by their organization, recounted that some Sacrifice students, after having beaten up their representative, had removed the large ring he wore in his earlobe, and then pushed their fingers inside the hole.

This is what a far-left militant who had taken part in the protest against Sacrifice told me:

"Our representative had a stretcher in his ear and . . ."

Sorry, what's a stretcher?

"It's a ring that you insert in the earlobe. You know what I mean?"

Are you talking about those rings that stretch the earlobe, creating a hole?

"That's right. The Fascists attacked him and then . . ."

What did they do? Did they punch him?

"No, they threatened him. They told him that the anti-Fascists must get out of Mussolinia, and then they slapped him hard and pushed him."

A small Italian communist group also intervened in support of the parallel world with a press release published on their website. The communist leaders asserted that Mussolinia is a town where Fascists beat up students while the mayor does nothing to stop them, that the Fascists now control all the streets in town and democracy has been put on hold.

The Sacrifice comrades also sent a statement to the press in which they declared that the left-wing students' representative had stated he would participate in the meeting only if the Sacrifice Fascists left the room. According to the document, this boy had even sung anti-Fascist songs to provoke and offend. The Sacrifice comrades had every right to participate in the meeting, since they had been regularly elected under the rules.

This is the English translation of the Sacrifice statement; it was published in a Mussolinia magazine and on the militia's Facebook page: "The left-wing students' representative had come to the meeting with a provocative attitude, asserting that he didn't acknowledge the Sacrifice members' right to speak, in spite of their election according to regulations. Not satisfied with this, during the voting he started to sing anti-Fascist songs from the 1970s. Following this, after leaving the building in which the meeting was held, the Sacrifice militants demanded an explanation, which gave rise to an exclusively verbal argument, as proved by the absence of medical certificates and diagnoses."

After the newspapers had published news of the clash between the young communists and Fascists, an elderly partisan who had fought against the Nazis and Fascists in 1944 publicly condemned Sacrifice solely on the basis of the left-wing militants' version of the facts. A few hours later, the entire National Association of Italian Partisans released a written statement that, besides condemning the alleged violence of the Fascists, recalled that the town of Mussolinia had received a gold medal for having fought against the Nazis during World War II. The partisans hoped that the Sacrifice comrades, whom they also described as criminals, would be arrested.

During the next several weeks, the far-left militants published dozens of comments on the Internet stating that Fascism was taking over the town of Mussolinia. A small far-left organization wrote on its Facebook page: "For some months we've been warning the Mussolinia citizens about the Fascist danger. After the violence against a young student, we can now say that the situation is as we all can see it. Fascism has taken over Mussolinia. Today more than ever, we need to rediscover the values of the partisans and anti-Fascist resistance. Long live the partisans!"

A few days later, unidentified people defaced with a Fascist symbol a plaque dedicated to the partisans in a Mussolinia square. The left-wing militants responded by posting online a series of articles that fueled the confrontation that was stirring up the parallel world.

5

LIVING WITH CONTEMPT

Our actions are influenced by what we think of others, by what others think of us, and by what we think others think of us. Social life is based on a chain of interpretations in which each of us is continuously engaged in interpreting the interpretations of others.[1]

To reconstruct properly the "paramount reality" of daily life in which Sacrifice militants live, we cannot only reconstruct what the comrades think of the people who are part of the bourgeois world. We must also reconstruct what the bourgeois think of the comrades and what the comrades think the bourgeois think of them.

In the first three chapters I tried to reconstruct what the comrades think of "others," then in the fourth chapter I reconstructed what "others" think of Sacrifice comrades. In this chapter, I deal with what the Sacrifice comrades think of what others think of them. Are Sacrifice militants aware of the "typificatory schemes" through which others perceive them?[2]

The Contempt of Women

When I first entered the Lenintown militia, my main purpose was to spend as much time as possible in their offices to make friends.

Since I had announced my real identity, I was in the typical situation of the "stranger" who is trying to be accepted by the group he is interested in.[3] To gain the trust of the comrades, I was prepared to speak on any subject, and I often employed a very useful investigative tactic that Jack D. Douglas calls "opening the members up." According to Douglas, it begins by being open with the members of the group, but it goes beyond—to sharing intimacies with them and, if possible, making oneself vulnerable in the same way they are in the interview, making oneself a hostage to their friendly trustworthiness, often by implicating oneself in the same things for which they are being studied.[4] Kathleen M. Blee has also used this technique in interviewing women in the "hate movement."[5]

My first meeting with Leonidas, to whom I had already spoken on the telephone, was in the Lenintown offices one Saturday after a meeting. This meant I could be introduced to nearly all the comrades at once.

Leonidas was polite and welcoming. Ethnographers know that some individuals love to talk about themselves while others are more reticent.[6] Leonidas, besides being loquacious, was excited about my interest in his story, and I asked him if I could take notes on the sheets of paper I had brought in my backpack.

After about thirty minutes of rapid note-taking, I asked Leonidas if I could record him. "You're telling me a lot of interesting things," I told him, "and I'm worried I won't be able to write them all down!"

For an hour Leonidas told me the story of his life. He talked about his relationship with his parents, of his mother's despair when she discovered her son had Fascist sympathies, of his becoming one of the Lenintown soccer team's "ultras," of his decision to join a group of skinheads, and about the end of this experience. He also talked about founding the Sacrifice militia and the fight in the bar in which he'd hit the young woman named Ashley.

He gave me confirmation that the comrades were fully aware of the contempt in which people held them when he spoke of their problems with the Lenintown girls. It is important to point out that Leonidas spoke about the sex issue spontaneously, without any prompting on my part.

According to Leonidas, Lenintown is a "crappy bourgeois town" where the young women are interested only in guys who drive around in expensive automobiles and wear fashionable clothes. The Lenintown men have no values, unlike Sacrifice comrades, who are fighting to achieve a revolution that will change the way people think, saving Italians from the poverty caused by immigration and corrupt politicians who are "all crappy thieves."

Leonidas is aware that the Fascist revolution may remain a dream, but what is important is the struggle against bourgeois society, because this is a noble action that makes individuals morally superior. Even if the final result won't be the installation of a Fascist dictatorship and the expulsion of all the immigrants from Italy, he asserts that the Sacrifice headquarters is a significant achievement. Leonidas becomes serious and sad when he talks about the difficulty of attracting women, which is caused by the contempt in which society holds men like him.

Let's listen to his words:

"We have founded this group because this town is sickening. Lenintown is a crappy bourgeois city. It is one of the most bourgeois in Italy. In Lenintown the girls only look at guys who have money and expensive cars. You know what the problem is?" Leonidas pauses, smiles, and gives the other comrades a knowing look.

"The problem is that . . ." Leonidas pauses again and continues smiling, as if he needs to think over what he's about to say. "The problem is that it's impossible to get laid in Lenintown. You can't fuck a girl here." Leonidas stops smiling and turns serious.

"Girls avoid us because they think we're losers. They think we're penniless scum, but we continue along our path. We want to change this society. It has a sick soul. We want to make a revolution. Perhaps ours is only a dream, but at least we have this hope. The hope that helps us to carry on. And if we don't succeed in starting a revolution? At least we can say that we tried to change this society. At least we have this apartment that is our refuge; it's our family, it's our home. This apartment is everything for us."

When framing questions, the interviewer has to avoid scientific jargon but must instead acquire and use the interviewee's own language as soon as possible.[7]

So let me get this straight: It isn't easy to screw Lenintown girls because they have a bourgeois mentality?

"Exactly! It's nothing to do with what you say or what you do. The Lenintown girls have decided whether they'll let you fuck them before you open your mouth, even before you say you're Fascist or communist. Get it?" With their head movements and facial expressions, the comrades who are listening to us show they agree with Leonidas. "The girls couldn't give a shit about your ideals. If you've got money and a nice car, then you can fuck them."

And if you don't have money?

"If you don't have money, they look at you as if you've got a dangerous disease. If a girl goes out with one of us, her parents get frightened, but we don't give a shit because we're better than the guys in this town. We don't have money but we have ideals; we're fighting to improve society."

I'm wearing an anonymous black tracksuit, a pair of old, broken-down sneakers, and a white T-shirt with a neck stretched by numerous washings. If I've understood the typificatory schemes through which the Sacrifice militants observe reality, I'm someone who has no chance of attracting Lenintown girls.

The comrades are listening to Leonidas in silence, and I try to involve them in the conversation.

Guys, does this mean it's impossible to get laid in Lenintown?

Leonidas replies in a serious tone, preventing the other comrades from joining in:

"If you're entering Sacrifice to get laid, then you've got the wrong idea. If you walk around Lenintown with us, you'll see how people look at us . . ."

How will people look at me?

"They'll look at you like someone with the plague."

And the girls?

"The girls too. Lenintown is a shithole town for two reasons: because it's bourgeois and because it's left-wing. You have to get out. This town has nothing good going for it. Mussolinia is better."

Mussolinia is better than Lenintown?

"Mussolinia is also a bourgeois town where the girls will only let you fuck them if you have money, but at least it's right-wing, it has a Fascist history. The Mussolinia comrades are much more organized and much more numerous, but you also have to consider that they've had more time to develop."

Are there girls in the Sacrifice militias?

"In the Mussolinia militia there's one girl, but she's ugly as sin." Leonidas and the comrades snicker. "She's the only female in the militia. There are no girls in Sacrifice; we're all men."

So you can't get laid either in Lenintown or in Mussolinia . . . ?

At this point Leonidas rises from his chair and exclaims:

"Wait! There is someone who fucks! It's Mithridates!

Who's Mithridates?

"He's one of the comrades. He couldn't come to the meeting today. I'll introduce you to him tomorrow. Mithridates is eighteen. You're sitting in Mithridates's chair."

When Leonidas says this, all the comrades look at me and laugh loudly. I get the feeling that I've said or done something ridiculous, but I can't understand what. I feel awkward and ask Leonidas:

Why are they laughing?

"You see this chair you're sitting in?"

Yes.

"Did you wonder why we let you sit in the only leather armchair, the only comfortable chair, while we're all sitting on these crap seats?" The comrades laugh.

Why?

Because that chair is full of jism! The comrades laugh.

I'm sitting on a chair full of jism? In what way?

"I'll tell you the story. One night, Mithridates met a girl in a bar . . ."

OK . . .

"Mithridates didn't know where to take her because he hasn't got a car . . ."

And so?

"And so he brought the girl here and fucked her in that chair, but he didn't have a condom. So when he came he drenched the chair in jism! None of us ever sits in that chair." Leonidas and the comrades laugh.

Contempt of the Family

The Sacrifice militants have to face the contempt not only of strangers but also, in some cases, of their family.

Leonidas described his mother's reaction when she found out that her son was reading Hitler and Mussolini:

"My parents aren't Fascists. My father is center-right, my mother center-left. They're both moderates. My mother is completely devoted to the family; she's a good person, she never argues with anyone. One day she came into my room, found Mussolini's and Hitler's books, and burst into tears. She asked: 'When did you start reading these books? What did I do wrong? Where did I go wrong as a mother?'" Leonidas, with a sad expression, imitates his mother's tearful voice. "My mother was always crying then, and even now she's always worried and sad."

Why is your mother always sad?

"She's sad because she thinks it's her fault that I've become a Sacrifice militant; she thinks she failed as a mother. She's ashamed."

How old were you when your mother came into your room and saw Mussolini's books?

"I was fourteen, but . . . my mother had understood for some time that I was reading those books."

What did you say to your mother when she cried?

"I said to her, 'Mom, I buy these books because I like Mussolini and Hitler, they were two great men and I want to learn more about them.'"

Contempt inside the Militia

Titus, a Mussolinia militant, was also a great help in understanding what the Sacrifice militants thought of what others thought of them.

Titus and I met when Harmatus, the political candidate, went to Mussolinia to give a campaign speech along with Commodus, one of the Sacrifice national leaders. There were ten police officers in front of the building where the meeting was held, there to protect Harmatus, who is reviled in extreme-left circles for his racist remarks.

I recorded the event, which lasted for eighty minutes.

In his speech, Commodus said that Sacrifice's political action was aimed at achieving four great objectives for the good of Italy: (1) to take money from rich Italians to give to poor Italians; (2) to give all Italians a home; (3) to block immigration immediately; and (4) to exit from the European Union and from the single currency and return to the lira.

Harmatus proved to be an expert orator. He said he had been on trial for making some racist remarks during a radio program and managed to draw applause three times.

The first time was when he said that Commodus had delivered a fine speech against Europe. Harmatus received a second round of applause when he declared his aversion to the European Union, and the third when he expressed his contempt for immigrants: "Chinese food should be placed in a special area in Italian supermarkets. It should be in front of the john!"

After the meeting, Harmatus left Mussolinia escorted by the police while I walked to the branch office with some thirty other people, including Commodus. While I was talking to two Sacrifice militants in front of the entrance to the office, a man with his arms covered in Fascist tattoos came over, saying he wanted to meet me. "Hi. I'm Titus," he said. "Marcus told me that you're writing a book on Sacrifice."

Sociable and smiling, Titus, aged forty-three, told me that he was very happy to learn that a professor was interested in writing a book about the Mussolinia militia and announced that he wanted to tell me his story. Titus had started to support Fascist organizations when he was fifteen and ended up in Sacrifice.

Titus, how come I've never seen you before in the Mussolinia branch?

"I've had a daughter. I don't have time to hang around with the militia the way I used to, but I do try to attend important events like this. Every so often I drop in to see the comrades, and we drink a beer together."

While I was explaining my research to Titus, a Sacrifice sympathizer called Urbanus passed by, greeting me without stopping. Titus and the other comrades looked at him and burst out laughing. Urbanus, whom I had met several evenings earlier, told me about his particular passion for a certain type of animal. (I can't say which one because it would make him easily recognizable.) After giving me his name and surname, he showed me photos of him playing with the animals he loves, which he had put on his Facebook page. He told me he hated immigrants, but he hadn't spoken about politics or history.

After Urbanus goes by, Titus becomes serious and says:

"This is one of the great problems of Sacrifice."

What problem are you talking about?

"Our problem is that a lot of strange people approach us, like that guy who greeted you. He has some very weird ideas. He's called Urbanus.

Every so often he comes to our branch to drink a beer with us. Don't think we're like him."

What ideas does Urbanus have?

"It's difficult to describe them because they're so absurd. He admires Hitler and believes in aliens. We listen to him because we're sorry for him, but then we laugh about him when he leaves. He's convinced that Hitler is an extraterrestrial." Titus and the comrades laugh.

Hitler? An extraterrestrial? In what sense?

"He thinks that Hitler was an alien and that the secret services know all about it. He says that the extraterrestrials once governed Hitler's Germany and that now they're in the White House and have taken over Obama's mind."

According to this theory, the extraterrestrials lost World War II?

Titus and the comrades laugh.

They lost the war and then sided with the winners?

The comrades laugh again.

So people think that Urbanus is one of you, and this damages your image. Am I right?

"Exactly."

After listening to Urbanus, people imagine that you're also convinced that our planet is governed by aliens.

"You've understood our problem perfectly."

Does Urbanus have a Sacrifice membership card?

"I don't think he has a membership card. You should ask Marcus, but every so often Urbanus visits us and drinks a beer."

Can't you tell him not to come to your office anymore?

"We have an unwritten rule not to turn away guys who have weird ideas. We try to reason with them and correct their view of Fascism. In some cases we can't do anything because they're people with psychological problems. Our difficulty is that we attract that kind of person."

Titus's last words seem important to me and I encourage him to explain them.

Do you mean to say that Sacrifice attracts these guys with psychological problems?

"Yeah."

Why are these people with weird ideas attracted to Sacrifice? Why do they come to you?

"Because people consider us a ghetto. We do all we can to shake off this label, but it's not easy. Some guys like Urbanus approach our group because they think they'll find others with the same weird ideas. They're hoping to find someone they can talk to, because everyone avoids them."

When I ask Titus to explain why the great majority of people have such a negative attitude toward Sacrifice, he replies that Hitler and Mussolini are considered absolute evil, and it follows that everyone who admires them is considered someone to be avoided. Titus starts to blame left-wing intellectuals who distort history to sling mud at Fascism as well as journalists. But, he says:

"We have to be honest and say that it's also our fault because sometimes . . ." Titus hesitates.

Because sometimes . . . ? Go on, I'm interested.

"Because sometimes comrades fuck up and, as you well know, the media are always ready to give us bad press."

I ask Titus to explain what he means when he says that some Sacrifice members "fuck up."

"Some comrades fuck up in the sense that every so often they start a fight and get arrested. When this happens, the TV and papers denounce Sacrifice because the return of Fascism is a real fear," Titus concludes. "It's a business that earns a lot of money for all those corrupt journalists who lie unscrupulously to sully the history of Fascism."

"Fascist Shit!"

I had another chance to see for myself the contempt in which Sacrifice militants are held and their awareness of being despised.

One of the comrades' most popular initiatives is the distribution of food. The militants donate five euros each to purchase the goods whenever the militia leaders decide to launch the program.

Marcus organizes three groups of comrades. The first group goes to the supermarket to buy the food, which is then taken to the militia headquarters. The second group prepares the packages. The third group distributes the packages in a Mussolinia square where there's a fruit and vegetable market. The packages are prepared at night and distributed the next morning.

I usually took part in the group that prepared the packages and the one that distributed them. The first time that Marcus and Lentulus allowed me to participate in the initiative, we prepared twenty-two packages, each of which contained a bag of pasta, a can of tomatoes, a can of lentils, a can of beans, some milk, and a bag of coffee. In some packages, instead of the coffee there was a bag of sugar or salt.

I returned to my place in Lenintown at four in the morning, slept a few hours, and at 9:30 arrived at the Mussolinia militia headquarters as agreed.

Lentulus greeted me by saying: "You wanted to be a militant? Now I'm going to show you what militancy means!"

There were nine of us.

While we were walking to the square, Lentulus explained to me that, after three years of doing this, he had succeeded in finding the best place to distribute the packages (the biggest market in town), the best time (when the market was busiest), the type of food poor people most appreciated, and last but not least, how to turn the packages into a tool for advertising Sacrifice. Lentulus had ordered us to staple a Sacrifice flyer to every package. "This way," he said, "the elderly will walk through downtown Mussolinia with our packages that display our name."

Having arrived in the square, I entered a market stall with three other comrades and placed the movement's flags alongside a table on which we set the food packages. We started handing them out at 10:22 after taking a group photo with the Sacrifice flag behind us.

My task was to stand in the median, distributing flyers with the Sacrifice symbol explaining our initiative.

I saw a girl of around twenty approaching, accompanied by an elderly lady. When she passed by, I asked, "Hi, can I give you a flyer?"

The girl looked at me with a disdainful expression. She left the flyer in my hand and walked away. She then turned her head, stared at me, and in a low voice said, "Fascist shit."

I looked at the comrade beside me, and after a few seconds said in amazement:

Did you hear what that girl said? She called me Fascist shit!

With the tone of one who is used to receiving these kinds of insults, the comrade said: "Don't let it worry you. You'll get used to it."

I called over to Lentulus and told him what had happened.

Lentulus, did you hear what that girl said to me?
"What girl?"
The girl who was accompanying that old lady.
"What did she say to you?"
I wanted to give her a flyer but she told me I was Fascist shit!

Lentulus said that these insults were "par for the course." He explained that in Mussolinia there are lots of people who condemn Fascism without realizing that the militia is fighting to defend the future of Italy.

Up till then I'd seen the great contempt in which society holds Sacrifice militants and realized that they are aware of it. But this wasn't the most important thing I'd discovered.

Leonidas thinks that a couple of his comrades are "losers."

In the previous chapter, I described my meeting with Leonidas in Gaugamela. After the exchange of texts with Fidel, Leonidas told me he has no faith in the future of his militia because his comrades are incompetent and unable to help him achieve anything important.

Let's listen to Leonidas:

"When I return to Lenintown, I'm going to find those communists in person. My problem is that I've got no one . . ."

Leonidas pauses briefly while he seems to think about what he's going to say. Then he smiles ironically, gives me a knowing look, and says: "Come on, you've seen what the comrades in my militia are like. Brutus and Cincinnatus are good guys. They go to the office every day, sweep the floors, and keep the apartment clean, but they're not capable of doing much else. They're just two born losers." Leonidas smiles in pity for Brutus and Cincinnatus.

I noted down what Leonidas continued to tell me about Brutus, Cincinnatus, and Camillus, but I'm not going to repeat his words here because I believe that Leonidas never imagined I would tell anyone what he said about comrades who devote time to the militia. Even though he never said "Don't tell anyone what I'm saying to you," Leonidas was obviously telling me all this in confidence.

While Leonidas was uttering his negative comments about Brutus and Cincinnatus, something happened that left a great impression on me.

Leonidas and I entered the office of the Gaugamela militia—located right in front of a bar—where Priscus, the head of the militia, was waiting for us.

I invited Priscus to play billiards in the hope of establishing a confidential relationship. I was insistent, and Priscus agreed to play, but he seemed very bored and easily beat me. Then we went into the courtyard of the militia office (a much bigger office than those in Lenintown or Mussolinia) and sat down.

Leonidas and Priscus sat down on the same bench, while I took a plastic chair from the room with the billiard table and placed it facing them, so I could observe both Leonidas's and Priscus's facial expressions while they talked.

We were silent for a few moments, and then Leonidas continued deriding Brutus and Cincinnatus. Priscus intervened with a mocking comment about certain aspects of their personalities. It now became important to me to learn if Priscus had ever met Brutus and Cincinnatus in person. I wanted to see if Leonidas had badmouthed at least three comrades to someone who wasn't part of the Lenintown militia.

Priscus, have you ever met Brutus, Cincinnatus, or Camillus?

"No, I don't know them."

Have you ever been to Lenintown?

"No, I've never been to Lenintown."

Before taking his leave, Leonidas told me that he thought highly of Mithridates and confided that he had decided to make him deputy leader, removing Camillus, whom he considered unsuitable for the position even though he acknowledged he was good at dealing with the cops, who "are always breaking our balls." I noted that Mithridates, the only comrade in the group who had boasted of getting laid, was also the person whom Leonidas respected most. I decided that I would study the link between the ability to get sex and prestige in the militia, but my expulsion from the group meant I wasn't able to look further into this question.

The conversation with Leonidas was significant because it helped me understand that the "chain of contempt" typifying the reality of everyday life in a Fascist militia is more complex than I have been describing.

I had learned that the Sacrifice militants despise the bourgeois, and the bourgeois despise the Sacrifice militants. But I had never imagined that Leonidas would judge Brutus and Cincinnatus using the same typificatory schemes and the same words that bourgeois and communists use to express their contempt for Leonidas and his comrades.

Contempt of Parents

I had first seen Luca while I was buying a slice of pizza with Brutus in a pizzeria located a few yards from the Lenintown militia office. It was lunchtime, and the place was crowded. Luca had entered immediately after us, greeted Brutus, and exchanged a few words with him about a person I didn't know. I realized that Luca and Brutus had some friends in common. It seemed to me that Luca was embarrassed at meeting Brutus, and I had the impression that he didn't want to talk to him. Brutus asked the questions and Luca just gave curt replies. I also noted that Luca and Brutus hadn't gripped each other's forearm in greeting as all comrades do when they meet.

I started to imagine that Luca had once been a Sacrifice militant, and I believed that I could obtain a great deal of ethnographic information if I became friendly with a man who had left the militia. During my career as a sociologist engaged in studying deviant groups, I have learned that ex-militants, no longer forced to abide by the group's rules, are often willing to reveal information that militants are obliged to keep secret. I've also learned that in many cases, former militants are willing to criticize the lifestyle of the group to which they no longer belong. Sacrifice militants have to be very careful about everything they say to strangers, and I would have given anything to speak with a defector from the Lenintown militia. He would have given me important information about the cultural universe of Sacrifice.

A few days later, I was sitting on a bench in downtown Lenintown with Neo, who was telling me he had decided to move in with his girlfriend.

Luca passed in front of me with two friends.

When I saw him, I remembered thinking that he was someone who used to be in Leonidas's militia. I kept an eye on him and saw him go into a small shopping mall where there's only a large abandoned store, a woman's hairdresser, a store selling children's clothes, a notary's office, a gym, and public toilets.

Luca had a bag over his shoulder and was wearing a tracksuit and sneakers.

Half an hour later I asked the girl at the gym reception desk the cost of a single visit to use the weight room. A package of ten visits would cost seventy euros, while a single visit costs ten euros. It was seven o'clock on a Monday evening, and I decided I would exercise at that gym every Monday beginning at 6 p.m.

After three weeks of working out together, Luca confided in me that he was in love with Carol, a girl who went to the same school he did in Lenintown: "I really liked her and we started to go out, but then we had to stop seeing each other."

Why did you stop going out with her?

"Our story lasted for a few weeks. Then someone told Carol's father that his daughter was going around with the Sacrifice Fascists and he got angry. I've never been friendly with the Fascists. Unfortunately, Lenintown is a small town full of mean people who talk a load of crap."

Did Carol's father think you were a Fascist?

"Yeah."

Have you ever been a member of the Sacrifice militia?

"Me? Never! A friend of mine is a friend of some Sacrifice militants. I've met some of them. When I come across them in the street, I greet them, but I don't know their names."

Why didn't you explain that you weren't a Fascist?

Luca replied that Carol's father was very strict. When some friends told him that his daughter was friendly with Fascists, he started waiting outside the school to walk her home, and he kept her from leaving the house for months.

Using the "opening the members up" tactic, I told Luca that I had lived a story similar to his:

I can understand. When I was fifteen, I went out with a girl in my school. Her father was also very strict and started to keep tabs on her to prevent her from seeing me.

"He didn't want his daughter to go out with you?"

He said she was too young to have a boyfriend. She was fourteen.

"And what did you do?"

We met secretly. She'd say she wanted to study at a girlfriend's house. Then her father discovered she was lying and beat her. Do you want to know something funny?

"What?"

The girl's father was a Fascist!

Luca laughs.

Why are the Sacrifice Fascists so despised in Lenintown?

"The Fascists are despised in all of Italy, and in Lenintown their leader ended up in the newspapers because he beat up a girl who reported him."

What are the Lenintown comrades like?

"Everyone speaks badly of them, as if they were dangerous. In fact they're just a group of dickheads. Their leader is different; he's the only one to watch out for."

In what sense?

"He's a boxer by profession. They say you have to be very careful around him. If you provoke him, he can lash out."

Luca isn't a comrade, but his testimony helps us understand the contempt in which the Sacrifice militants are held. Carol's father forbade her to go out with Luca simply because some people had told him they had seen Luca talking to some Sacrifice militants.

The Contempt around Me

One Saturday, at one in the morning, after a few games of billiards in the Mussolinia militia branch headquarters, I left with two comrades and went to the main bar in town, where hundreds of young people were gathered outside listening to loud music.

Jonathan, the forty-two-year-old engineer we met in the first chapter, was inside standing near the bar, and I went over to him. Jonathan introduced his two friends. One was an aerobics instructor in a Mussolinia gym, while the other, Marilyn, was a lawyer whom Jonathan had described to me with great enthusiasm: "Alessandro, I hope one day you'll meet a friend of mine, Marilyn. She's the most beautiful girl in Mussolinia. Everyone knows her."

I too was struck by her beauty.

Marilyn politely noted that my accent was different from the Mussolinia one, and I told her I'd been living in Rome for twenty years.

"You live in the most beautiful city in the world and you spend Saturday evening in Mussolinia? I'd like to escape from Mussolinia and spend every Saturday evening in Rome!" Marilyn said, laughing.

The music in the bar was at high volume and I had to yell:

At the moment I'm in Mussolinia full-time. I go out with a group of friends . . .

"Who are these friends?"

That's them over there. They're the Sacrifice guys.

I pointed to the two comrades, who were looking at us from about fifteen feet away.

"Sacrifice? Are you serious?"

Yes, I'm serious.

Marilyn stopped smiling and her face clouded over.

"You're a Sacrifice militant?"

I told her I was a sociologist writing a book about Sacrifice, and I started to explain what my work involved. Marilyn didn't seem interested and interrupted me:

"You moved from Rome to live in Mussolinia with the Sacrifice militants?"

Correct. I'll introduce you to them.

With a rather ostentatious movement of my hand, I gestured to the comrades to come over. I noticed that Jonathan was observing all my actions. The two comrades politely introduced themselves to Marilyn. She listened to their names, shook hands with them both, and left immediately, preventing any attempt at conversation.

I went over to Jonathan to say good-bye, but I got the impression that he was rather distant with me.

While I was driving back to Lenintown, Jonathan texted me on WhatsApp:

"Alessandro, why did you tell Marilyn you were friendly with Fascists?"

I opened the door of my house, threw myself on the bed, and texted Jonathan that I had explained to Marilyn that I was a sociologist.

Jonathan's reply read: "Alessandro, I told you that the Sacrifice people are considered criminals in Mussolinia. Everyone remembers the story of the guy who lost an eye. Marilyn was angry with me. She said I had made her meet Sacrifice Fascists and she thinks you're one as well. People can't understand why you moved from Rome to live among the Mussolinia Fascists. It might be all in a day's work for you, but other people think it's strange."

My mother also helped me to better understand the reality of everyday life in a Fascist militia.

During a dinner at my parents' apartment in Rome at which one of my two brothers was present, my mother got up from the table and refused to continue eating after I'd explained what my new research involved. "Alessandro," she said, "I've never been so ashamed in all my life! And if a friend of mine should see you? Or someone who knows your father? Do you realize how much shame you're bringing on your family? Why do we all have to pay the price for your absurd choices?"

Over the next three days, my mother called me three times and sent me eleven messages on WhatsApp accusing me of damaging my family's image. Then she asked my father to intervene and persuade me to give up my research. In the end, she said she would explain to her women friends in Lenintown why I was associating with the Sacrifice Fascists. But I asked my mother not to speak to anyone about my research for a number of reasons linked to my personal safety.

During the first telephone call, which lasted seven minutes, she accused me of having caused her great suffering at what was already a difficult time because of my father's cancer. In the second call, lasting nine minutes, she told me that she had started to feel ill because of me. In the third call, lasting fourteen minutes, she urged me to realize I was being selfish. During this last call she also told me that my research was dangerous and that it could ruin my life.

Four Types of Insults

During my research in Lenintown, I recorded eighty-nine insults against the Sacrifice militants, which I've divided into five categories.

The first category includes insults prompted by the idea that the Sacrifice comrades are "social misfits" seeking a group of people like themselves.

The second category is prompted by the idea that the militants are by nature violent people who are looking for others who are just as violent.

The third category is based on the idea that the comrades are ignorant of the history of Fascism because they have a low level of education or because they have a very low IQ and don't really understand the meaning of what they're saying. Accordingly, it's ignorance or stupidity that makes people knock at Sacrifice's door.

The fourth category of insults is prompted by the idea that Sacrifice militants are people with serious psychological disturbances.

The fifth category includes insults that don't express any anthropological concept. One example is the Lenintown politician we met in the first chapter who said that the Sacrifice militants were comparable to shit without explaining why he despised them: "Sacrifice is a Fascist organization and shit is the essence of Fascism."

I was able to use two kinds of approaches, central to qualitative sociological research, with thirty-one insulters in order to understand their view of the Sacrifice militants. "Talk in action" refers to accounts or patterns of talk formulated in a naturally occurring situation that is part of some ongoing system of action; "informal interviewing" involves asking questions *in situ* during the course of naturally occurring activities, as John Lofland explained in his guide to qualitative observation.[8]

In the other cases I wrote down the insults without being able to conduct an interview because the situation did not permit it. For example, I wasn't able to interview the girl who called me "Fascist shit" while I was handing out flyers in downtown Mussolinia.

Insults of the First Type

A few days after I had been accepted into the Lenintown militia, my good friend Neo informed his closest friends—who had also become my friends—that I had become a Sacrifice militant for research reasons. Not long after, six of us met in a Lenintown bar.

Rachel, aged thirty-seven, told me that she knew the sister of Brutus, one of the Sacrifice militants, who was ashamed of having a Fascist brother.

"Alessandro, those Fascists you're studying are a group of social misfits. One of them is the brother of a girl I've known for a long time. He's called Brutus. He's thirty and has always been a guy with a lot of problems, ever since he was young."

What problems did he have?

"He had lots of problems. You know those guys whom everyone avoids and who don't have friends? Brutus was like that. He was . . . kind of limited."

Rachel told me that Brutus got low grades at school and everyone said he wasn't very bright. He failed his exams more than once even though he was enrolled in a low-level school. Ever since he became a Sacrifice militant, his sister has been ashamed of him and has even unfriended him on Facebook.

Why did Brutus become a Sacrifice militant?

"I told you, he's a misfit. Before he didn't have any friends, and now he has a group of people he can go around with. Every so often I see him downtown with his Fascist friends. He feels important for the first time in his life. He's finally found someone to have a pizza with. I feel sorry for him."

Neo joins in the conversation, pointing out that he doesn't know Brutus personally. Neo's testimony is important because it comes from a person who judges another without knowing him or her. And in such cases the typificatory schemes become more evident to the sociologist. "I've never met this Brutus personally," says Neo, "but you can tell he's an asshole just from his face. No normal person would mix with the Sacrifice militants. They're a group of social misfits."

Insults of the Second Type

Just as Buddhists seek out groups that practice Buddhism, so violent young men seek out groups that use violence. This is what I was told by Laurie, a teacher whom I met in the Lenintown municipal library, where I spent many hours studying and writing. Laurie, who doesn't look much more than thirty (I didn't ask how old she was), teaches history and philosophy in a high school.

"I think the papers publish too many articles about these Sacrifice cretins," she said. "They make out there's a lot of them but there are actually very few."

How many are there?

"Four or five."

Who are these Sacrifice militants? Do you know them?

"They're guys who have violence in their DNA. They're violent people who attract other violent people. It's easy to understand the mechanism. If you're a Buddhist, you look for a Buddhist group. If you're a violent person, you look for violent people like you. Do you know that animal who beat up a girl in a Lenintown bar?"

A Sacrifice militant beat up a girl?

"The head of the Lenintown militia hit a girl in the face. Have you ever seen anything like that? He's like an animal. He has the face of a monkey. He's probably mentally handicapped. Someone like that can only hope to be noticed by a woman by punching her in the face. I figure these Fascists are sexually frustrated and have psychological problems with women."

Insults of the Third Type

I was distributing packages for poor Italians in downtown Lenintown.

Massimo, a man who looked to be around eighty, approached the plastic table to ask about our initiative. Leonidas had left for a moment to speak with some police officers who were checking up on us. Brutus replied that Sacrifice was a political movement that was trying to help needy Italians, but he didn't say we were a Fascist organization and didn't mention the campaign against immigrants. Massimo said to us in a paternal tone, "You could be my sons; in fact you could be my grandsons!" then he complimented us on our initiative: "Italy needs young people like you!" But he didn't take the food package because he said he only wanted to ask about us and wasn't in need at the moment. He took his leave affectionately, shaking our hands one by one. (There were five of us.)

As Massimo was leaving, I said in a clear voice:

We're Fascists.

Massimo looked at me for a few moments, then said:

"I'm sorry, I didn't quite get what you said . . ."

I said that we're Fascists.

"You're Fascists?"

Massimo continued to look at me in silence with an embarrassed and bewildered expression. This kind man had just praised us, and I wanted to observe his reaction after being told that he had praised a group of Fascists.

I went on the offensive:

We're Fascists. Sacrifice is a Fascist organization. We distribute food to poor Italians, but only to Italians and not to immigrants because we're enemies of immigration. Italy spends too much money on immigrants and not enough on Italians, who are becoming increasingly deprived. Italians should be more important than immigrants who come to steal our jobs. We're here to do what the Italian state hasn't done for some time: help the Italians!

Massimo, who was still holding a Sacrifice flyer, looked at the four comrades next to me as if he didn't believe what I was saying, and asked them: "You're Fascists? Really?"

The comrades nodded their heads without uttering a word.

Massimo looked at the flyer and said: "You're Fascists? But it doesn't say so on your flyers . . ."

I explained to Massimo that it was dangerous to write the word "Fascism" on the flyers because the police could arrest us.

Massimo explained that Fascism had been a very bad experience that had devastated Italy. Then he started to tell us the history of Fascism and the bombing that had destroyed many Italian cities during World War II. From the way he spoke, he seemed to take it for granted that we knew nothing about the history of Fascism. He ended his historical overview by saying: "I'm eighty-six. Fascism was a terrible experience for the entire world. History books are important. You have to study history."

Massimo didn't insult any of us, but his way of confronting us helped me understand the perception prompting the insults I've classified as the third category.

Here are twelve insults I heard based on the idea that people join Sacrifice because they're ignorant:

"The Sacrifice militants are a group of ignorant shits. Everyone knows that."

"The Sacrifice militants are ignorant people who don't know history. That's why they only talk bullshit."

"The Sacrifice militants have never read a book in their life. There's a lot of empty space in their heads that they fill with shit."

"The problem is that, besides being mentally deficient, the Sacrifice militants are also ignorant."

"The Sacrifice militants vote. Unfortunately democracy recognizes the right to vote for ignorant people and dickheads too."

"I heard the Sacrifice militants talk during a student demonstration in Mussolinia. They're so ignorant that I felt ashamed for them."

"It's a scientific law that Fascism is founded on ignorance. The Sacrifice militants, like all Fascists, are ignorant."

"Sometimes I amuse myself by visiting the Facebook page of the Sacrifice militants to read what they write. I don't know if they're total dickheads or just ignorant."

"Unfortunately, the Sacrifice militants only read Hitler's *Mein Kampf.* If you read bullshit, you think bullshit and you talk bullshit."

"A friend of mine, who went to high school with a boy who has now become a Sacrifice militant, told me that this asshole talked about Fascism without knowing anything about the history of Fascism and everyone made fun of him."

"If you're a Fascist, you're ignorant. It's taken for granted."

"All Fascists are ignorant, whatever organization they belong to."

Insults of the Fourth Type

Insults of the fourth type are prompted by the idea that some people become Sacrifice militants because they are mentally deficient. Unlike other insults, which acknowledge that Sacrifice militants have the capacity to act in a rational and intentional manner, insults in this category associate Fascism with mental disorders.

Here are seven examples:

"The Sacrifice militants are mentally ill."

"Young people who enter groups like Sacrifice need to go to a psychiatrist."

"The Sacrifice militants should be removed in an ambulance and not by a police car."

"The Sacrifice militants are guys with serious mental problems."

"These young people [Sacrifice militants] should be shut up in a mental home. Sooner or later one of them will take a gun and shoot some immigrant. They're crazy; politics has nothing to do with how they act."

"If, in 2014, a fifteen-year-old boy says he's a Fascist, it means he's insane."

"I wonder what kind of mental problems the Sacrifice militants have. Maybe their mother beat them too hard when they were children?"

6

FROM A FASCIST PERSPECTIVE

When someone spits in your face, it is disgusting. Saliva stinks. But spit in your mouth is even more repulsive.

The journey from my apartment to the Lenintown militia headquarters was always the same and took about fifteen minutes. At the beginning I preferred to go on foot, so that the Sacrifice T-shirt I wore could be seen by the greatest possible number of people. Later I started using a bicycle that I tied to a lamppost some two hundred yards or so from the office.

I'd walk past the shops, ring the bell, and wait for a comrade to open the door.

After about two weeks, I found a note in the bicycle basket that read, "Fascist shit, we're following you."

My body stiffened.

I remained there for a few seconds holding the note while I looked around me in confusion. It's unsettling to learn that you're being watched and followed by a hostile and unknown group of people. Prompted by fear, your imagination makes you magnify the danger. I told myself that

I should keep calm, they're just a bunch of cretins incapable of hurting anyone. A few second later I changed my tune, asking myself if I was really in danger. I shouldn't be too sure of myself. Those who underestimate danger always end up badly.

What should I do? Perhaps Leonidas would be able to tell me who had written that note. Putting a face on your enemies is always reassuring. But Leonidas had told me that he'd never even found out who had dumped the shit outside the door of the militia's headquarters. Why would he know who had written that note?

In the end, I decided not to say anything to the comrades because that would have inevitably set off a fight with the extreme-left groups. My task wasn't to provoke battles but to study them. Also, if there had been a fight, I would inevitably have been involved, since the note was addressed to me. Leonidas would have gone to the communists and said, "Which piece of shit wrote this?"

When I entered the militia offices, Leonidas asked me why I had such a long face. Then he told me to pack the Sacrifice flags in a cardboard box. "Come with us," he said. "We're going downtown to distribute food to poor Italians." Leonidas told me that four cops would be coming to check on us and that they would remain with us the entire time: "You're about to meet the Lenintown special police squad that keeps an eye on everything we do."

It was a fine day, and the downtown area was full of people calmly strolling around.

I was not calm.

We set up the stall, placed the food packages in it, and then I saw one of the cops coming toward us. I knelt down behind the plastic table pretending to look for something in a box in the hope I wouldn't be noticed.

"Look out, guys," said a comrade in a low voice. "Here come Carlo's ballbreakers."

Carlo, chief of the special police unit, greeted the comrades and congratulated Leonidas on his latest victory in a boxing match a few days earlier. He good-naturedly said that he'd seen the photos of the match on Leonidas's Facebook page and started to recount that when he was young . . .

Suddenly he stopped talking, creating an unnatural silence. I lifted my head and saw that Carlo and the comrades were peering down at me.

I got up. Not taking his eyes off me, Carlo scolded Leonidas: "Leonidas, who's this? I've never seen him before. Why didn't you tell me that you had a new militant?"

Leonidas didn't reply, and I stayed silent to express my respect for the militia leader. No comrade ever took the liberty of speaking in Leonidas's place. The first rule of a Fascist militia is respect for the leader and submission to his authority. As long as I was a Sacrifice militant, I scrupulously followed this law.

Leonidas's silence irritated the officer, who said in an aggrieved tone of voice, "It's not OK, guys, it's not OK." Carlo paused and shook his head in disapproval. "Leonidas, why didn't you tell me that you had a new militant? Why wasn't I informed?"

From Leonidas's answer, I understood that the comrades had agreed, in an amicable way, to give the police the names of those who joined their militia. I say "amicable" because Italian law does not require political movements to register the names of new members with the police, so Leonidas was not obliged to inform them: "You're right, I forgot to tell you. Our group has a new member. He's a sociology professor who's writing a book about us."

Carlo turned to me with a smile and, in enthusiastic tones, said something he should never have said: "Of course. I know who you are! They told me about you!"

My heart started beating fast.

I was very frightened.

The only person who could have talked to Carlo about me was the Lenintown chief of police. If Leonidas were to learn I had met him, it would be the end for me. Suddenly the roles were reversed. Now it was Leonidas who was asking the questions and it was Carlo who wasn't answering. Leonidas asked Carlo who could have talked about me: "How do you know who he is? Who told you about him?"

Idiot!

Asshole!

Shut up!

It's what I wanted to shout at Carlo, stamping my feet on the ground and waving my fists, but the only thing that came out of my mouth was a few words accompanied by an extremely nervous laugh:

The police know about me because I'm a famous professor!

Ha ha ha . . .

Isn't that so? Everyone knows about me. I'm famous!

Carlo, who probably realized the mistake he'd just made, didn't utter a word and shifted the comrades' attention to the cardboard boxes, which he started to riffle through himself. Leonidas, looking at him with annoyance, commented with a resentful smile, "Don't worry, Carlo, we haven't brought any bombs with us!"

Although he continued to smile, Carlo was genuinely searching us. He read what we had written on the flyers and then left, saying, "Behave yourselves." Instead of getting into the car with his men, he joined the people milling around the streets of Lenintown.

When I was sure that the cops were far enough away, I started to rail against them in the attempt to remove any possible suspicion of having had interactions with Carlo and his men:

These asshole cops! How do you put up with them? Look at them sitting in their car watching us! Haven't they got anything better to do?

Leonidas explained, with a patient expression on his face, that Carlo and his special squad were detailed to observe all our initiatives:

"My lawyer told me that we have to keep a low profile because we're being investigated since the fight in the bar. The police are keeping watch on everything we do. They're relentless; they never let up."

When Carlo returned to our stall, I realized that he hadn't gone off just for a stroll. A group of extreme-left militants had gathered on the other side of the square.

The Lenintown militia, like that of Mussolinia, has a very active Facebook page on which it announces all its initiatives in the hope of involving sympathizers in them. When I was conducting my research, the Lenintown comrades' Facebook page had 1,049 likes and was the best tool for collecting information on the life of the militia.

Carlo, worried that the Fascists and communists could come to blows, said in the tone of someone used to being obeyed: "Guys, don't move from here, OK? Stay put. Is that clear?"

Leonidas, who had just instructed me to keep calm, became irritated and replied angrily: "Fuck! Why is it that the communists are allowed in the busiest street in Lenintown while we have to stay here? It's not fair!"

Leonidas complained to Carlo that he had gone to the Lenintown police station to ask if he could put up his plastic table in the precise spot the communists were occupying, but the cops had said no, offering him another space. The place where the communists were now gathered had always been occupied by Sacrifice, and Leonidas felt that he had been wronged.

The situation became tense.

Carlo had searched our boxes as if we were criminals. He had demanded, without having the right, that Leonidas give him the names of new militants, ordering him around in front of all the comrades. And he had examined our flyers. In addition to all this, he was preventing us from moving, confining us within ten square yards while everyone else was free to walk around. Carlo repeated himself, sounding like a commander addressing his subordinates, while Leonidas became increasingly irritated: "Leonidas, I said that you mustn't move from this place. Do you understand?"

Leonidas spoke over Carlo's words and openly challenged his authority with the addition of some profanities: "Why should the communists occupy our position? I don't give a shit! You've favored the communists! It's not right."

Carlo exploded: "ENOUGH!"

The eight comrades around me closed ranks, creating a kind of blockade behind Leonidas, while passers-by stopped to see what was happening.

Increasingly agitated, Leonidas tried to walk away from our booth, but Carlo stood in front of him to block him. A policewoman around thirty with an aggressive expression, wearing close-fitting jeans and with the handle of her gun in plain sight, got out of a police car and came over, but Carlo stopped her with a gesture of his hand. Then he took a step back from the comrades and relaxed his posture, clearing the way for Leonidas.

The policewoman didn't move.

We didn't move.

The people around us didn't move.

Very slowly—the slowest movement in the world—Carlo took off his dark glasses and allowed silence to fall for a few seconds while he looked down, avoiding the comrades' gaze.

Then he did an extraordinary thing.

He stopped commanding.

Politely and considerately he said: "Guys, it's not my fault, believe me. You and the communists decided to organize an initiative on the same day and at the same time."

Carlo then assured Leonidas that he had always tried to do what he could for him: "Leonidas, you know very well that I'm always willing to help you if I can. I'm not the one who decides who gets which space. I didn't make that decision. I've always tried to meet you halfway, haven't I?"

Carlo promised Leonidas that in the future he would try to assign him the space he wanted. What up to a few seconds earlier had been a peremptory order now took on the guise of a favor asked of a friend: "Leonidas, please don't move from here, OK?"

Leonidas immediately calmed down and didn't utter a word. The policewoman returned to the car, the comrades started distributing food packages again, the people moved away, and I pretended to speak on the phone to record my account since I couldn't take notes while everyone was looking.

After about an hour, showing my respect for the militia leader, I told Leonidas I was thirsty and asked his permission to go and buy a bottle of water and take a walk. In fact I needed to step away to write in my notebook. Leonidas agreed, telling me that Carlo wouldn't have stopped me from walking around: "Carlo knows that you're a professor. He won't give you any problems. Go."

In the other part of the town center, I saw that the communists had set up a plastic bench with a stack of flyers on it. Since I was wearing a black T-shirt with the Sacrifice symbol, I tried to keep my distance, but I needed to see what they had written on their poster. It was a protest against the Italian government, but I didn't see any anti-Sacrifice slogans. The problem was that coming close enough to observe the communists meant that they could also observe me, and from the way they were staring at me, I realized that I had become a member of the parallel world.

The police knew that I was a sociologist. The Fascists knew that I was a sociologist. But what about the communists?

The Mussolinia Chief of Police

The next day I went to a bar with Leonidas, who wanted a beer. While we were walking there, he didn't speak for a few seconds and then said, in a serious and portentous tone: "We're a drop of lead that slowly slips into your tortured conscience."

Leonidas didn't know it, but I had already read that phrase. He had published it on his Facebook page, and I had transcribed it in my notebook before I met him. Leonidas didn't know that I had spent the last several years of my life collecting information on him and on the Mussolinia and Lenintown militias.

A drop of lead in your tortured conscience . . . That's a great saying!

"It's an excellent saying."

What does it mean exactly?

"The drop of lead represents our militia and our values."

And who has the tortured conscience?

"It's the conscience of the people who live in this crappy bourgeois society. They're people who don't think. They're people who live a life without living."

Leonidas, can I tell you something?

"Go on."

Yesterday the chief of the special police squad wanted to piss us off. At a certain point I was scared that a fight would break out . . .

"A fight? Never. The cops have the task of hiding us, not hitting us. The cops have to ensure that people don't notice us. A fight downtown with the police? Everyone would have noticed us. That's not what the system wants."

As Leonidas continued, I began to see the borders of the parallel world more clearly. According to Leonidas's reasoning, influenced by revolutionary Gnosticism, the Lenintown militia was the "drop of lead" that for him signified the essence of truth. Thanks to their books on revolutionary Fascism, the Lenintown comrades were the only ones who understood the ultimate meaning of historical development. The history of a civilization, Leonidas explained to me, develops as long as a warrior race exists capable of fighting, because war is the mainspring of historical development. As Mussolini said, the history of humanity is nothing but the history of the domination of a few men over other men. Bourgeois society, with its pacifism, is creating the conditions for the destruction of European civilization. The only people who can stop this disaster are Sacrifice militants, but they cannot broadcast their ideas because if they were to do so, they could provoke a revolution that would lead to the fall of bourgeois society and capitalism.

Leonidas explained his thinking in ungrammatical Italian, accompanied by profanities, but his ideas were clear and showed he had internalized the political culture of revolutionary Fascism. Leonidas thought Carlo's task was to maintain not so much the so-called public order but rather the "mental order" on which bourgeois society is based: "Carlo couldn't give a fuck about respecting us. He just didn't want people walking around downtown Lenintown noticing us. The cops want to keep us enclosed in a little world so no one can see us."

I tried to encourage Leonidas to continue his account by enthusiastically telling him that his ideas were original:

A little world? Fuck, I like the idea! What do you mean exactly when you say that the cops want to keep us enclosed in a little world?

"There's the world of the bourgeoisie, where millions of people live without awareness, and there's our world, which is a small world because in the end we're just a few comrades, but we're more frightening than a million people in revolution. That's why they try to keep us hidden."

The next day, Leonidas texted to tell me that the meeting scheduled for that evening wouldn't be taking place. A few hours later, an unknown telephone number lit up on my display. A man, after saying he hoped he wasn't disturbing me, told me he was Mario, the chief of police in Mussolinia. I knew that the police had created two special units to monitor the Sacrifice militants, one in Lenintown and one in Mussolinia, and I also knew that the chief of police in Lenintown answered to the chief of police in Mussolinia, who outranked him.

I realized I'd been lucky. If the Mussolinia chief had phoned me while I was walking with Leonidas, I'd have been in serious trouble.

I should point out that Mario had my telephone number because I had told the Lenintown chief that I would like to meet his Mussolinia counterpart to ask him about the fight in which Joe had lost an eye. I should also point out that, when I made this request, I was still in the initial stage of my research, the "approach stage." Immediately after entering Sacrifice, I'd decided that I shouldn't have any further contact with the police, and I hadn't.

After telling me he had gotten my telephone number from the Lenintown police chief, Mario said: "Professor Orsini, the Lenintown police chief told me that you wanted to speak to me. I would also like to meet you in Mussolinia to have a chat."

I thanked Mario for having phoned me and told him that I would be very pleased to meet him, but I had to refuse his invitation: "It's too dangerous for me. If the Sacrifice militants were to see me with you, I would be in trouble and my research would be finished. I've devoted too many years to it for this to happen. I hope you can understand."

Mario politely insisted and tried to reassure me: "Professor Orsini, don't worry, I know a bar in Mussolinia where we can speak without being seen by anyone."

I suspected that Mario had suggested meeting in a bar so as not to reveal over the phone the place where he really wanted to take me, but not being able to verify my intuition, I had to take his suggestion at face value. If I accepted his invitation, there would be at least one witness to my meeting with the Mussolinia police chief: the bartender! One witness was one too many, so I said firmly: "A bar? No, no, it's too dangerous!"

I suggested meeting in Rome, in my office at LUISS University. Mario told me that was impossible and tried again to persuade me to meet in Mussolinia: "Professor Orsini, trust me, I'll take you to a very safe place. No one will see us. I have total control over the situation in Mussolinia." I repeated that I couldn't meet him in Mussolinia and I said good-bye. Mario gave me his office telephone number and said: "Professor Orsini, if you change your mind, call me anytime at this number. Thank you. I hope to hear from you soon."

A few days later, Mario called me a second time to try to persuade me to meet him. He was just as polite as he had been before. Our conversation was identical to the previous one, and I again refused to meet him.

As the days passed, I had the impression of being shadowed, and I imagined it was by Mario's agents. I had studied for years how people tail someone to kill them and I had also studied the so-called counter-surveillance techniques, those that enable you to know if someone is shadowing you. I had learned a lot about these practices from the lengthy interviews I had conducted with extreme-left terrorist groups responsible for multiple murders. Some of these people used to enter and exit a number of subway stations before entering the right one.

To return home, a person normally gets on and off the subway just once. A terrorist, before returning to his hideout, may get on and off the subway a dozen times to discover if he's being tailed by the police. When he enters and exits the subway car, he looks around and tries to memorize the faces of the people who enter and exit with him.

I had been affected by the paranoia of those living in the parallel world, especially when violence was about to be carried out. I had become like Cincinnatus, who was frightened of driving his car because he had Hitler's *Mein Kampf* in the trunk and thought he was being followed by the cops.

For three consecutive days, before returning home, I entered and exited various bars and clothing stores a dozen times.

As I mentioned earlier, it usually took a quarter of an hour to walk from the militia headquarters to my apartment. During those three days, the journey took more than two hours.

And no cop was shadowing me.

It wasn't the police that was my problem.

The Worst Day of My Life

When I was sure that I wasn't being tailed by the police, I realized I was entering a paranoid universe and I decided to take an evening off.

Instead of spending the evening in the Mussolinia militia offices, I went to a pub with Neo and some of his friends.

I have to confess I felt guilty.

I felt that my duty as a sociologist was to spend as much time as I could with the Sacrifice Fascists, and I was also aware that I could be expelled at any moment, but that evening I really needed a break. Behaving like a member of a far-left terrorist group who fears he's being followed by the police meant that my mental processes were no longer normal. Since I had entered Sacrifice, my private life had disappeared. I had spent every Friday, Saturday, and Sunday evening studying the comrades, and I was starting to understand how repressive the lack of female companionship could be.

I took my leave of Neo and walked toward my bicycle, which I had parked in an alley behind the pub. During the summer, the street in front of the entrance to the pub is crowded with young people, whereas the alley behind is badly lit and almost always deserted.

While I was taking out my key to unlock the chain, I heard someone say behind me, "Hi, Fascist!"

I turned around and saw that some youths were approaching from different directions. I tried to make out the face of the person who had spoken and was coming toward me.

Did I know him?

The alley was dark, and his face was partly hidden by a red baseball cap. I searched my memory but I didn't recognize him. When I realized I was surrounded, I got on my bike and grabbed the handlebars, making two mistakes in one move.

There are two fundamental rules to be followed if you think you're about to be attacked. The first is to have both hands free, to protect your face. The worst thing that can happen when you're being attacked in the street is a blow to the face. A punch in the stomach or a kick in the shin will pass, but damage to your face remains for life.

Injuries to your face are terrible from a psychological point of view. When you look at yourself in the morning and see a smashed-up face, you also see the face of the person who hit you. As Antonio Iosa, a victim of extreme-left terrorism whom I had interviewed, told me: "Unfortunately, you always remember the face of the person who ruined your features. The person who injured you carries on with his life and forgets your face. But you are condemned to see the face of your torturer for the rest of your life."

The second rule when being attacked is to look for an escape route to get away as quickly as possible. Generally, those who plan an assault expect the victim to remain motionless and cry out for help. They never imagine the victim will start running away without saying a word.

I broke both rules.

Instead of starting to run, I got on my bicycle and put both hands on the handlebars. I squeezed the brakes with both my hands to keep my balance since the saddle was very high, and I could touch the ground only with the tips of my toes.

I couldn't protect my face, I couldn't run away, and I had difficulty maintaining my balance.

No one can escape under these conditions.

The guy who had called out to me, probably referring to my blond hair and blue eyes, said, "Fuck, you've come straight to Lenintown from Nazi Germany!"

After hearing these words, I opened my mouth to explain that I was a professor of sociology when, from my left side, a gob of spit arrived so large and powerful, and from such close range, that it covered my nose and entered my mouth.

I could smell the spit and could taste the disgusting warm saliva that had come from the mouth of another male. The youths around me ran away, and I never had time to recognize the person who had spat in my face. The only words I managed to say were "Listen, I'm a profe—"

Spit in the face come in two types: spit from far off and spit from close up. From the victim's viewpoint, spit from far off is preferable to that from close up since it has farther to travel and tends to open up and fragment. If the victim is lucky, he gets only a small spray of saliva on his face.

Spit from close up reaches your face in a compact mass.

I, unfortunately, was hit by spit from close up. Strong, abundant spit, coming from very near me.

After everyone had left, I got down from the bicycle and started to spit on the ground ten, twenty, thirty times with such violence that I felt a stabbing pain in my ribcage. I continued spitting until I no longer had a drop of saliva in my mouth. I swore to myself that I wouldn't swallow, to prevent the spit from ending up in my stomach. While I clasped the area in which I felt the stabbing pain, I felt an abrupt movement in my gut, then I bent over and vomited. I held my breath and remained motionless for a few seconds. As I returned home pushing my bike, I realized that when you remove spit with your finger, the odor remains on your skin and the saliva forms a sticky coating that has to be washed off with water.

What should I do next?

If I were to tell Leonidas about the episode, he would inevitably start a chain reaction that would lead to a fight with the communists. But there were three reasons why I didn't want to find myself in the midst of a brawl.

First, if I were to drive Leonidas into another fight, I would definitively ruin his life. Although it is true—as Laud Humphreys wrote—that any conceivable method employable in the study of human behavior has at least some potential for harming others, the task of ethnographic research isn't to intentionally ruin people's lives.[1] It's one thing to find yourself in a brawl; it's quite another thing to create it.

Second, I remembered the warning the Lenintown police chief had given me, telling me I wouldn't receive any favorable treatment from him if I broke the law.

Third, a fight can have unpredictable outcomes. In some cases, you return home with a black eye. In other cases, you return home without an eye.

I decided I wouldn't tell anyone what had happened to me. I was more fortunate than other sociologists such as Bill Buford, who was violently beaten by three policemen,[2] and Alice Goffman, who had seen much worse violence than I had suffered.[3]

In any case, that spit in the face was useful because it aroused hate, which is one of the most important emotive components in the parallel world. The feeling of hate increased my sociological comprehension of the social universe in which I was living.

That night I was very worked up and didn't get much sleep. As the hours passed, my desire for revenge against that gang of bastards grew and filled my body with tension.

How dare they spit in my face?

Fucking cowards!

Bastards!

I got up, took a shower, and started shaving. Violent fantasies were running through my mind.

Without having any control over my thoughts, which flitted relentlessly though my head, I relived the scene in that dark alley a thousand times. At lunch, at dinner, while I was riding my bike, when I was with friends, while I watched television, when I was driving my car. My hate constructed a fantasy world full of violence, in which I beat up those youths, humiliating them as they had humiliated me.

I wrote down the violent scenes produced by my imagination in my notebook. Later I realized, rereading my notes, that my hate was aimed not at the person who had spat in my face but at all the members of the group to which the spitter belonged.

I didn't hate "that" bastard.

I hated "those" bastards.

Even though in my violent fantasies I was a superhero who beat up everyone, I hated my hate because it filled my days with negative emotions. It took away my smile. I didn't laugh anymore, and I was full of anger. As I walked through the streets of Lenintown, I was always tense because I feared other attacks.

They follow me, observe me, leave notes on my bicycle, and then spit in my face.

Damned bastards!

I was upset because I had lost my greatest asset: my peace of mind.

I was a man full of anger, with a great desire for revenge. So I told myself that I was different from the Sacrifice militants; I would free myself of that hatred and I would once again become the composed, kind, and peaceful person I have always been.

I'm not a Fascist!

I returned home, put on my sweat suit, and stopped to admire my beautiful racing bicycle. It's such a beautiful bike that people turn around in the street to admire it. Riding my bicycle is my great passion. I can manage 125 miles in one day, pedaling up to nine hours. The bike I used to go to the Lenintown militia office was old and ugly, but this is a Wilier Triestina, a historic Italian brand, a bicycle made entirely in Italy by expert craftsmen.

It's a jewel that I keep inside my home.

I opened the door, went down a flight of stairs with my bicycle over my arm, and set off for a peaceful medieval hamlet, famous for its fantastic panoramic view. It's "one of those places that puts you in contact with God," as Neo, who had first shown it to me, said. I traveled a hundred miles there and back, stopping just once to enjoy a gigantic chocolate McFlurry in a small McDonald's with tables outside.

I returned home at ten in the evening.

I had detached myself from all that hatred and had proved to myself that I was a better man than the Sacrifice militants.

I wasn't like Leonidas.

I wasn't like Cincinnatus.

The next morning I woke up proud and satisfied because I felt no pain in my leg muscles despite the long bicycle ride the day before.

I was in great form!

I went to my usual café to have breakfast, and while I was waiting for my crepe with apricot jam, those scenes of violence ran through my mind again.

All I wanted to do was rip the shit out of those bastards. I didn't just want to punch them; I wanted to humiliate them. I wanted to hit them so hard and for so long that they would plead with me to stop. In that moment, I understood that hatred is an objective force that enters our daily life independently of our desire and our will. Hatred is a hot fluid that invades your heart, lungs, blood, and arrives at your brain. It's a stream that comes from the outside, like a dose of poison injected into your vein. Once it enters your circulation, it follows its course without asking for authorization.

I didn't want to hate, but I hated, and I was frightened.

If I really were to meet those bastards? Would I really rip the shit out of one of them? Would I be able to punch a guy younger than me?

No, I couldn't do it.

My values were telling me that it's wrong to hit another man, and yet my mind continued to produce those violent images.

I was hating.

I had entered the parallel world not only with my body but also with my mind, destroying all my enemies through my imagination. But my mind didn't understand that. In the parallel world, violence isn't used to destroy your enemies. Such a "little" world cannot allow itself the luxury of driving anyone out. In that moment, I clearly saw the difference between the two types of violence that characterize the parallel world and I recorded the thought in my notebook. I'm talking about the difference between "destructive violence" and "integrative violence." The first consists of eliminating political adversaries from the social space by killing them and is very rare in the parallel world. The second involves letting your enemies into your daily life to bring them closer, increasing the exchange of text messages and occasions for meeting. Integrative violence also includes threats and insults; it is widespread in the parallel world.

After breakfast, I received a call from my mother asking me to come back to Rome immediately. I got in my car and raced toward the worst day of my life.

For some weeks my father, who seemed perfectly fit, had developed a pain in his hip that he attributed to a false step during a yoga exercise. It took me two hours to persuade him to go to the hospital and undergo tests. When my parents left the doctor's office to get something in the hospital cafeteria, I was left alone with the young doctor who had examined the X-ray.

"You're his son?"

Yes.

"Alessandro Orsini?"

Yes.

"They told me that you're a colleague?"

Yes, I'm a colleague.

By the term "colleague," I meant that I was a professor at the same university, the University of Rome Tor Vergata, as the young doctor. She understood it to mean that I was a physician like her. Convinced of this, she said in a detached and unguarded manner: "Your father has developed three metastases in the brain and a large metastasis in the hip. He has a few months to live." When she saw me start to cry with my head between my hands, she asked me in bewilderment: "But aren't you a colleague? Aren't you a doctor?"

When we returned home, my mother told me I should tell my father the truth. I went into the living room and saw my father calmly sitting on the couch, watching television. "Alessandro," he asked. "What do the tests say?"

I told him that I had to return to the university to collect them. I went down the steps, got into my car, and returned after an hour, when I had found the strength to tell my father he was dying, even though he continued to feel well and lead a full life.

I opened the door and saw my mother crying in a corner of the hallway so as not to be heard. My father was still sitting on the couch, in the same position in which I had left him. I was carrying a large white envelope bearing the name of the hospital where we had been a few hours earlier.

I remained standing. We looked each other in the eye and neither of us spoke. Then I started to talk, with an anguished expression and pronouncing every word very slowly:

Dad . . .

Pause.

Unfortunately . . .

Pause.

I don't have good news . . .

Long pause.

The pain in your leg is a metastasis.

"A METASTASIS? It's impossible! I feel fine!"

Dad . . .

Pause.

Unfortunately there's also a problem . . .

Long pause.

In your brain . . .

"In my brain?" There was astonishment on his face.

Yes, Dad, unfortunately there's also a problem in your brain.

My father looked at me with the gentle and serene expression of someone who is aware that he has arrived at the end of his life.

The doctors have said that you can't drive anymore because you could suddenly feel ill. From today on, I will accompany you to the university, but I think it would be better if you stopped teaching. But I'll accompany you anyway if you wish. Don't worry.

My father told me that he didn't fear dying and that he was happy to have refused chemotherapy: "Don't worry, I'm OK. Don't be anxious about me. The chemotherapy would have destroyed me like it destroyed my father. At least I've lived well all these months."

While I was talking, my brother Andrea, the youngest son, entered the room after rushing home in response to my mother's telephone call.

My father got up from the couch, and they hugged each other for five minutes, eyes closed.

Desperation is a sentiment that cannot be described.

The terrible thing about a tumor that has run its course is that you are looking at a person who seems perfectly fit but who is about to die. There's time to say good-bye, to hug him, to look at photos, to remember the past, and even to talk about sociological research.

That evening my father was serene. He said that he was happy to know that the metastases had affected the part of the brain that governs motor activity without damaging the parts involving cognitive processes: "For someone who's a scholar it's important to remain lucid. I must hurry up and finish my last book."

When we were alone, he asked me about my research into Sacrifice. Referring to Leonidas, he told me that, as a psychological matter, being despised is one of the most distressing experiences: "The experience of being held in contempt is very painful, especially when the contempt becomes permanent. It is one thing to be surrounded by contempt for five minutes; it's another thing to be surrounded by it every day of your life."

My father's words about the significance of contempt recalled an episode that Leonidas had told me about and that, up till then, I hadn't really given much thought.

Looking depressed, Leonidas, in the presence of four other comrades who listened in silence, had told me that a few weeks before his clash with Ashley at the bar, he had run into some guys from the W La Rivoluzione party: "I was walking along and I suddenly saw them coming toward me, right here on the street where our militia is. When I came up to them, since we already knew each other, I greeted them and held my hand out to the group leader. I was polite and respectful with him, but he didn't shake my hand . . ."

He didn't shake your hand?

"No, he didn't. While I was standing there with my hand held out, a girl said, 'We don't shake hands with Fascists.'"

The expression on Leonidas's face became even more depressed as he said: "Does that seem normal to you? You don't shake my hand because I'm a Fascist? You don't shake my hand because my ideas are different from yours? I think this behavior is ridiculous. They're the intolerant ones. This is intolerance!"

As I read these words with new insight, I began to see Leonidas in a different light. That young man, whom everyone described as a monster, seemed to me to be very fragile in his desire to be accepted by other people. But my new feeling of compassion didn't last very long. As soon as I returned to Lenintown, I discovered something that shook me.

Leonidas, a month after beating up Ashley, had attacked a fifty-year-old man. He had beaten him so violently that his face had split open. The man had lost consciousness and was immediately taken to the hospital, where he underwent surgery. The fracture was so serious that the doctors had to insert titanium plates and screws in his face.

My reaction was twofold.

First of all, I was shocked at the level of violence that Leonidas had committed.

Second, I was angry with myself. How could I not have seen this coming?

I was now faced with two tasks. The first was to investigate what had happened between Leonidas and the fifty-year-old man.

The second was to understand what had failed in my system of collecting information on life in the Lenintown and Mussolinia militias.

Leonidas's Second Fight

Once again, my friend Neo played an important role in my research.

Neo invited me to a Lenintown pub to watch a soccer match in which his favorite team was playing. On that occasion he introduced me to a friend of his, Stefano, who said as soon as he saw me: "Fuck, I know you! I always see you walking around Lenintown with the Sacrifice Fascists!" Neo hastened to explain that I was a sociologist, and Stefano, reassured, started to talk about Leonidas: "These fucking asshole Fascists. I really hope that this Leonidas ends up in prison." Neo told him that, for reasons having to do with his work, he had met Leonidas's father: "He's a good man, very polite and educated. Poor man, they all badmouth him because of his son."

Neo's friend spoke again, and this was how our conversation went:

"It's understandable. That man's face has been ruined. Fifty years old. I'd be mortified too to have a son like that."

A fifty-year-old man? With a ruined face? What are you talking about?

"Some time ago Leonidas quarreled, for pointless reasons, with a fifty-year-old man. They were in a bar. They came out and Leonidas knocked him down and started kicking him in the face."

While Stefano was talking, I started to Google the episode, but I couldn't find anything. There was nothing about it on the Internet. How was it that the communists hadn't written even one piece to deplore such a serious act of violence? Stefano told me that the communists, with whom he was friendly, hadn't published anything on Leonidas's attack because, after the fight with Ashley, many of them had been called as witnesses in his trial. Their lawyers had told them not to write any more articles against Leonidas so they would not seem unreliable witnesses on account of their resentment against the accused.

I left the pub for a few minutes to call a Lenintown politician with whom I had become friendly, and I made an appointment to see him the next day. Thanks to the information he gave me, I managed to narrow down my Google search and found two short items that mentioned the attack on the fifty-year-old man. The detail in which I was most interested was Leonidas's line of defense. He claimed that he hadn't been there. His defense can be summarized as: "I didn't do it. When the man was being beaten up, I was somewhere else."

To back up his claim, Leonidas needed witnesses. Who were they?

Leonidas can count on his comrades, Stefano told me.

Leonidas, during an interview that he gave in the presence of the militia members, told me that the comrades were prepared to testify on his behalf in the trial against Ashley, and the comrades confirmed this: "Of course, we're willing to testify on behalf of Leonidas."

I realized that I had an extraordinary opportunity to observe directly the sociological dynamics of a revolutionary sect.

In all the interviews I have carried out, the comrades always uttered this pledge with eyes full of passion: "I would be prepared to sacrifice my life to defend my militia." I thought that if a comrade was ready to die to defend another comrade, he would have no problem perjuring himself.

If the fifty-year-old man was found to have made a false accusation, many people would have had to apologize to Leonidas and to his comrades. But if Leonidas was found guilty?

Perjuring yourself in a criminal lawsuit means risking prison. Would the Lenintown comrades risk so much for their leader?

Anyone can be brave when it just means repeating a slogan, but this time it involved passing from the didactic principles contained in Codreanu's books to the facts. If the comrades were to perjure themselves, they would run the risk of ruining their lives, putting the interests of the militia before their own. For me it was not easy to investigate the attack against the fifty-year-old because Leonidas had never talked to me about it, and I couldn't suddenly say: "Leonidas, I've heard that you're about to go on trial because you destroyed the face of a fifty-year-old man. Can you give me your version of the facts?"

If Leonidas didn't bring up the matter spontaneously, I would be forced to remain silent and resign myself to being unable to gather information.

It was a serious problem.

7

THE GREAT FIGHT

I couldn't ask questions about the attack on the fifty-year-old man, but I could continue my research into the meaning of violence in the parallel world, attempting to understand why the threats, the insults, the provocations, the fights, the clashes, and the arrests were so frequent in this particular cultural universe.

The spitting in my face had prompted me to focus on attacks in which Fascists were the injured parties, not only on those for which they were responsible. I felt I hadn't done anything to deserve being spat at. My anger and the feeling that I was the victim of an injustice helped me widen my sociological horizon.

I asked Lentulus if we could meet, and I caught up with him and his girlfriend in downtown Mussolinia.

After talking for nearly an hour about communist provocations, we walked toward the militia offices.

When we arrived at the door, Lentulus exclaimed: "Fuck. Not again!"

The door of the headquarters was jammed. Someone had put a nail in the lock. They must have used a hammer to ram it in so deep.

I was astonished and said, "The communists!"

Lentulus didn't reply. I saw that he was dejected but not angry. The way in which he shook his head, the look on his face, and his hand movements seemed to say: "The communists are just unfortunate cretins. Since we comrades are more intelligent, we simply have to put up with their stupidity."

Together with his girlfriend we went to a locksmith, since—as Lentulus said—the only way to get the door open was to break the lock. It took only about ten minutes to walk there, but as it was nearly closing time, the locksmith told us to return on Monday. Clearly it wasn't the first time that Sacrifice militants had asked him to break open the lock: "Again? No, guys, it's Saturday evening! I'm about to close the shop. Come back on Monday."

During the walk back, I began a conversation by saying that the communists seemed very aggressive and well organized. I was hoping that sooner or later someone would say something about Leonidas's attack on the fifty-year-old man.

In a world in which everyone was extremely careful when speaking about ongoing police investigations, my task was to stimulate conversation and to insert myself in the flow by asking the right questions.

Lentulus answered, "The communists live for us."

In what sense?

"The difference between us and the communists is that we have plans and we're trying to carry them out, whereas they have no ideas and exist to be a pain in the ass for us."

They exist to be a pain in the ass for you . . .

"Exactly. If we were suddenly to disappear, the communists would be desperate; they'd no longer have any reason for living."

Meanwhile, the Mussolinia headquarters would have to remain closed on Saturday night and Sunday. I figured the communists had caused the comrades considerable damage.

A few days later I was walking through Mussolinia's main square. I heard my name called. I turned around and saw four young Sacrifice comrades approaching in a friendly manner.

The lock had just been broken open and the locksmith had been paid with the militants' money. I immediately started to talk about the communists and their act of sabotage.

The youths told me that, when Leonidas inaugurated the Lenintown branch, the communists dumped a load of shit in front of the building and smeared on the wall the words "Fascism = shit." I knew all about this, but I let them talk in the hope of acquiring new information. Ten different people can provide ten different versions of the same incident. When people recount events in which they are emotionally involved, they add personal comments and refer to other actors, enabling the ethnographer to contact new people to interview.

The youths repeated the same idea that Lentulus had expressed: "The communists do fuck all and spend all their time trying to stop us from carrying out our initiatives."

Then the conversation about the communists became more impassioned and led me to one of the most important documents I found in all my years of work devoted to Sacrifice. It was a video, lasting twenty-five minutes, of a battle between Sacrifice militants and extreme leftists taking place in a major Italian city. It turned on its head the official accounts of a huge fight, involving a hundred or more youths, in which Sacrifice militants were entirely to blame. The main Italian TV networks and the major newspapers had dealt at length with this violent encounter, and it had also been the subject of a parliamentary debate, in which left-wing members had warned against the dangers of a return of Fascism. On the basis of the journalists' stories and the politicians' statements, everyone was convinced that Sacrifice Fascists had attacked a peaceful march of left-wing militants without provocation. Public opinion had been horrified by the comrades' violence, and many had asked why the magistrates, under the Italian constitution, hadn't ordered Sacrifice to be dismantled and its leaders arrested.

When I saw the video, I understood why.

As soon as I entered the militia premises, the young comrades greeted me with enthusiasm, saying: "Come! Sit here!" indicating a chair in front of a table with a computer on it. "You'll see what bullshit the journalists say about us! They're all corrupt and on the side of the communists."

One of them started the video, and I saw everything clearly.

Two groups of university students are facing each other, the comrades on one side and the extreme-left activists on the other.

Both groups of demonstrators have come to the square to protest against the government, but the left-wing faction is much more numerous than the Fascists, at a ratio of what looks to me to be approximately one Fascist for every ten left-wing activists.

The situation is quite embarrassing for the communists, who find themselves protesting against the government for the same reasons as the Fascists. A left-wing sympathizer of around fifty picks up a microphone and starts to yell that the Fascists are disgusting and have no right to be present in the square. A Fascist shouts through a megaphone from the rear of a van that the Sacrifice militants want a peaceful demonstration and have no intention of fighting with the leftist contingent. The fifty-year-old man starts chanting an anti-Fascist slogan that echoes throughout the square. All of a sudden, the left-wing militants transform the demonstration into a platform for expressing solidarity with the partisans who, seventy years earlier, had fought against the Fascists.

For some minutes, the video shows the two groups of demonstrators involved in a competition over who can shout the loudest. The communists chant threatening and aggressive slogans against the Fascists, while the Fascists reply with peaceful responses in which they proclaim their right to be present in the square. A left-wing marcher aged around thirty raises a cardboard box on which he had just written "This is an anti-Fascist demonstration." The Sacrifice militant once again grabs the megaphone and yells: "We're all students! Everyone has the right to demonstrate in this square, whatever their political party. We're not against you. Leave us alone to demonstrate freely!"

Those in the Sacrifice contingent are all young students. The left-wing side includes dozens of thirty-, forty-, and fifty-year-olds.

Cries of panic are heard from the left-wing marchers.

Numerous anti-Fascist militants have joined the left-wing group armed with sticks and glass bottles. Some have covered their faces with scarves, while others are wearing helmets. Upon their arrival, dozens of well-turned-out girls marching in the same group start running away, yelling in fear. Many very young demonstrators, who look to be minors, also flee.

A clash is imminent.

The parallel world has opened its doors, and an entire political culture appears before my eyes. The leader of the Fascist group steps forward. He's a young student whom I recognize. I had talked to him in Rome at the end of the ceremony in honor of Dominique Venner.

With the comrades motionless and silent behind him, the young leader yells as if he were an officer addressing his soldiers on a battlefield: "Clooose raaanks! No one moooves!"

Submission to the leader.

Behind him, the comrades all take up the same position as if they had received military training. Their legs are slightly apart, their arms tense and lowered, and they hold out the plastic pole with the Sacrifice flag as if it were a spear.

The myth of the soldier.

The Fascists number around forty. There are many more communists.

Courage.

The comrades prepare themselves for the communists' challenge.

Honor.

They know they have no chance of winning, but they accept the fight all the same.

Sacrifice.

They are lined up beside one another in mutual protection.

Love for the militia.

The voice of the comrades' leader sounds anxious, or at least full of emotional tension. I get the impression he's scared. Not moving, still in the position I described, he yells: "You are many! You're bigger than us! We're just a group of young people."

The fight begins.

The communists, armed with bottles, stones, and sticks, advance with helmets on their heads.

The cries of the fleeing girls become louder.

The tension grows.

The parallel world is about to explode.

A girl, who can't be seen on the video, cries out in fear: "It's dangerous! It's dangerous!"

The communists charge.

Glass bottles, sticks, and stones are thrown at the Fascists, who don't retreat despite the objects flying toward them.

The comrades' leader shouts like the captain of a ship in a stormy sea: "Clooose raaanks!"

The communists are now running toward the Fascists. Suddenly the screen goes dark, and I imagine that the person filming the action alongside the Fascists has been hit and has dropped the camera, but the audio continues, and I can hear the noise of bottles breaking on the ground. The images return, and it seems that the person holding the camera is running, because the lens is pointed at the ground as arms follow the movement of legs. For a few seconds I can see only the pavement passing rapidly under his feet. Then he finds some protection, stops, and resumes filming.

All hell has broken loose.

Dozens of people continue to flee but get trapped in the narrow alleys around the square. The Fascists remain steadfast. Some are hit and fall to the ground.

Cries, yells, agitated images.

The communists destroy everything around them. When they have thrown all their bottles, they start hurling the plastic chairs and tables from the bars in one of the most beautiful squares in the world. Then hand-to-hand fighting begins. The Fascists have broken ranks and are engaged in physical encounters with extreme-left militants. Some of them have removed their belts and are hitting one another with them, but I can no longer distinguish the Fascists from the communists.

The video comes to an end.

The young comrades seemed full of adrenaline. One of them said to me: "Did you see? It was the communists who attacked! There were many more of them, but our comrades fought with honor! We were outnumbered, but we didn't retreat!"

We started talking about the way the mass media represent Sacrifice to the public at large. The comrades explained to me that Italian journalists are biased and corrupt. They're concerned not with reporting the truth but with hiding it to damage the image of Sacrifice. One of them said something that caught my attention because it reminded me of the parallel world concept that I was trying to develop in my ethnographic notes:

"The journalists describe us as criminals because they're frightened of our ideas and want to keep us shut up here."

Here where? In this headquarters?

"Here in the sense that they want to put us in a ghetto to keep us from influencing society."

I don't understand. Do you think that Sacrifice lives in a ghetto?

Before the comrade could answer my question, Marcus opened the door, entering the room and interrupting my interview just when I was waiting for the young comrade's answer.

He asked, "What are you doing?"

Since we were talking about the communists' attacks on the Sacrifice militants, I took the opportunity to ask him:

Did you see? The communists put a nail in your lock. I was with Lentulus when we discovered it . . .

"What communists?"

What do you mean, what communists? The communists, the ones who hammered a nail into the keyhole . . .

Marcus's reaction, and what he told me next, seemed incredible.

Up to that moment I had been certain that the communists had put the nail in the lock to prevent the comrades from meeting in the militia headquarters. After the emotional tension created by the images I had just seen and all those bottles that had been thrown right before my eyes, I had no doubt that it was the communists who had pounded that nail into the lock.

Who could be so stupid as to question such an obvious truth!

The truth about that nail was astonishing and reminded me of Luigi Pirandello's essay on "the comic" that tells us about the difference between appearance and reality. Humor is different from "the comic," says Pirandello: The comic is when you feel that something is the opposite of what should be, and that provokes laughter. Humor, by contrast, is a feeling that comes from reflecting on why a person or situation is the opposite of what should be.[1]

It was the first time in my whole career as a sociologist that I risked laughing in the face of a social actor I was observing. In the tone of someone talking to a simpleton who hasn't understood anything that has happened, Marcus said: "What communists are you talking about? After the fifth time we found a nail in the lock, we decided to set up a camera above the door. Five times! Come, I'll show you the camera."

Marcus pointed out the security camera, which I had already noticed but didn't think belonged to the comrades. Since the Mussolinia militia headquarters are in a small old building containing other apartments, and the Fascists have few financial resources, I thought it had been put there by one of the other residents.

You're telling me that it wasn't the communists who put the nail in the lock?

"Who told you that it was the communists? Lentulus?"

At that moment I realized that Lentulus had never actually said that it was the communists but had let me believe it. Like an idiot, I stammered in embarrassment:

No . . . Lentulus . . . Lentulus didn't tell me that it was the communists. I thought it was . . . I thought that . . .

"Lentulus couldn't have told you that it was the communists because it wasn't them who stuck that fucking nail in the lock!" said Marcus, sounding tense and irritated.

So who was it?

"The camera recorded everything, and some months ago we went to the police, but they couldn't do anything. The cops even burst out laughing when they saw the video!"

All right, who was it?

"We also thought it was the communists. You know our code of honor. You can't go to the police to settle a score with the communists. You do that personally with them. But then we looked at the video . . ."

So who was it?

"It was a fucking eighty-year-old woman who lives next door! She goes out at night, with a fucking bag in which she carries a fucking hammer and nail. She goes over to our front door, pulls out the hammer, and starts driving the nail into the lock!"

At Marcus's words, all the emotional tension that had built up on the faces of the four young Fascists during the viewing of the video suddenly vanished.

An eighty-year-old woman who goes out at night with a hammer in her bag? Are you fucking serious? Is this really true?

"Yes, she's over eighty!" he said, still sounding tense and irritated.

It's incredible! And what did you do? I found it difficult not to laugh. I tried to control my facial muscles, but a wide smile was breaking out.

With the same expression of forbearance that I'd seen on Lentulus's face, Marcus told me that the cops had said that the only way the Fascists could defend themselves against the old lady was to report her.

And did you report her? From the tone of my voice it was obvious that I was trying not to laugh.

"How could we report an eighty-year-old lady? Can you imagine what the papers would say? 'The Sacrifice Fascists are taking an eighty-year-old lady to court for putting nails in their lock!'"

What luck that you set up the camera; otherwise you would've had another fight with the communists for no reason!

"Exactly."

OK, you didn't report the old lady . . . So what did you do?

"One day, Lentulus and I waited for the woman to come out of her apartment and we said to her, 'Lady, why do you put nails in our lock at night?'"

Fuck, you had to ambush an eighty-year-old lady . . .

"I know. It makes me furious to think about it."

And the old lady?

"The old lady denied it! We told her that we had a video. Then we felt sorry for her and we let her go."

But she continues to put nails in the keyhole . . .

Marcus doesn't reply. He opens his arms with an expression that seems to say: "What can we do? We're the object of this abuse and we have to put up with it."

Who Observes the Observer?

I would have liked to ask Marcus a few questions about the brawl I had just seen in the video and start a debate on the violence of the communists against the Fascists to involve the young comrades. But my inability to control my facial muscles had destroyed all the emotional tension needed to develop such a delicate matter.

When I returned home, I noted down that ethnographers should be more willing to recount situations that reveal their errors or their lack of professionalism. I had been unprofessional, and I had committed a serious error.

It wasn't professional to laugh at Marcus, who was the leader of the Mussolinia militia. It wasn't even expedient, since Marcus was the person who defended my presence in the militia while others were asking for me to be removed, fearing that I would reveal confidential information.

I believe that readers would find ethnography much more interesting if they knew how many strange, embarrassing, and even comical situations are created in the process of doing research inside deviant groups. In some cases, ethnographers can compromise the success of the interview or an entire research project. In other cases, they are simply ridiculous, blundering, and incapable of doing their work well.

It has happened to me more than once.

It would be interesting to observe ethnographers while they observe others: Who observes the observer?

As I developed these reflections at my computer, two incidents came to mind that were even more comical than the one I had just experienced with Marcus. I amused myself searching through an old ethnographic notebook while comfortably sitting in my splendid apartment in Lenintown, with the window open and the sound of the sea to keep me company, hoping to recover the sense of serenity that life in the parallel world had taken from me.

The two incidents occurred during my research on Satanic sects that I had to suspend for safety reasons.

In Italy, one of these sects had committed a series of horrendous homicides. The bodies of the young victims had just been discovered in a wood, and I wanted to approach these devil worshippers to understand their way of seeing the world, but also to reconstruct their daily life and the types of interactions that occur in their sects.

Why does a person decide to become a devil worshipper?

I went to a very beautiful place called the Tuscolo Archaeological Park, not far from Frascati, southeast of Rome, which Goethe had praised in his book *Italian Journey*.

I was in the company of an elegant and sophisticated engineer who at that time had been my girlfriend for some years.

Thanks to the Italian newspapers and several television programs, I had learned that at night, Satanic groups gather in Tuscolo Park to celebrate black masses. Arriving in front of the ancient Roman amphitheater, which is the main attraction of the place, we met a man who was both a superintendent and guide at the park, with whom my girlfriend, interested in archaeology and unaware of my research, had made an appointment by telephone for a guided tour. The man was knowledgeable and courteous and told us that he was over seventy.

While he was telling us the history of the amphitheater, I tried to steer the conversation around to Satanic sects. This dialogue with the guide is drawn from my ethnographic notes dating back to the summer of 2011:

This is a beautiful place . . . Have you worked here for long as a tour guide?

"Yes, many years now."

I read something about this place that struck me . . .

"What?"

I read that Satanic masses are celebrated at night in this beautiful place.

"It's true, unfortunately."

Have you ever seen anything strange here?

"You see many strange things here. I've seen a lot of weird happenings over the years . . ."

I was very happy to hear this because I was sure that he would reveal invaluable details for my research into the world of the Satanists.

What did you see, exactly? I'd love to hear all about it.

"One evening I was driving home from the park when I realized that I had left my bag behind. It was getting dark as I came back and . . .

You came back and what did you see?

The guide to the archaeological park spoke slowly in a deep, grave tone of voice that captured my attention. He paused for a while, then pointed to a tree not far from us.

"You see that tree?"

Yes. What did you see there?

"I saw a woman of around fifty leaning on the tree. Behind her there was a man of the same age who was having sexual intercourse with her. The woman's head was banging against the tree, but the man continued to penetrate her from behind."[2]

I'm sorry, I don't understand. Were they two Satanists?

"No, they were two secret lovers who had gone into the park so as not to be seen, but I recognized them because they live near me."

My girlfriend and I looked at each other in shock and embarrassment. I hid behind her because I had started to laugh and I didn't want the guide, who was walking in front to show us the way, to see me.

But it didn't end there because the man added: "I've seen worse in this place. When night falls, anything can happen here."

I encouraged him to go on. I'd have been happy for even a small detail that would help me understand the Satanists who gathered in this place.

What have you seen? Can you tell us anything else?

"One evening, around sunset, I went to the park to take some photos of a tree that I wanted to cut down because there was the risk of its falling. I was here, where we are now, and the place was closed to the public."

What did you see?

"I saw a man lying on the ground wearing a camouflage combat outfit. You know, the ones that soldiers wear?"

Yes . . .

"He was hidden among the leaves, motionless, holding a rifle and taking aim. I took a wooden stick, approached him from behind without being heard, and hit him violently on the arm holding the rifle. The man cried out in pain: 'Ow! Are you crazy? What are you doing? Stop it!'"

A man with a gun! Who was he?

"He was playing a game I didn't know the name of. It's a game in which two groups of friends meet in the woods and shoot fake bullets at each other." He was describing paintball!

I passed from a state of emotional tension—I thought I was about to acquire information about Satanists—to an unexpected account of paintball players. I couldn't control myself, and I started to laugh.

Should Violent People Be Protected?

Once I had written down my thoughts about ethnographic errors to avoid, I was relaxed enough to return to my reflections on the Sacrifice militias. I realized that the comrades had an ongoing need to be involved in clashes and tension so as to be able to feel that they were living like soldiers at war.

It is important to clarify this point because, from the video I saw, it would seem that the Sacrifice Fascists wanted to give the impression that they were peaceful, accusing the press of unjustly describing them as violent hooligans. I reflected on this for a few days, but then I realized that my interpretation was contrary to everything that I had learned up to then.

The Sacrifice militants are against violence?

The Sacrifice militants battle in order to let everyone know that they are peaceful?

What did those young comrades hope to tell me by showing me that video?

I was confused and asked for an appointment with the person who could clarify my ideas better than anyone else: Augustus, the philosopher, the organization's cultural mentor, the person who had given the speech in honor of Venner.

Augustus helped me to a clearer sense of the relationship between Sacrifice and violence. To summarize: The Sacrifice comrades didn't use that video because they wanted to show that they were against violence. They wanted to show that the communists were cretins who spent all their time attacking Sacrifice militants, who have very important projects to implement.

The meeting with Augustus was a great stroke of good fortune for me. Augustus is a very distrustful person who thinks that everyone wants to badmouth Sacrifice, and he tends not to meet either academics or journalists unless they state that they are Sacrifice sympathizers.

The meeting occurred on one of the three campuses of LUISS University, the Libera Università Internazionale degli Studi Sociali Guido Carli in Rome, and lasted for about an hour. Knowing Augustus's mistrust of the outside world, I tried out a technique that I've called "interviewing by contrast." This consists of making a statement attributing an idea to a social actor that is the opposite of what he or she believes. When this occurs, social actors react impulsively and, out of fear of being misunderstood about something that's important to them, explain their thinking, repeating the same idea and giving the ethnographer a better understanding of the way their mind works.

While I was walking with Augustus, I uttered these words in the confident tones of someone who understands everything:

The journalists always blame you for all the clashes. Instead you're against violence . . .

Augustus reacted immediately.

"No, it's not true! It's wrong to say we're against violence. On the contrary, we believe all militants must be prepared to employ violence at any time. When it's necessary, violence is useful and must be used."

So those who say that you recruit violent youths are right?

"We don't recruit violent youths. We recruit little hoodlums and we try to turn them into political soldiers; we try to discipline them and to educate them in the values of revolutionary Fascism."

Augustus explained to me that the task of the Sacrifice militias is to train the "little hoodlums" to use their anger and their energy to fight against bourgeois society, rather than brawling in the street for trivial reasons. When I told him that some Mussolinia comrades had shown me a video to prove that the communists had attacked the Sacrifice militants during an anti-government demonstration, Augustus told me that Sacrifice used that video not to assert that Sacrifice is against violence but for three purposes.

The first purpose is to show that journalists are all corrupt and in the service of the bourgeoisie. The second is to show that the communists are idiots who spend all their time trying to break the Fascists' balls. The third is to show that the Sacrifice militants are political soldiers who do not fear anyone and who would risk their lives to defend their ideas and their militia.

Augustus couldn't have been more clear. He was better educated than Leonidas or Marcus, and I was disappointed that he didn't want to meet again. I would have liked to ask him about my interpretation of the facts, but I gave up because I was sure he would react badly, labeling me an enemy of Sacrifice.

As Jack D. Douglas put it, "No one gives anyone anything for nothing, especially truth."[3]

The interpretation on which I wanted Augustus's opinion was this:

You say you recruit little hoodlums to teach them discipline, but sometimes this operation doesn't succeed and, for petty motives, one of these little hoodlums breaks a bottle, thrusts it into a guy's eye, and blinds him. When this happens, instead of reprimanding your militant, you defend him because, on the basis of Codreanu's philosophy, the comrades must always protect one another, even at the risk of their lives. True?

I wasn't able to ask Augustus this question, but I was able to talk to Caligula about it, the only Sacrifice militant who disproved Douglas's maxim.

Caligula told me the truth about the relationship between Sacrifice and the recruitment of the "little hoodlums" without asking anything in return.

Once again my interpretation was limited, and I needed additional interviews to obtain a broader perspective.

I have already briefly discussed Caligula (see chapter 2), but now it may be useful to explain more about the profile of this militant. I first met Caligula when I started to use the weight room of a sports center owned by two well-known Sacrifice militants respected by all the Italian militias. The gym, which I'll call gym X, is neither in Lenintown nor in Mussolinia. In my approach to the Lenintown and Mussolinia militias, I had to move twice. First I left Rome and rented an apartment in the same city as gym X, where I lived for some years, and then I rented another apartment in Lenintown.

Caligula, one of the coaches in gym X's weight room, has a university degree and had recently had a child. His grandfather was a Fascist, his father and brothers are Fascists. When I asked him about the path he had taken to become a Fascist, he replied, "In my case, Fascism is a family tradition."

Caligula is greatly respected by all the comrades. He has started a process of de-radicalization, which he says he has spoken about only with me, prompted by the following perception: "I'm not arguing about the importance of Mussolini, but after many years of militancy, I've realized that in Italy the word 'Fascism' is so discredited that no Fascist movement can ever leave the ghetto. There's no future for Sacrifice."

All our conversations occurred in the weight room, usually in the morning, when there were fewer people in the gym and Caligula was less busy.

In five years I had twenty-two conversations in which I managed to get Caligula to talk about Sacrifice. We've had many more conversations, but they have been about other topics.

Caligula told me that he had great respect for me, both as a person and as a sociologist. In most cases it was Caligula who asked the questions, about terrorism and international politics in the Middle East. He addressed many more questions to me than I did to him. Since we talked about Sacrifice in many conversations involving different topics, I can't say exactly how long I spoke to him about Fascism, but all in all, they covered several hours. In some cases, especially in the final stages of my research (I also met with Caligula after my expulsion), we even talked exclusively about Sacrifice for an entire hour without interruption. Caligula told me that the books by Codreanu, Degrelle, and Giani were essential to him: "[They] have been a point of reference in my life, as a man, as a father, as a husband, and not only as a militant."

It was very easy for me to take ethnographic notes on my conversations with Caligula since gym X has numerous restrooms, and one of these, which is particularly large, is situated in the weight room. This enabled me to record the notes on my phone a few seconds after each conversation ended. The only problem was that the restroom didn't lock, and anyone could have suddenly opened the door, so I had to lean against it to keep it closed.

Of the great quantity of notes I made about my conversations with Caligula, I select only the parts that concern relations between Sacrifice and the "little hoodlums." Caligula has what you might call a contrary attitude toward the militants in prison. He believes they were wrong to attack their victims, but he also thinks that it's his moral duty to defend them.

The dialogue I report here occurred in response to a question I asked about some Sacrifice militants who were in jail for organizing, and participating in with twenty friends, a very violent act of aggression against a group of left-wing militants, attacking them with iron clubs and sticks. The newspapers had reported the fight.

Caligula told me that Sacrifice would always remain in the ghetto, for two reasons. The first reason, as we have seen, was cultural: the word "Fascism" has such a negative connotation that anyone who uses it will always be held in contempt. The second was that Sacrifice always defends militants who are arrested for committing offenses that shock ordinary people.

Does Sacrifice know that these militants are guilty?

"In some cases Sacrifice knows they're innocent, in other cases it knows they're guilty, but it defends them all the same. I defend them as well, but . . ."

But?

"But the problem is that this closes up the organization even more in a ghetto, because people then . . ." He left the sentence unfinished.

What does Sacrifice actually do to defend these guys?

"It publishes press releases and in many cases pays for their lawyers."

Why does Sacrifice protect these militants, even though it knows they are to blame?

"In Sacrifice there's a rule that you can understand only if you read Codreanu's books. The rule is that the militia is more important than anything else in the world."

Then Caligula went into a lengthy discourse on Codreanu's book, re-iterating that all the Sacrifice militants know they always have to defend one another, even if someone has committed a crime: "Everyone defends the others, because he knows that the others would defend him."

How many Sacrifice militants are currently in prison?

Caligula's response gave me information that I could never have gained from the Mussolinia or Lenintown militants. I could thus investigate further and reconstruct some stories that would better explain the connection between Sacrifice and political violence.

He didn't know them all, he told me, but he knew for certain that four were in one prison, three in a second prison, one in a third, and another in a fourth. A tenth man had just come out of prison and was now under house arrest. Sacrifice had nominated this comrade to run for mayor of his town.

"Some militants commit minor offenses and leave prison after a couple of days. Others commit more serious crimes and are sentenced to several years."

What offenses are they arrested for?

"They're always offenses linked to brawls and beatings. We have a code of honor. If one of our militants is arrested for drug dealing or for theft, the organization will abandon him. That has never happened."

At the time Caligula gave me this information, a Sacrifice leader had in fact been accused of helping a member of an international drug-trafficking organization obtain a false document in order to throw the police off his trail. The story had received extensive coverage in the newspaper *La Repubblica,* so this information was in the public domain. The legal pro-ceedings were still under way, but the magistrates had finished their in-vestigation, and the accused now had to defend themselves. This Sacrifice leader, before being investigated for drug dealing, had been the victim of an attack one night during which he had been shot in the legs. The victim had declared that he hadn't recognized his attackers but said he was sure they were extreme-left militants. The judges considered the incident a set-tling of scores inside a drug-trafficking ring. This attack was to have very negative consequences for the image of Sacrifice because it was a Mafia-style form of punishment.

This is the only case I've heard about of a Sacrifice militant being investigated for something other than a physical attack; and anyway, it remained possible that he might be acquitted. Even though Caligula neglected to mention this case, his testimony is otherwise reliable. On the basis of my experience, I, like Caligula, am convinced that both the Mussolinia and Lenintown comrades would immediately expel—perhaps even beat up—any militant who had anything to do with drugs or with people linked to the drug-dealing world.

I told Caligula that a comrade whose name I didn't remember had told me that Sacrifice recruits little hoodlums to turn them into political soldiers. Caligula replied that this type of recruitment was one of the organization's main merits. Sacrifice, he told me, recruits many different people, including some little hoodlums, whom it recruits in order to educate them, giving them a spiritual mission.

The Role of the Media

I realized that the interpretation I'd wanted to put to Augustus was based on a rather negative idea: that Sacrifice's national leaders were protecting their militants in prison even though they knew they were guilty.

The conversation with Caligula helped me to see that this opinion was not entirely correct.

More specifically, Caligula helped me understand the relationship that exists between the journalists' manipulation of information and Sacrifice's decision to protect hoodlums who were arrested.

The problem, he explained to me, was that in the great majority of cases, journalists unjustly accuse Sacrifice militants of wrongdoing, reporting a lot of things that aren't true: "I can assure you, because I've seen it with my own eyes, that many comrades have been attacked by left-wing militants or by the police, but then the journalists turn the truth around." The Sacrifice militants are so used to being unjustly accused by the media, Caligula continued, that a strong and immediate camaraderie develops among them. The result—and this statement is important—is that "when journalists accuse a comrade of having committed a crime, everyone immediately figures he's innocent."

This produces a result that is also important for understanding the Sacrifice leaders' attitude toward militants who have been arrested. Knowing that journalists distort the truth, the Sacrifice leaders instantly defend their militants, assuming that they've been unjustly accused. When, months later, they discover that their comrades were actually guilty, "they can't turn back," explains Caligula, "and they have to continue to defend them so as not to lose face, even if they don't personally know the comrades involved."

What Caligula told me also helped me understand one of the strategies local Sacrifice leaders use for bonding with the national leaders. The former know that, in the case of arrests, the latter will pay the lawyers and, if possible, also make bail for their comrades' immediate release. Thanks to Caligula, my ethnographic notes became a lot clearer. I remembered what Marcus had told me after a game of Risk—the military strategy board game—when we were in the Mussolinia headquarters.

Marcus related that, a couple of years earlier, he had gone to another town to see the Mussolinia soccer team play. He was already on the bus to return to Mussolinia with the other fans when he was harassed by a police officer, who ordered him to get off the bus, accusing him of being disrespectful. Marcus got off quietly, but the police officer started hitting him, then arrested him and had him put in jail on a charge of insulting, resisting, and assaulting a public official. Marcus showed me the articles published in the press after his arrest. The journalists had described him as a violent youth who assaulted an officer. One headline read "SACRIFICE MILITANT PUNCHES POLICE OFFICER IN THE FACE!"

As a consequence, the cops in Lenintown and Mussolinia had increased their pressure on the militias. The police officer, however, was unaware that the incident had been recorded on the stadium video camera. Marcus's lawyer asked for the tape, thanks to which Marcus was acquitted. The most embarrassing revelation never appeared in the media: the video images showed that the aggressor was the cop, who was subsequently tried for police brutality, since he had hit Marcus and arrested him for no reason.

Marcus told me all of this while we were sitting on an old, broken-down couch next to the front door of the militia headquarters. It was late at night, and we were both very tired.

"Now do you understand the bullshit the journalists invent about us and the prejudice we have to put up with? They threw me in jail without any reason. Can you imagine what my parents went through? I owe everything to the Sacrifice leaders. I'll never forget what they did for me. I'll remember it forever."

What exactly did they do for you?

"When they put me in prison, I was allowed to make a telephone call to a lawyer. Do you know who I called?"

No.

"I didn't call a lawyer. I phoned the Sacrifice national headquarters. The Sacrifice people went into action immediately and paid for a lawyer, who got me out of jail in twenty-four hours."

Is this something they did just for you, or do they do it for everyone?

"If the head of a militia is arrested, the Sacrifice national leaders pay for a lawyer and send out all the press releases defending him. While the journalists were destroying my reputation, the only people standing up for me were the Sacrifice national leaders. Could you ever forget someone who had defended you when the whole world was saying you were a thug and instead you were the victim of injustice?"

No, I wouldn't forget.

"Has anything ever happened to you like that?"

What do you mean?

"Have you ever found yourself in a situation like mine?"

Using the "opening the members up" technique, I said:

I've never been arrested, but I had reason to be grateful to my parents just as you were grateful to the Sacrifice leaders. I was fourteen and I was leaving school. My teachers said I wouldn't gain any more benefit from education. It was a psychological blow, but my parents said that they believed in me and that I had important qualities.

"What does that have to do with my story?"

I think it's similar because you also found someone who believed in your innocence when everyone else had given up on you. I didn't go to prison, but I experienced the trauma of being abandoned by everyone and, at the same time, the joy of having two people to defend me from the bad things in the world. The experience I had at fourteen helps me to understand why you're so loyal to the Sacrifice leaders.

Marcus paused and then started to tell me another very interesting story that once again showed the one-sidedness of the major Italian newspapers when reporting anything involving Sacrifice.

"I once risked being burned alive."

Are you joking?

"No, I'm serious."

Marcus got up and went to a stack of newspaper articles.

Marcus, who's a tall, robust young man, to such an extent that some people call him "the giant," went to a university in a beautiful Italian city where there's a Sacrifice militia, where Marcus attended meetings when he was living away from Mussolinia. The city has a large number of left-wing voters. A series of terrible homicides were carried out there by the radical group known as the Red Brigades, which includes a number of particularly violent and well-organized extreme left-wing militants.

"At that time," Marcus told me, "we had received a lot of threats from left-wing extremists, who told us that if we didn't close our branch, they would kill us. So we started to sleep in the office to protect it and to show we weren't afraid."

While he was in the militia office, Marcus heard the cries of a female Sacrifice militant. "I didn't even have time to understand what was happening when the door burst into flames. They had started to throw Molotov cocktails. It was a terrible scene because this girl was in the throes of a panic attack, but none of us could get out of the place because the door was on fire."

So what did you do?

"I started yelling: 'There's a woman! There's a woman in here!' Then I tried to open the door, but they started throwing large stones, so I had to retreat."

And then? What happened then?

"What happened was that the journalists didn't write anything about that attack. Just try to imagine what they would have written if the Sacrifice militants had assaulted the headquarters of a left-wing group."

At this point, something unexpected occurred. For the first time, Marcus wanted to know my opinion and started to ask me questions. I think that the dialogue clearly shows my inability to manage the cross-examination:

"What do you think of this story?"

What story?

I pretended not to understand.

"The story that I've just told you. What's your opinion of the behavior of these far-left militants?"

Why are you asking me these questions?

I was trying to find a way not to answer.

"I'm asking you this because you ask all of us a lot of questions. Just for once, I'd like to find out what you think. What are your ideas? I want to know what you think," he said, in the insistent tone of someone determined to receive an answer.

I don't have political ideologies. I'm a sociologist. I identify with sociology and not with a political ideology.

I was still grasping for a strategy for not replying.

"Really? On the Internet I found an article about you that Roberto Saviano [a well-known Italian journalist] wrote. The article was published in *La Repubblica,* which is a left-wing paper that hates Sacrifice. Roberto Saviano writes that you had written one of the finest books on left-wing politics he had ever read. He said that you'd written a book about the left. On the Internet I also found other articles that say you're a man of the left."

I think I know what you're referring to.

I was feeling great emotional tension and became agitated.

"So you say you don't have a political ideology?"

It depends what you mean by ideology . . .

I was still trying to get out of having to reply.

"You haven't answered my question. You don't need an ideology to reply."

What question?

I pretended not to understand.

"The question I've just asked you."

I think that you were right and they were wrong. I believe in the sanctity of human life. No man can kill another man. If they threw firebombs, then they committed a crime. These left-wing militants should be charged and put in prison.

Marcus stopped speaking and remained silent without any particular expression on his face. I felt the tension rise in my body. Perhaps Marcus thought I was pretending not to understand his questions to hide my true ideas. In a world in which courage is everything, I felt humiliated.

A few seconds later Marcus said: "The communists have this fucking habit of wanting to burn Fascists. Do you know the story of the Mattei brothers?"

I knew all too well the story of the Mattei brothers, who were burned alive by a group of extreme-left militants on April 16, 1973.

Given that I wanted Marcus to tell the story, I replied:

No, I don't know it.

"It happened in Rome, in the seventies. It's a famous story. You really don't know it?"

What happened?

"One night some members of an extreme-left group poured gas under the Mattei family's door while everyone was sleeping. The father, Mario, was a highly respected Fascist. His young sons were burned alive."

Marcus didn't tell the whole story. It is important in understanding the parallel world, and I want to report all the most significant facts.

During the night of April 16, 1973, some left-wing extremists, who were many years later tried and found guilty, poured gasoline under the door of the apartment of the family of Mario Mattei, consisting of six children—Virgilio (age twenty-two), Stefano (eight), Antonella (nine), Giampaolo (three), Lucia (fifteen), and Silvia (nineteen)—and his wife, Anna Maria. They all saved themselves by jumping off the balcony except for the eldest, Virgilio, who hung back to help his younger brother Stefano. By the time Virgilio arrived at the window, Stefano was already in flames. While a crowd that had assembled in the street watched, Virgilio tried to leap out of the window with his brother, but he slipped, stood up, and also caught fire. Both brothers burned to death before the eyes of the people below.

A message found outside the house bore the words "Death to the fucking Fascists!"

Soldiers Who Fight and Soldiers Who Don't

The great majority of Fascist militants are nothing like what we imagine.

The typical Fascist militant doesn't resemble Arno Michaelis, who was a leader of a worldwide racist skinhead organization and lead singer of the hate-metal band Centurion. His band sold twenty thousand CDs by the mid-1990s and is still popular with racists today.[1] In "Reflections of a Former White Supremacist," Michaelis tells how he lost some skinhead comrades to street violence and admits that he lost count of how many of his friends had been incarcerated. Finally, "it became clear that death or prison would take me from my little daughter if I did not change my ways."[2]

The typical inhabitants of the parallel world aren't like Anders Breivik, the Norwegian far-right terrorist, who on July 22, 2011, massacred sixty-nine young people on the island of Utoya.[3]

They're not even like Timothy James McVeigh, the American extreme-right terrorist who detonated a truck bomb in front of the Alfred P.

Murrah Federal Building in Oklahoma City on April 19, 1995, an assault commonly referred to as the Oklahoma City bombing.[4]

The parallel world isn't a sudden, momentary eruption of violence but a symbolic universe that is built up day after day. The construction of the parallel world requires calm, patience, sacrifice, love for your comrades, self-abnegation, and dedication to the cause. It also requires a capacity to survive humiliation, people spitting in your face, shit dumped outside your door, pressure from the cops, the falsifications of journalists, police investigations and arrests, the contempt of women, discrimination in the workplace, offensive slogans on walls, threats from communists, nails driven into your door locks. The construction of the parallel world is a symbolic undertaking that covers 365 days a year and not just the few minutes needed to create havoc.

The parallel world is open only to those who are willing to renounce their values and their ideas to embrace a radical ideology; but embracing a philosophy that proposes to overturn dominant values means entering into war with the world around us. And war, as we know, is always a traumatic experience because it produces victims.

This may help to explain why I never saw anyone except militants and sympathizers enter the Mussolinia and Lenintown militia headquarters. And yet it's easy enough to enter the parallel world physically; you just have to knock on the door and step over the threshold. But as soon as you start walking past walls hung with posters praising Mussolini, your mind enters a cultural system that glorifies Fascism.

The parallel world is an open space in physical terms but segregated in cultural terms. After you observe the world in the militia offices, the borders between the parallel world and the crappy bourgeois society become clear.

Lenintown and Mussolinia militants assert that their premises are "pubs" where anyone can come for a drink or a sandwich at moderate prices. The website managed by the national leaders of Sacrifice gives the names of the towns where the organization's offices can be found. "Sacrifice," the site asserts, "has numerous pubs all over Italy." Marcus, Leonidas, Lentulus, and all the other Lenintown and Mussolinia militants refer to their offices as "pubs."

These are the words with which Marcus ended our first telephone conversation, which I wrote down in my notebook immediately after I hung up the phone: "You can come to see me in Mussolinia whenever you want. We have a pub that's open to everyone. If you ever want to drink a beer with your friends, you can come to our pub. Anyone can come."

The Mussolinia militia has two Facebook pages. One is its official page and the other that of what I'll call Pub X. Mussolinia militants have created a Facebook page to publicize their "pub" without explaining that it is located inside the offices of a Fascist militia, with a bar and a fridge containing beer bottles. The Mussolinia pub page contains no references to Fascists because, as Marcus explains, "unfortunately, Fascist symbols push people away instead of bringing them closer to us. We have to work to make people understand that the word 'Fascism' means love of Italy."

This is what Leonidas said during our first telephone conversation, before he gave me permission to enter the Lenintown militia: "I'm often away from Lenintown these days, but you can go to our headquarters whenever you want, even if I'm not there. We have a pub that's open to anyone."

Marcus and Leonidas assert that the door of their "little world" is always open, but the members of the "big world" never enter it. The Lenintown "pub" is in a small building where you have to climb some stairs to get to the bar, while the door to the Mussolinia "pub" is on a downtown street, just like at a "real" pub. Nevertheless, the young people of the "big world" never go in. When individuals are forced to make a distinction between good and evil, cultural boundaries become insurmountable barriers.

It's easier for a camel to pass through the eye of a needle than for someone belonging to the "big world" to enter the "little world."

Readers may remember Marilyn, the lawyer whom Jonathan described to me as "the most beautiful girl in Mussolinia" (in chapter 5). Marilyn was a very charming and kind young woman, and with the help of Jonathan, we became friends. While walking with her and Jonathan in downtown Mussolinia, I asked both of them to accompany me to the militia offices, where the comrades were waiting for me to play Risk.

Marilyn replied in words that I transcribed in my notebook five hours after hearing them. (Unlike the ethnographer Thomas S. Eberle, who could move freely about the hospital where he was conducting his research, I couldn't take notes whenever I wanted.)[5]

"I understand that you're a sociologist, but I'm a normal person and I wouldn't go into that place even if you tortured me."

Why?

"You have to ask me why? Anyone who thinks that Hitler was a great man should be locked up in that place and never allowed out."

But we're not talking about just one person. There are at least twenty young people. You can't lock them all up in one room!

"OK, then someone should lock the door and hang up a notice with 'MADHOUSE' written on it."

To provoke Marilyn to describe how the inhabitants of the "crappy bourgeois society" construct a wall around themselves, I tried to irritate her by saying things I knew to be false. My aim was to prompt a reaction that would help me see the "emotional wall" that impedes contact between people who define good and evil in different ways. In some cases, "mundane phenomenology"[6] requires us to resort to a sociological stratagem in order to understand the "subjective meaning"[7] of social actions.

Marilyn, you're exaggerating. I'm only going to the militia offices to play Risk. It's all the same to me if the posters are Mussolini or Mickey Mouse. I just don't look at them and the problem is solved . . .

"If becoming a sociologist means no longer feeling revulsion in front of a poster of Mussolini, then I wouldn't want to do your job."

No offense, but lawyers often have to defend criminals and maintain that they're innocent . . .

"Hitler was much worse than a simple criminal. Although I'm a lawyer, I'd never defend someone who admires Hitler."

The conversation is interrupted when Jonathan says firmly, "Alessandro, stop it, please!"

The Soldiers Who Fight

The horror that the big world shows for the little world is fed not only by street fights but also by shootings involving extreme-right militants. Periodically journalists invade the parallel world to exhibit it to the crappy bourgeois society through videos, photographs, and interviews.

Marcus told me many times that shootings by extreme-right militants had disastrous consequences for Sacrifice: "Our problem is madmen like Gianluca Casseri, who ruin all the work we do to persuade young people to believe in us. Gianluca Casseri's actions in Florence caused us enormous damage. People saw us as criminals, and we were even in danger of having to close down the militia. It was a very bad time for us."

On December 13, 2011, Gianluca Casseri, a fifty-year-old accountant from Pistoia and a long-standing Fascist militant, fatally shot Samb Madou and Diop Mor, two street vendors from Senegal, and then wounded Moustapha Kieng, another vendor, in the throat in the Piazza Dalmazia market in Florence. He then fled in a car and seriously wounded two more vendors, Sougou Mor and Mbenghe Cheike, at the San Lorenzo market later that day. He finally shot himself dead as he was approached by police in a parking lot. At the time of the shootings the mayor of Florence was Matteo Renzi, later the Italian prime minister, who was shocked by the racist-inspired shooting of Senegalese vendors in a city famous for its cosmopolitan culture.

Casseri, an admirer of Mussolini, dreamed of living in a society in which all the blacks and Jews had been exterminated. He was highly respected in Italian extreme-right circles, where many called him an "intellectual" and an "educated man." He had been invited to speak in various public debates. In 2010 he had written a book, *La chiave del caos* (The Key of Chaos),[8] and had published articles on the website of a Fascist organization.[9]

The shootings aroused hardly any interest in the international media. The *New York Times* gave them only ten lines,[10] in part because, on the same day that Casseri killed the Senegalese vendors in Florence, Nordine Amrani was carrying out an even more deadly assault in Belgium—the 2011 Liège attack that left six dead and 125 wounded.[11] Amrani, who used a machine gun and grenades, then committed suicide by shooting himself in the head.

Then there is the story of Jeff Hall, a plumber in Riverside, California, and the regional leader of the National Socialist Movement, who, on May 1, 2011, was shot dead with his own gun by his ten-year-old son Joseph at 4 a.m. while he was asleep on his couch.

These stories help us to understand why so many people think that all Fascist militants are violent. It has to be said, however, that daily life in the parallel world is dominated more by Fascist militants who know nothing about fighting than by racist murderers like Gianluca Casseri, who are a very small minority compared to the total number of Fascist militants.

In the construction of the parallel world, those whom I call "the soldiers who don't fight" play a fundamental role. Their importance can be understood only if we stop thinking that all Fascist militants are like Dylann Roof, who, on the evening of June 17, 2015, killed nine people at the Mother Emanuel African Methodist Episcopal Church in downtown Charleston, South Carolina, in hopes of igniting a race war.

Daily life in the parallel world is typified not by "soldiers who fight," like Dylann Roof and Gianluca Casseri, but by "soldiers who don't fight," like Brutus and Cincinnatus. To understand the parallel world, we have to focus more on the daily life of the militia than on the actions of individuals operating without militia backing, the so-called lone wolves.

The Soldiers Who Don't Fight

To escape the crappy bourgeois society, Sacrifice militants try to construct a social order in which they are courageous soldiers. This symbolic and cultural undertaking, what I have called the construction of the parallel world, rests on three pillars: the ideological organization of sports, clashes with left-wing groups, and street brawls that allow militants to prove they have the same courage as soldiers at war. Yet most Sacrifice members know nothing about fighting.

The question is this: How can militants who don't participate in street brawls and who don't fight in the MMA cage matches prove they are real soldiers? The clashes that result in police investigations and arrests offer the chance to all militants, even those who don't know how to fight, to sacrifice themselves for the militia, just as ancient Roman legionnaires did. Sacrifice members have copied not only the legionnaires' form of greeting but also the idea that the militia is a sacred place.

The word "militia" comes from the Latin *miles,* which means "soldier."

"The true soldier," as Leonidas, Marcus, Augustus, and Lentulus always say, "is someone who loves the militia." None of them ever told me that the true soldier is someone who fights in the street or inside an MMA cage.

Let's listen to part of an hour-long interview with Marcus—we had agreed on subjects some days earlier—which took place at the Mussolinia headquarters:

"The first thing that a youth has to learn when he enters this place is love for the militia."

How do you show love for the militia?

"Love for the militia is shown first of all through sacrifice. For example, it's shown by sacrificing your Saturday evening. Instead of spending Saturday night in downtown Mussolinia with your schoolmates, our comrades know they have to spend it here. Everyone accepts, taking turns cleaning the premises."

Can you give me some other examples of love for the militia?

"I could give you hundreds of examples." Marcus pauses briefly as if reflecting on how to answer. "You should read Codreanu's book . . . You mustn't think that love for the militia is always shown through heroic feats." Marcus is silent for a moment. "Love for the militia is shown by running to help a comrade who wakes you at night because he has a problem. The true Fascist is the person who loves the militia. This is the first fundamental rule. The Roman legionnaires were ready to die to defend the militia. We consider ourselves the Roman legionnaires of the twenty-first century. For us the militia is everything. Sacrifice for the militia is demonstrated every day in many little ways."

I understand that the word "sacrifice" is very important for you. Am I right?

"It's an extremely important word. Fascism is sacrifice. The first words that a militant has to learn are 'sacrifice' and 'militia' because living in a militia means sacrificing yourself."

What would you be willing to sacrifice for the militia?

"I would be willing to sacrifice my life to defend the militia," Marcus replies resolutely. "I'd be willing to die to defend the young people who belong to this militia."

Can you explain to me the rule that Sacrifice militants have to spend Saturday evening here?

"The rule is that all militants must spend Friday and Saturday evening here in the militia office. We have a bar where you can buy alcoholic drinks and sandwiches."

What happens if a fifteen-year-old boy tells you that he has to go to a birthday party?

"If he asks our permission, we'll give it to him, but there are turns to be respected."

There are turns? In what sense? Do you have a logbook in which the names are written—

Marcus interrupts me.

"This Saturday it's your turn to run the bar, next Saturday it's me, and so on. If a militant has to go to a birthday party on the day of his turn, he has to make an arrangement with another militant to substitute for him at the bar. For example, next Saturday I'll be here as usual, but it's not my turn to work at the bar. I'm free to go for a walk in downtown Mussolinia if I want."

You just have to tell the other comrades that you're going out to get a beer. Is that it?

"That's it. You must always tell the other comrades that you're leaving the office."

But if it's your turn to keep watch, you can't leave. Right?

"Correct. It's through the little things that the young militants learn discipline and sacrifice for the militia."

Why do you establish these rules? To make the group more united?

"These rules are necessary for many reasons."

I'll give you my impressions. Please tell me if I'm wrong. Lentulus told me that these rules serve to make the young militants understand that the militia comes first and that the group is more important than any single militant. He said that these rules serve to uproot the bourgeois individualism that is inside all of us . . .

"Lentulus is responsible for education in this militia. He's the one who decides what books the boys have to read. I'm not very good with philosophical discussions," Marcus says, laughing, "but I agree with Lentulus. The militia comes first. The militia is more important than having fun on Saturday evening. If you're not willing to sacrifice a birthday party, how do you think you can become a Fascist soldier?"

I'd like to ask if I can interview Lentulus on the subject of education. Will you give me permission?

"Of course. No problem."

Unfortunately I never managed to interview Lentulus on the topic of education in the militia because—this is what Marcus told me while I was out walking with him in downtown Mussolinia—Lentulus feared that my research would be harmful to the organization. He would talk to me only about certain subjects, and he wanted to be free to decide. Nevertheless, thanks to the participant observation technique, I did get Lentulus and another militant to talk about education. I copied their words into my notebook twenty-five minutes later, sitting in my car before leaving for Lenintown.

When taking notes, I wrote as quickly as possible. Although I use quotation marks, the dialogues are based on my recollections. I used the present tense because, in Italian, that means using fewer words than the past tense, so I can write my notes down faster. In the passage that follows, I haven't changed anything I wrote while sitting in my car:

Over these past months, I've spent almost every Friday and Saturday evening in the Mussolinia headquarters, and I've noticed that no one except the Sacrifice militants and their sympathizers ever entered this "pub." In fact the militants find it impossible to spend every Saturday evening shut up in these two rooms, as the militia rules say they should, and they take turns going for a stroll in downtown Mussolinia. About an hour ago, at the end of a game of Risk, I say to Marcus, Lentulus, and two other comrades that I would like to go for a walk with them in downtown Mussolinia. Marcus replies, "OK, let's take a walk, but we have to decide who remains here." Marcus turns to the other comrades and says: "Guys, we're going out for a walk. We'll be back soon."

On the way back, I'm beside Lentulus while Marcus and the other two militants are walking in front of us. Lentulus often speaks of the way in which the young militants have to be taught. He always says that the first objective to achieve is education in "sacrifice."

I start the discourse with this question:

Lentulus, I've noticed that on Saturday evenings you militants are all together in the militia offices. Marcus told me that it's a rule of yours . . .

"Yes, it's one of our rules. The militants have to spend Saturday evening in the headquarters. But we're flexible. If a boy has something else he has to do, then we can discuss it."

So, if a boy wants to spend Saturday evening with his friends, he has to inform you, and you give him permission. Am I right?

"It could be that there are only a few comrades in the headquarters and so he isn't given permission, but that hardly ever happens."

Have you ever told a boy that he couldn't go out with his friends but had to spend Saturday evening in the militia?

"Yeah, sometimes this has happened."

Why have you established this rule?

"Because first of all the Fascist militia teaches sacrifice. A boy of fifteen has to learn to sacrifice himself for the group. This is the basis of all Fascist education."

While Lentulus continues speaking, Marcus and the other two comrades join us.

I say jokingly, "Sorry, guys, I'm giving Lentulus a hard time with my usual questions."

The guys smile. Lentulus, however, remains serious and says: "Our comrades have to be shaped, and this requires time. It's not easy to mold a boy."

When Lentulus says "mold," Priscus, who belongs to the militia's leadership group, says he disagrees with the use of this verb: "I don't like the word 'mold.' We have to teach our boys to destroy everything that is bourgeois in their minds, but I don't like the word 'mold.' I prefer to say that we have to educate the boys."

Lentulus doesn't agree with Priscus and says: "When you speak of teaching revolutionary Fascism, 'mold' is the exact word. A boy of fifteen or sixteen is like clay, and we have to mold his personality. You don't educate clay. You mold clay. These boys come to us because they're confused and have a spiritual problem to solve. They are seeking a point of reference in a society that has lost its moorings. That's why these boys come to us, and we must have very clear ideas about what we're doing."

Lentulus explains that everything the militia does, from sports to fairs, from camps to soccer tournaments, must always have the aim of putting Fascism in the boys' heads.

Priscus insists: "I don't think that 'mold' is a suitable description. To 'mold' is a word that gives a negative image."

Lentulus becomes even more determined: "You're wrong, Priscus. The boys have to be molded through sacrifice. Fascism is a strict doctrine that you learn through sacrifice." Then Lentulus clarifies his thinking by talking about the educational function of putting up posters illegally at night: "For example, when I take three fourteen-year-old boys in my car to put up Sacrifice posters in the Mussolinia streets at night, with the danger of being stopped by the police and with glue that sticks to you, the boys learn to sacrifice themselves for the militia. When a fifteen-year-old boy returns home at night tired, his clothes sticky with glue, and knowing that he has to get up early the next morning to go to school, he learns to sacrifice himself for the militia. This is teaching sacrifice!"

Marcus's and Lentulus's words about the importance of the militia help shift our focus from street fights to the dynamics that develop in the Fascist militia when the brawls are over. Through brawls, the small world enters the large world. Through police investigations, the large world enters the small world. When fights break out, the heroes of the parallel world are the militants who know how to fight. When the clashes are over, the heroes of the parallel world are "the soldiers who don't fight." Contrary to appearances, the lifeblood of the revolutionary militia comes not from the violent actions of the leaders but from the nonviolent actions of the militants who don't know how to fight.

The militia is the place where the weak can play a heroic role. To understand the functioning of the revolutionary militia, which constitutes the foundation of the parallel world, we have to focus on the enormous importance it gives to its members' existence.

Alessio Sakara, the Legionarius

In the second chapter we saw that Sacrifice militants set great store by the book *Militia* by Léon Degrelle and *The Nest Leader's Manual* by Corneliu Codreanu, who on the very first page states that the militia is the supreme good and that comrades must love one another like "brothers," in addition to demonstrating total submission to the leader. It is no coincidence that one of the most popular tattoos among the Sacrifice militants is the word "MILITIA" and their favorite mixed martial arts fighter is Alessio Sakara, called "the Legionarius."

The tattoos covering Sakara's body are a text in cultural anthropology, and they help us understand better the significance of the figure of the soldier and the role of the militia for the Sacrifice militants.

I first heard the name Alessio Sakara from Severus, one of the four young Mussolinia militants who, in the previous chapter, showed me the video recording the clash between Fascists and communists.

While we were walking together in downtown Mussolinia, Severus said to me:

"In this shitty society, people my age worship the wrong idols. Dolce and Gabbana, fashionable clothes, expensive automobiles . . . These are the idols that encourage people to do drugs."

Do you think that it's Dolce and Gabbana's fault that young people take drugs?

"Youths do drugs because they have no values. Their lives are empty because their idols are empty. We have other idols."

What are your idols?

"My idols are the warriors of ancient Rome like Alessio Sakara."

I haven't heard of him. Was he a Roman soldier?

"Alessio Sakara, called the Legionarius, is one of the greatest MMA fighters."

What do you like about Alessio Sakara?

"I like everything about him. I like his tattoos and the way he dresses when he's going into the ring. I like the values he believes in."

How does he dress when he enters the ring?

"He dresses like an ancient Roman legionnaire."

Born in Rome in 1981, Alessio Sakara is an athlete with better technical skills than most other MMA fighters, and this is one of the reasons for his popularity with the Sacrifice militants, who can identify with an Italian combatant who—for as long as his sponsors allowed it—went into the ring dressed like a soldier of the Roman Empire.[12]

Severus explained to me that the tattoos on Sakara's body are copied by numerous Sacrifice militants. When he showed me photos, I noticed that all the tattoos exalted the figure of the soldier, the value of war, and love for the militia. The names that Sakara gave his two sons are also linked to the cult of war. The elder is called Leonida, in honor of Leonidas, the king of Sparta who went heroically to meet death against the Persian army in the Battle of Thermopylae. The younger is called Marco Valerio, in honor of Marcus Valerius Maximianus, considered one of the greatest generals in the history of the Roman Empire, who lived during the reign of the emperor Marcus Aurelius.

There is a large imperial eagle on Sakara's chest, which, says Severus, "was a symbol of the Roman army, much loved by Mussolini and even by Hitler." Tattooed above the eagle is the same motto flaunted by gladiators who fought in the Colosseum, as well as by Roman soldiers: "USQUE AD FINEM," which means "to the very end."

On the right is a Spartan soldier's helmet. Sparta was a society of warrior-heroes who were the living exemplars of such core values as duty, discipline, self-sacrifice, and extreme toughness.[13] Inscribed around the Spartan helmet is "NULLI SECUNDUS," which means "second to none."

On the left is the face of Julius Caesar surrounded by the famous Latin phrase he supposedly used in a letter to the Roman Senate around 46 BC, after he had achieved a quick victory in his short war against Pharnaces II of Pontus at the Battle of Zela: "VENI, VIDI, VICI," meaning "I came, I saw, I conquered."

Severus points to Sakara's neck, on which are tattooed the heads of soldiers fighting. A few centimeters higher, on his Adam's apple, is the phrase "HIC ET NUNC"—"here and now"—summarizing the existential philosophy of those who, like soldiers, are mindful that the human condition is finite and uncertain and decide to live their life in the most intense and conscious manner possible, never putting off till tomorrow what they can do today.

The larger tattoos on his back consist of two words. The first, "LE-GIONARIUS," spans his shoulders. The second, "ROMA," spans his waist. Above the word "ROMA" there is one of Fascism's most famous sayings, a quotation from the poet Gabriele D'Annunzio: "MEMENTO AUDERE SEM-PER," which means "Remember always to be daring." Above the word "LEGIONARIUS" there is an imperial eagle with its wings spread.

On his dorsal muscles between the words "LEGIONARIUS" and "ROMA" are two faces. On the right is King Leonidas; on the left is General Marcus Valerius Maximianus. Between the faces of Leonidas and Marcus Valerius is a *gladius,* a small two-edged sword with a broad blade and tapered point that was carried by the legionnaires of the Roman army. The triangular point, very sharp on both edges, was designed to penetrate the enemy's flesh during hand-to-hand fighting. The *gladius* tattooed on Sakara's back is surrounded by a laurel wreath, also known as a triumphal crown because it was given to the generals of ancient Rome who returned home as victors from war. A little lower down, on the left, is a tattoo of the Colosseum.

There are two small tattoos between the *gladius* and the triumphal crown that I couldn't make out clearly. A small tattoo with three columns perhaps represents the remains of the Temple of Apollo Sosianus in Rome, adjacent to the more famous Theater of Marcellus. The original Temple of Apollo Sosianus, rebuilt several times over the centuries, dates back to 431 BC. Its present name derives from that of its final rebuilder, Gaius Sosius.

The second small tattoo closely resembles the papal Basilica of St. Peter in the Vatican, but it's difficult to imagine that Sakara would have wanted the most representative symbol of Catholicism on his body. Catholic culture represents the negation of all the legionnaires' values.[14]

There are two mottoes on his right hand: "MILITIA" and "ROMA CAPUT MUNDIS."

When I asked Severus which tattoo he liked best, he answered that it wasn't easy to choose because "they're all fantastic." I pressed him and he finally said, "The 'LEGIONARIUS' one." Then Severus showed me three important documents.

The first is a video on YouTube, lasting just under seven minutes, in which Sakara comments on the significance of a tattoo while a man is drawing it on his arm.[15]

The second is an interview with him that appeared on the Internet on July 21, 2011, which—says Severus—"is what made me a fan of Alessio Sakara." While we were sitting in front of the computer in the Mussolinia office watching the interview, I asked Severus to tell me exactly what had turned him into an admirer. Severus explained to me that many youths get tattoos simply for aesthetic reasons, "because they want to seem cool with the girls," unlike Alessio Sakara, who uses tattoos to promote the values of Roman soldiers.

Here is the part of the interview with Sakara that Severus likes so much:

Who is Alessio Sakara, and what does he conceal behind an athletic body and a collection of tattoos that recount our past?

"I look on my tattoos as a code. Each phrase and each image represents a stage in my life. The words written on my body are all in Latin because I'm inspired by the ancient Roman world. Roman history is my passion, but I don't like showing my tattoos. I think that sometimes I avoid going to the beach so as not to let people see them. The words on my body have been written by the great men who have given me my philosophy of life. The symbols are always inspired by stories of the past. I don't like showing them. These symbols and my body are a single thing."

Where does the name Legionarius come from?

"At the beginning, when I was training in Brazil, everyone called me 'the Gladiator,' but the gladiators were slaves. Studying the history of ancient Rome, I learned that the legionnaires were the soldiers of the Roman Empire. The legionnaires created the colonies of the greatest empire in history. I don't feel like a slave. I feel like a soldier of Rome, and I fight for my family, for my friends, and for my fans who believe in me. Without them I could do nothing!"

Before I could ask him other questions about the interview, Severus typed in "Alessio Legionarius Sakara Tribute" on YouTube and enthusiastically presented me with a third document that he called "the best video of all!"

I have to admit that, among the many videos devoted to Alessio Sakara, this has the most cultural content and the strongest educational message. The images are clear, and almost all the tattoos can be clearly seen.[16] As the tattoos slowly pass across the screen, the following words appear: RESPECT, HONOR, COURAGE, HUMILITY, MORAL INTEGRITY, PERSEVERANCE, SACRIFICE, DISCIPLINE, LOYALTY, VIRTUE. Immediately after, the deep and resonant voice of a professional actor pronounces these lines from the poem "Invictus" by William Ernest Henley, which appear on the screen:

I AM THE MASTER OF MY FATE.
I AM THE CAPTAIN OF MY SOUL.

Unfortunately, by the time I finished my study of Sakara's life and was ready to enroll in the gymnasium where he was an instructor, I had been expelled from the militias and forbidden under threat of punishment to approach any comrade. From that moment on I avoided any of the places that Sacrifice militants frequented, and I didn't go into any kind of Fascist environment, including Romulus's bookshop. If a Sacrifice militant had encountered me in a Fascist bookshop, I would have aroused suspicion. I imagine the comrade would have thought: "This sociologist prick isn't a Fascist! Why is he continuing to visit our hangouts even after we've expelled him?"

When a sociologist decides to study a deviant group that uses violence, he has to accept that he runs some risks, but he must also be prudent and realize when the moment has arrived to drop out of circulation. In any case, not interviewing Alessio Sakara also had positive consequences, since I didn't have to reveal to him that I was writing a book on Sacrifice. An interview would have enabled me to gather a lot of information, but I consoled myself with the knowledge that I can give his real name, describe his tattoos, and tell of his fight in 2012 against Brian Stann—a former U.S. Marines captain—which Sakara described as "the most important match of my life."

It was Macrinus, the comrade who thinks that blacks are "pure shit," who had invited me to watch the fight. Macrinus is the only Sacrifice militant who spoke to me about Alessio Sakara with scorn, describing him as a mediocre fighter. From what he said, I got the impression that he was envious. Macrinus, though a combat sports instructor, has never won a match.

Macrinus told me, "Go to YouTube and see how many beatings Alessio Sakara took from Brian Stann!" Whenever a Sacrifice militant urged me to see a video on YouTube, I rushed to find a computer with the speed of a man who has been told the precise spot where buried treasure is hidden.

When a mixed martial artist floors his adversary, he continues to kick him in the face, even if he realizes that his opponent is now unconscious. If the referees were not so quick to stop the matches, there would be numerous deaths.[17]

The fight between Alessio Sakara and Brian Stann was well balanced for the first fifty-nine minutes. Then Sakara took a kneecap to the face and hit the floor. Stann stood over him, raining down punches that Sakara managed to parry by covering his face. After seventy-five seconds of hand-to-hand combat, Stann managed to get in an elbow strike on Sakara's temple and two punches to his face. Sakara apparently lost perception of what was happening around him and covered his face to protect it from further punches. Rather than continue the abuse, Stann pulled back, looked at the referee, and invited him to stop the fight as Sakara writhed in pain on the mat. Instead of rising to receive the public's applause, Stann stayed with Sakara to ensure that he was all right while seven medics ran into the cage to provide first aid.

In previous fights Sakara had behaved very differently, continuing to hit an adversary who had passed out, as you can see in another video on YouTube.[18]

I'm Not a Fighter

Alessio Sakara is a true fighter, a legionnaire, a gladiator for our times. But what can we say about soldiers who don't fight? Hundreds of Sacrifice militants state they are "soldiers," but they have never come to blows in their life.

What I discovered through participant observation can be summarized as follows:

1. A small number of Sacrifice militants engage in street fights.
2. An even smaller number step into the MMA cages.
3. All the others demonstrate their military valor by protecting their comrades who have participated in fights.

When police and journalists erupt into the parallel world, the existence of the militia is in danger. This became clear to me on the day when the bathroom fixtures in the Lenintown militia offices finally broke down. The toilet flush had been out of action for a long time, but the Lenintown comrades didn't have sufficient funds to call a plumber. So there was a bucket beside the toilet to hold water for flushing, but it was difficult to fill because the sink faucet was also broken and only a dribble of water came out.

When Leonidas arrived, I clasped his forearm in greeting like the ancient Roman legionnaires. Leonidas smiled and said: "You learn fast! You sure you're not becoming more Fascist than me?" We went into the bathroom and tried to repair the faucet, then went to the room with the fridge containing drinks, the so-called pub.

Leonidas, who had just spoken with his lawyer, said he was worried about the police investigation and started to show me some photos of Ashley that he had downloaded from his Facebook profile the day after the brawl. I noted down these conversations in my Lenintown apartment an hour after they ended.

"This is a close-up of her face when she was at a party with a girl-friend," Leonidas told me. "Do you see any bruises on her face? She looks fine. Look how she's smiling!"

While he ran through the photos on his cell phone, Leonidas continued to comment on them, asking: "Where are the bruises? How can you go to a party if the day before you've been punched in the face? Anyway, they'll testify in my favor," said Leonidas, indicating the comrades around us.

They'll testify in your favor?

"Sure! They're my only witnesses!"

The comrades, who up to that moment had remained silent, now spoke with passion: "Of course we'll testify! We've already given written testimony to Leonidas's lawyer."

I told Leonidas that he was lucky to have such loyal friends, but Leonidas corrected me in a serious and dramatic tone: "A comrade is much more than a friend. A comrade is a brother, and our militia is like a family."

Are there other people who are willing to testify but who aren't your friends?

"Yes, unfortunately there are."

What do you mean 'unfortunately'? Who are you talking about?

"I'm talking about that scumbag, the owner of the bar and his wife."

What have they done?

"The owners of the bar were Sacrifice sympathizers."

What do you mean by sympathizers. Are they Fascists?

In an increasingly grave tone of voice Leonidas told me that he and the comrades had been frequent customers at the bar where the brawl took place and that the owners had always treated them well: "They weren't Sacrifice sympathizers, but we had a good relationship with them. It was our bar, a place we used to meet in."

After Ashley reported him to the police, however, things changed.

"When I learned that the girl had reported me, I went to talk to the bar owner and asked him to testify in my favor. That scumbag told me: "I'm sorry. You were out of line and now you have to pay for it.""

He said that to you? He said that you were out of line?

Leonidas replied that he remembered perfectly the words of the bar owner. The other comrades confirmed Leonidas's account and added that the bar owners had decided to testify in favor of Ashley. In brief, the bar owners claimed that Leonidas was to blame for the brawl, whereas the comrades asserted that he was innocent.

Leonidas then started to show me photographs of banners bearing his name that had been put up in Lenintown. The banners accused Leonidas of being a "dwarf" (Leonidas is relatively short) and of being psychologically disturbed because of his presumed hatred of women.

Written on the largest banner was "LEONIDAS, MISOGYNIST DWARF."

Leonidas told me that for a period of time his parents were ashamed to leave the house because the banners included his surname, identifying the whole family. I tried to bring the conversation back to the bar owners. I asked the comrades if they had tried to improve relations with them, since in the meantime the mayor of Lenintown had issued a regulation ordering all the bars in the area to close early to prevent any more fights. The owners of the other bars (I interviewed four of them) were also angry with the Sacrifice militants, whom they considered responsible for starting the fight, which had not only damaged the town's image but also damaged them financially. "That bastard of a mayor," said Leonidas, "has made things more difficult for me. The bar has been forced to close early every evening."

Leonidas asked me to help Cincinnatus prepare a large banner protesting the Lenintown mayor and then go with the other comrades to do something, without telling me what it was.

Left alone with Cincinnatus, I was thinking that the best way to get more information on the fight was to contact the friends of the young woman who had clashed with Leonidas, or even to contact Ashley in person, but I realized it was too risky. If the comrades found out that I was trying to meet their enemies, they would expel me from the militia. For the same reason I couldn't even try to talk to Leonidas's attorney. I had no other options, so I resigned myself to the fact that my only informants on the brawl would be the comrades. I didn't think that this situation would affect my ethnographic research because, as time went on, my sociological interest had shifted from the violent militants to those who didn't know how to fight.

One of them was sitting next to me.

Cincinnatus, a laborer who at the time of my research was thirty years old, was a very timid and self-conscious man, but he was also one of the militants who loved the militia most. He devoted all his free time to militia activities and to taking care of the premises. He was forever dusting the shelves of the "library" and, just like Brutus, almost daily washed the floors, the windows, the bathroom, and everything else that could be washed to keep the apartment, which he called "our world," clean. More specifically, he used certain expressions that I noted down scrupulously in my notebook: "This apartment is our world," or "The police are always after us but we're safe in our world." When he spoke of the communists, he never used violent expressions or offensive phrases, nor did he claim he wanted to beat them up. Once, in reply to a question of mine about their provocations, he said: "The communists will never change. They have their world and we have ours," without realizing that, in fact, both were the architects of the same parallel world.

One Saturday afternoon, while we were on the balcony of the apartment, which looks out on one of Lenintown's main streets, we saw a striking woman pass by wearing a black skirt, white shoes with five-inch heels, and a white blouse that was unbuttoned enough to show prominent breasts encased in a bra that was also white. Cincinnatus gazed admiringly at the woman until she disappeared from our view, but he made no comment. When standing on the balcony looking at attractive women, almost all the comrades usually made the same comments. Even though they knew nothing about these young women, they always described them lewdly as willing to have sex with anyone: "Guys, come and see this whore!" "She's someone who'd give a dog a blow job!" "She's someone who's had a lot of pricks in her ass!"

I looked at Cincinnatus and said enthusiastically, "Did you see that woman?"

Cincinnatus replied in a resigned tone, typical of those who know how relations between the sexes function in society, "That woman has her world and we have ours."

I replied jokingly: "What is her world? Tell me so I can go and find it!"

"Her world is completely different from ours. It is they who decide who can enter their world, not you."

Cincinnatus's attention to the material aspects of the militia headquarters was a reflection of the spiritual love he felt for the comrades who filled his daily life with meaning, especially since Leonidas had given him the task of managing the militia "library" I spoke about in chapter 2.

I don't know if it's permissible for an ethnographer to express himself in this way, but I've always felt pity and human compassion for Cincinnatus. I imagine that, like all the other comrades, he would have been prepared to give false testimony to help Leonidas during his trial. I also imagine that he probably would have concealed any other offense to protect the militia, but at the same time, I've always felt human solidarity with him throughout my research.

Cincinnatus was an incredibly kind and polite person, with a very meek disposition, entirely without violent or aggressive tendencies. He spoke little and always in a low voice. He had an erratic gait and often couldn't manage to walk in a straight line.

Every time I traveled with the group to visit comrades in other towns, I would go in the car with Cincinnatus, who was a great fan of rock bands that praised Fascism. During our journeys in his old, broken-down car, I'd sit next to him and ask him a lot of questions about the meaning of the songs. I could write a very long book if I wanted to analyze everything we said to each other while we listened to the Fascist music. I have always had great respect for Cincinnatus, and I believe that, when Leonidas convened the comrades to decide whether to expel me from the militia, he must have been one of the four who said they had no problem with my remaining in the group.

While I waited that day for Leonidas to return with the other comrades, I was smoothing the banner on which Cincinnatus was about to spray the black paint so that the fabric wouldn't develop creases and spoil the writing. I started to talk about the brawl and obtained information that seemed important:

Leonidas told me that his attorney contacted Ashley's attorney to reach a settlement, but Ashley didn't want to drop the charges . . .

"Ashley will never drop the charges. Her friends are all anti-Fascists. They want to make out that they're heroes who are fighting against Fascism."

Did you know Ashley's friends before the brawl?

Cincinnatus answered that Lenintown isn't a big city like Rome and that the Fascists and communists recognize each other, even if they don't know each other personally. Then he concentrated on the banner and said: "Take your hands away. I'm going to start to spray."

I wanted to talk more about the brawl but decided not to ask any more direct questions, fearing to appear too inquisitive.

I wanted to prompt Cincinnatus to say something more about the relationship between the militia and Leonidas. I tried to provoke an emotional reaction by touching on a subject that all the militants had at heart:

One of the best things that I've seen since I've been studying this militia is how you stick together. You defend one another like brothers. Leonidas is right when he says that your values are different from those of bourgeois society.

"It's true. That's exactly right."

What would you be willing to do to defend Leonidas?

Cincinnatus stopped spraying, looked me in the eye, and said, "I would be willing die to defend this militia."

In what sense would you be willing to die?

"I'm not a fighter, but if someone wants to hurt a comrade, he first has to kill me."

My Expulsion

The story of my expulsion can be understood only if I explain how I originally approached the world of Sacrifice and managed to be accepted in the Lenintown and Mussolinia militias. As I described in the introduction, my research was divided into three stages: approach, entry, and departure.

The approach stage started on May 28, 2010, at 7:36 p.m., when I first emailed the national Sacrifice leaders asking for an appointment. This is the text of the message I wrote along with Maria, a colleague who wanted to work with me:

> We are two professors in the Faculty of Literature and Philosophy at the "Tor Vergata" University of Rome interested in reconstructing the history of your association and your social and political profile.
>
> We would like to meet you to plan research that should lead to the publication of a book and one or more articles in academic journals.
>
> Hoping to hear from you soon.
>
> Yours sincerely,
> Alessandro Orsini

The answer arrived on May 31 from the official address of Sacrifice:

    I will try to arrange a meeting for this week. As soon as I have specific
news we'll be in touch to see if we can fix a date.

Sincerely,
Lucretia

The meeting took place on July 5, 2010, at 10:30 a.m. and was a disaster. Maria was a statistics professor who had no familiarity with deviant groups. We entered the building in which the Sacrifice national headquarters was located and as we climbed the stairs, we saw walls hung with Fascist posters. Maria and I were received by Terentius, who said he was one of the members of the national executive committee, and by Lucretia, who said she was Sacrifice's communications manager.

I introduced myself, trying to be as polite and respectful as possible. I said that Maria and I were very interested in studying Sacrifice and that we wanted to base our research on a series of interviews with their national leaders. Terentius, who took a somewhat hostile attitude and seemed to be playing the tough guy, said to me rather rudely: "I saw on the Internet that you deal with terrorism. Are you capable of understanding that we have nothing to do with terrorism? I don't want you to write that we have something in common with the terrorists. Is that clear?"

While I was trying to reassure him, Maria asked Lucretia a question, which seemed to me too direct, about how Sacrifice was organized. Lucretia replied that Sacrifice's organization was based on a strict hierarchy. This was the dialogue between Lucretia and Maria, according to notes I took at the time:

Can you explain how the decisions are made inside your organization?

"Sacrifice is based on a hierarchical principle. The leaders make the decisions and the militants carry them out."

Maria let her moral contempt for that type of political culture show, increasing Lucretia's hostility and Terentius's paranoia.

You're saying that all the decisions are made by your leaders without any internal debate?

"Yes, that's right."

So there's no democracy inside Sacrifice!

"We're Fascists. Democracy is an invention of the bourgeoisie that has to be eradicated."

Sorry, but what education are you giving young people? Are you teaching them to submit?

"Perhaps you haven't understood. We're Fascists."

I tried to interrupt the duel with these words:

I'm well aware that you're Fascists, and I have the greatest respect for your ideas. I'm very interested in interviewing you because I'm sure there are many people who don't understand what your ideas are and perhaps get the wrong impression about you . . .

Terentius said that Sacrifice had no need of my research to explain their ideas to people, and Lucretia dismissed us with these words: "Listen, we'll talk to the other members of the national executive and we'll let you know if we're interested in your research."

On July 7, 2010, Lucretia sent the following email to me and Maria:

> I don't have good news. We've discussed your project. For the time being we don't consider it interesting for us. Let's hope we can have an opportunity for working together in the future, perhaps even to see you at a conference organized at our headquarters next fall.
>
> In any case, it was a pleasure meeting you.
>
> Regards,
> Lucretia

The Dinner Party

In May 2010 I had started collecting a great quantity of information on Sacrifice, but I hadn't planned to enter one of its cells because, in addition to studying a Nazi political movement, whose leader I interviewed for an hour in front of twenty militants, I was conducting research on some extreme-left terrorists responsible for multiple homicides, which I later published in the academic journal *Studies in Conflict & Terrorism*.

On November 1, 2011, I moved to the town where my girlfriend lived—she was the engineer we met at the Tuscolo Archaeological Park—and I found I had a choice of two gyms. The first gym had an underground weight room, whereas the second one, gym X, seemed much nicer because it was in the middle of a park. My girlfriend told me to be careful, however, because "the owners of gym X belong to a very violent Fascist organization called Sacrifice."

I recognized the owners' Fascist tattoos, and I immediately tried to become friendly with them in the hope of learning something about the world of Sacrifice, and also to create a cordial atmosphere in a place where I was paying to relax and feel good. My first conversation with Arcangelus, an owner of the gym, was one of the most comical in my career as a sociologist because of a faux pas I committed in attempting to be friendly.

One time when the weight room was almost deserted, Arcangelus, a taciturn character, was sitting on a bench next to mine while I was catching my breath between one exercise and the next. I was looking out at a splendid hillside through a glass wall that filled the weight room with sunlight, and I noticed that there was a two-story house some fifty yards away in the gym parking lot that rather spoiled the view. As a friendly overture, I said these words to Arcangelus (copied from my notes):

You're the owner of the gym, aren't you?

"Yeah."

Hi, I'm Alessandro. I enrolled a few days ago . . .

"I'm Arcangelus."

This gym is fantastic. And this view is also fantastic . . .

Arcangelus gave me a big smile and thanked me. Then we returned to looking at the view. After a few seconds, in a very serious voice, as if I were saying something important, the result of deep spiritual reflection, I spoke these words very slowly:

You see that house in front?

"Yes."

You know what I would do?

"No, what?"

I would take a bomb and raze it to the ground. A big bomb and . . . BOOM! *No more house.*

Arcangelus remained silent, gazing at the house as if he were imagining the scene I had described. He was bent slightly forward with his elbows resting on his thighs in a relaxed pose. Then he uttered three sentences, punctuating each with a short pause:

"It's my house."

Pause.

"It's my parents' house."

Pause.

"I've lived in that house since I was born."

It was not a great start. But after a few weeks, my relations with the gym owners, the two secretaries who worked in reception, and the instructors in the weight room were excellent. Whenever I entered the gym, everyone greeted me hospitably.

In December 2011, there was a second defining moment in the history of my ethnographic research. I'm talking about the murders of the Senegalese street peddlers committed by Gianluca Casseri in Florence, something that convinced me I had made a good decision in choosing to study Fascist movements in Italy. A young woman I'll call Clarissa, then a student in my sociology course and now completing her doctoral thesis, told me she was very interested in ethnography and in particular in participant observation. We decided that she would carry out research in a high-security prison where four extreme-left terrorists had been sentenced to life for several homicides committed in the 1980s. I wrote to the four prisoners, and on February 23, 2012, I received a letter from a high-level official in the Ministry of Justice, who informed me that the four inmates had said they didn't want any kind of contact with me.

Clarissa was very disappointed, and I proposed something that she accepted with enthusiasm: "Clarissa, would you like to do ethnographic research on Sacrifice? I know some important militants, and I could get them to meet you . . ."

I attended the first meeting between Clarissa and Masculus, which took place in a bar. Masculus said he understood what participant observation consisted of and accepted Clarissa's proposal. But a few days later she phoned me to say there was a problem: she had the impression that Masculus was interested in her sexually. Masculus is an example of extreme masculinism; he supports the cult of war and is notorious for having beaten up a lot of people. All those who know him assert that when he was younger, he was always involved in street fights. A woman I became friendly with had a relationship with Masculus based only on sex; she told me that, during a dinner party at a friend's house, Masculus continually wanted to have sex with the women.

A few days after their first meeting, Clarissa had already received several invitations to dinner from Masculus, so she sent him an email stating clearly that she was interested only in ethnographic research. Masculus told her not to contact him anymore and accused her of being a stupid, conceited woman who had misinterpreted his noble intentions. He stopped greeting me when we met at the gym.

It was some months after Casseri's rampage when Caesar shoved a broken bottle in Joe's eye in central Mussolinia. This gave further confirmation that Sacrifice was an important phenomenon, but I hadn't yet planned to try to enter a militia. While renting an apartment in Lenintown, I started carrying out in-depth investigations into the brawl.

In November 2012 I experienced a third defining moment, if you can call it that, which created the necessary, albeit still insufficient, conditions for entering the Lenintown and Mussolinia militias: the end of the story with my fiancée. If I had continued that relationship, I wouldn't have been able to do the research that I did.

In December 2012 I organized a dinner party at my home and invited the owners of gym X, their Fascist friends, and their girlfriends. I also invited Masculus, though he didn't come. It was the first time in my life that I had hosted a dinner party, and I got the entire organization of the evening wrong, inviting two groups of people who had never met each other before. Each group was very self-contained.

The first group of ten people consisted of university graduates and their girlfriends, sophisticated and elegantly dressed. This group also included the woman who had had a sexual relationship with Masculus. The second group of nine people was mostly Sacrifice Fascists and their girlfriends, pretty, polite, and well dressed. None of them had ever gone to college, with the exception of one woman.

The college graduates, taken aback by the appearance of Macrinus and Arcangelus, pulled me aside and said: "Alessandro, are you crazy? What on earth were you thinking of, inviting these Fascists? They're positively primeval!" The Fascists and their girlfriends, by contrast, seemed willing to be friendly with the college graduates, but when they realized they were being laughed at they stopped being sociable, and the two groups separated into two different rooms. A friend of mine in the graduate group, who at the time of these events was pregnant, seeing that I was going back and forth from one room to the other to be hospitable to everyone, proposed an idea to make the atmosphere more relaxed: "Guys, let's play Taboo."

The idea was good, but the consequences were disastrous.

Taboo is a card game played by two opposing teams, A and B.

A member of team A takes a card from the pack and has to help one of his teammates guess the secret word on the card. This game is based on the use of a great variety of synonyms and metaphors and requires a large vocabulary that Macrinus and his friends didn't possess.

The college graduate team racked up a lot of points. Then came the turn of Macrinus's girlfriend, who took a card from the pack and chose Macrinus as her partner. Macrinus was supposed to guess the secret word, but he committed a series of grammatical errors that created an embarrassing situation for all present. Soon he started to stutter because of his bad grammar, while his teammates urged him to answer more quickly because the hourglass was running out.

Given the disdain shown them by the graduate group, Macrinus's friends wanted to win at all costs. They cried, "Come on Macrinus! Get a move on! Come on! Fuck! Time's running out!" The more his friends shouted at him in encouragement, the more confused Macrinus became and the more he committed the logical and grammatical errors typical of someone with little formal education. But the cries became louder and louder as the sand in the timer started running out. It was like being in a small stadium.

Finally Macrinus, who was a very muscular man with his body covered in tattooed slogans such as "NULLI SECUNDUS," turned red, contorted the muscles of his face, and in a voice full of anger yelled, "WHO THE FUCK SUGGESTED PLAYING THIS FUCKING GAME?"

The little hourglass was still running, but now everyone shut up. It was as if the stadium had been transformed into the Widener Library at Harvard. The absolute silence was interrupted by Macrinus, who repeated his question, creating even more embarrassment, since his voice was the only one echoing through the apartment: "WHO'S THE ASSHOLE WHO SUGGESTED PLAYING THIS FUCKING GAME?"

Two days later, while I was dining at a well-known restaurant in central Rome, thieves broke into my apartment and stole all my computers. The morning after, on my way to the police station to report the theft with a list of the stolen objects, I ran into Arcangelus, who thanked me for my hospitality but didn't say a word about the contemptuous attitude shown by my university graduate friends toward his group. My graduate friends, with whom I've remained in touch, still laugh about Macrinus's grammatical errors.

The Final Decision

Some months after that dinner party, the Lenintown militia was founded. The day of the launch, some members of the extreme left threw a great quantity of shit at the front door of the building and wrote "Fascists = shit."

I can't publish a photograph showing all that shit, but I can say that, from the calculations I made and the interviews I carried out, there was more than forty pounds of shit on the sidewalk. At that time I was living in Lenintown. I was thinking I would love to do ethnographic research on Sacrifice, but I still believed that my project was unfeasible, and above all, not knowing the Lenintown militants, I couldn't assess whether they were a threat to my personal safety. So I planned a book on Sacrifice with an approach similar to what I had done for my *Anatomy of the Red Brigades.*[1]

I wrote and wrote, and then I deleted what I had written. Things went on like this for a few weeks until I realized I had no original ideas. The more I wrote, the more I could see that the paradigm used in *Anatomy of the Red Brigades*, based on the concept of revolutionary Gnosticism, didn't allow me to make any new discoveries. I wasn't writing a new book about Sacrifice. I was simply writing a new chapter of *Anatomy of the Red Brigades*. I came to the conclusion that I could observe the phenomenon from a new perspective only if I committed myself to ethnography. I reread an article I had written, called "A Day among the Diehard Terrorists," and an anonymous peer review for the journal that said the approach was original.[2] Perhaps it would be a good idea to repeat that type of research with the Fascists, although in a more complex manner? But I was still convinced that it was impossible to enter one of their militias.

The final defining moment came when the Lenintown newspapers reported on the brawl between Leonidas and Ashley. At that moment I decided to risk approaching the militia. But first I had to observe its militants to decide if they were dangerous. One of the most frequent questions I'm asked is "Aren't you frightened of getting close to this type of person?" The answer is yes, I'm frightened. An ethnographer who specializes in studying violent people has to be very cautious and, before establishing direct contact, must collect information on the people he or she intends to work with. In ethnography, gathering information means observing. To observe the Lenintown Fascists, I went to a bar that has tables set out in front of the militia's front door. I always had a computer with me, and I left good tips, so I could sit there for hours on end without causing comment. When I left the bar, I continued to observe from my car, which I parked in a place that was hidden from view.

I must admit that I was very lucky.

The two-story building, which I am looking at as I write now, thanks to Google Earth, is quite old, and only two of its apartments are inhabited (the ground floor is a store). It was easy for me to distinguish the members of the middle-class family who lived there from those of the militia, who closed the balcony window when they left and opened it when they entered. If the window was closed, I waited until the Fascists arrived. If it was open, I waited until they left. After a while I got to know their schedules and their faces.

Naturally, this approach to a deviant group does not tell you if the people you are observing will punch you in the face. But it does allow ethnographers to understand the people they want to study and to decide whether to be frightened of them.

If you're frightened, you need to give up your research.

I passed on to the entry stage.

The Entry Stage

I rang the doorbell of the militia offices and a comrade observed me attentively from the balcony.

"Who are you looking for?"

I replied with a big smile: "Hi! I'm a friend of Arcangelus! Can I come up for a moment? I want to ask about something."

I identified myself as a friend of one of the most respected militants in all the Italian militias to reassure the comrade that I wasn't a cop or an enemy. I climbed the stairs and shook hands with the comrade, who said, "Hi, I'm Camillus." I immediately told him that I was a sociology professor who was interested in conducting some interviews with the Sacrifice militants.

Camillus, who was very polite and hospitable, said: "Sure, come in. We're in the middle of a meeting. Unfortunately our leader isn't in Lenintown today." Then he said: "I'm sorry if I didn't open the door immediately when you rang, but this is a rather complicated time for us because . . ." He smiled and didn't finish his sentence.

The comrades were sitting in the room containing the library managed by Cincinnatus, with seats arranged in a circle. Through tone of voice and body language, I tried to appear shy and gauche.

The message I was trying to communicate was *Don't be frightened of me. I can't do you any harm. I'm a weak and insecure person.*

Camillus offered me a seat and invited me to explain more clearly what I was hoping to obtain from them. The best technique for gaining the trust of a deviant individual who is wary of you, and who is surrounded by a society that condemns him, is to make him believe you think he is who he likes to think he is.

If he thinks he's an idealist, describe him as an idealist. I said: "I'm a sociologist who studies youth movements, but I'm interested only in young people who are political activists because they have big ideals. You know better than me that politicians think only of making money, and I'm not interested in studying that kind of person. I want to write a book about you because your way of being political is based on ideals and not on economic interests. To write this kind of book, I need to get to know you, to talk to you, to understand better your ideals and what you don't like about this society."

There were no questions after I finished my explanation. The comrades looked at me in silence as if I were a ghost. I felt like an intruder, just like Clifford Geertz when he arrived in the Balinese village described in his famous essay "Deep Play: Notes on the Balinese Cockfight."[3] Later I would learn that, in important situations, the comrades never speak, out of respect for their leader. Accustomed to receiving a lot of questions from my students, I thought they were not speaking because they weren't very intelligent. I came to understand that the reason had to do with their political culture.

Camillus thanked me for my interest and said: "I promise I'll speak to our leader about your proposal. If you give me your name and telephone number, I'll call you and tell you what has been decided, even if it's a no."

Once I had given Camillus my name, I'd passed from the role of "observer" to that of "observed."

What did I do? Remembering that, four years earlier, Terentius had been frightened off because of my studies on the Italian Red Brigades, I rushed home to delete the word "terrorism" from my university Web page. Since the Sacrifice militants loved the words "rebellion" and "revolution" and hated "bourgeoisie" and "capitalism," I wrote a presentation of my academic profile that corresponded to the contents of my books, in particular *Anatomy of the Red Brigades* but also *The Rich Revolutionary: Cognitive Strategies for Feeling Superior to Others*.[4]

Interpreting the extreme-left and extreme-right terrorist movements as forms of organized hatred toward capitalism and bourgeois society, I wrote: "Alessandro Orsini is a professor of Political Sociology. His research mainly focuses on revolutionary youth movements fighting against capitalism and bourgeois society."

The Negotiation

Camillus never phoned me, and I couldn't knock on the door of the militia headquarters to insist.

I asked for help from my friend Jonathan, who put me in contact with the Mussolinia councilman whom I had met through him (in chapter 1). Three days later, while I was alone in the LUISS University faculty room in Rome, I telephoned Marcus, the head of the Mussolinia militia, and answered all his questions on the type of research I intended to carry out.[5] The telephone call lasted forty-six minutes.

Marcus said: "I'm sorry to ask all these questions, but we're very paranoid because we're always afraid that someone is trying to harm us. This is why we never give information to anyone and we don't trust anyone."

With these words, he gave me three fundamental items of information I could use to manage my relations with the Sacrifice militants:

1. "We're always very paranoid."
2. "We're always frightened that someone is trying to harm us."
3. "We don't trust anyone."

Marcus said that he was "flattered" that a university professor was interested in his militia. In my notes, which I have in front of me as I write these words, I recorded that Marcus treated me with great respect: "His voice seems insecure. It's like the voice of someone who thinks he's talking to a very important person. Sometimes he doesn't finish his sentences, as if he were afraid of getting the construction wrong."

Marcus told me he was in favor of my entering the militia, but he had first to obtain the permission of the national leaders. This was our dialogue, which I copied onto a piece of paper as it was happening:

"My leaders will ask me what Sacrifice will gain from agreeing to your requests. They'll ask me what . . . Do you see? What you can offer."

What do you think I could offer the national leaders?

"The national leaders will certainly want some sort of political benefit. It's not about money. I'd like to let you enter the militia but . . . Do you understand what I mean?"

You want to know what I can offer Sacrifice as a university professor?

"Correct."

I think that the Sacrifice national leaders would be interested in increasing their members, entering places where they can't go.

"Right!" Marcus laughed.

From that moment on, a negotiation began that allowed me to reply to the question everyone was asking: "Why would a Fascist militia like Sacrifice, with such a high level of paranoia, decide to let a sociology professor enter its organization?" The answer is that Sacrifice's national leaders hoped to gain access to my department and use me to launch a strategic penetration of Italian universities.

The cause of my expulsion was linked to this negotiation, which became more complicated as weeks went by. As I'll show, we agreed on everything, but later on problems arose, and I received a demand that I couldn't accept. A Cornell University Press editor and a senior MIT professor—the only people I asked for advice besides my father—reminded me that there were rules that I couldn't break.

In an exchange of emails, the MIT professor told me that I would have to abide by two fundamental rules during my research.

The first was to respect the people I was studying. I had to reveal my identity and the purpose of my research.

The second rule was to respect what Thomas S. Kuhn, in his fine book *The Structure of Scientific Revolutions*, calls the "scientific community," that is, my colleagues.[6] The MIT professor was also concerned about my personal safety.

The initial negotiation with Marcus ended with a deal: in exchange for authorization to enter the Mussolinia militia, I agreed to:

1. Urge my students to read my book on Sacrifice after its publication.
2. Invite one of the Sacrifice national leaders to my sociology class so that he could talk to my students.

Marcus thought he had closed an excellent deal, but in fact I hadn't conceded anything, for two reasons.

First, when I write a book that costs me years of work, I always ask my students to read it and discuss it in class.

Second, every year I seek out a violent political activist, perhaps even someone who has committed homicide for ideological reasons, to come and talk with my students. On April 8, 2014, for example, I invited to LUISS University an extreme-left terrorist who had killed seven people but who, after having served thirty-two years and six months in prison, had become a fervent Catholic. He never repented publicly for the homicides he had committed, but he had written essays criticizing his role in the Prima Linea terrorist group, of which he had been a leader.

A lengthy exchange of texts, emails, and telephone calls began between me and Marcus. Marcus talked to the national leaders and then told me what they had said. In the end, he said, the national leaders had decided to accept my proposal because they thought it was advantageous for Sacrifice. The only problem was that they weren't happy about my entering the Mussolinia cell. "The national leaders want you to go to the organization's national headquarters," he told me, "and not the Mussolinia militia."

I replied that from a methodological angle, it was essential for me to study Sacrifice in a small town. Marcus asked me if I could provide the name of a Sacrifice militant who could put in a good word for me with the national leaders. I told him, "Tell them to call Arcangelus from gym X." Marcus said that Arcangelus had spoken highly of me but the national leaders were still very suspicious and wanted to be sure they could control me: "They say that if you enter the Mussolinia militia, they won't be able to keep an eye on what you do. Personally, I'm sorry, because it's as if they didn't trust me, but unfortunately that's how things stand."

Then Marcus sent me an email in which he said: "I told the national leaders that I'm in favor of you entering my militia because, if you were someone who wanted to badmouth us, you could write a pack of lies behind a desk, like the journalists do. Someone who has bad intentions doesn't act like you. He doesn't ask for authorization and he doesn't spend his own money renting an apartment in Lenintown." As time went on, a relationship of trust and respect was created between me and Marcus; it would save me the night when Leonidas expelled me from the Lenintown militia.

A few days later, Marcus put me in direct contact with Augustus, one of the Sacrifice national leaders who had celebrated Venner's suicide, who came to see me at my university. Augustus told me that he had asked for information about me from Arcangelus and also from a student of mine, a Sacrifice militant who was taking my political sociology course.

At the end of the meeting, Augustus asked me to confirm that I accepted the conditions of the Sacrifice leaders—that I would have my students read my book on Sacrifice and that once a year I would invite one of the Sacrifice national leaders to talk to my students. (Augustus would be that Sacrifice leader.) In addition, I told him that I would show the national leaders those parts of my manuscript in which their interviews appeared and they would be able to ask for corrections or additions.

I accompanied Augustus to the bus stop in front of the university and phoned Marcus to inform him that we had come to an agreement. Marcus first phoned Augustus, who confirmed my words, and then Leonidas to tell him about the agreement and ask him to treat me well.

Once I had entered the Lenintown and Mussolinia militias, I faced two problems.

The first was Lentulus's attitude. He didn't like the fact that I was being received like a real militant because that meant I could see or hear things that should have remained secret. Moreover, he was convinced that the national leaders would punish the Mussolinia militia if my book damaged the organization.

The second problem was that Dux, the founder of Sacrifice, whom no one was allowed to contradict, said that an eye had to be kept on everything I did and that I would have to agree to have my manuscript read before publication. This was the condition that I refused and that, in the end, caused my expulsion.

Although Augustus was a member of the Sacrifice national executive committee, he was accountable to Dux, who could have expelled him from the organization in a second. Augustus phoned me as I was passing through the Piazza Navona on my Vespa Piaggio on a day that reminded me that Rome is the most beautiful city in the world. Since I had missed the call, I phoned Augustus back and, using the language of the Sacrifice militants, told him that I needed to talk to "my leaders" to see if I could accept this request to have the manuscript read prior to publication. In fact, I don't have "leaders" in the Sacrifice sense, but I couldn't explain to Augustus how the scholarly world functioned. Augustus told me he was in favor of my research and tried to persuade me to accept the request of Dux, whom I had met only once, at the end of the evening in honor of Venner.

This was my response:

Augustus, I get what you're saying, and I'm very grateful for your help, but like you I also have leaders and I can't do everything I want. I don't believe that my leaders would allow me to accept, but I'll ask them all the same.

Augustus asked me to put myself in his shoes and I asked him to put himself in mine. Then he asked:

"Where are these leaders of yours?"

They're in the United States.

"I don't understand you. No one will ever know that you let the book be read before publishing it. None of us will ever tell anyone that we've read it. The problem is solved. These guys are in the United States!"

I gave Augustus the most Fascist answer I could think of:

Augustus, the problem is that, like you, even though I'm not a Fascist, I profoundly believe in honor and loyalty. My leaders are my leaders, and I could never betray their trust. Perhaps they'll never find out that I let you read the manuscript, but I would lose honor, and I could no longer look at myself in the mirror.

Augustus continued to say that he couldn't understand me and repeated that my leaders would never know anything. I continued to be very polite with him and replied that I had already agreed to show all the parts of the manuscript that quoted Sacrifice leaders, who could ask me to make corrections or additions. Augustus told me that he would try to find a solution, but he didn't tell me that I had to leave the militias. From that moment on, I did the simplest thing in the world: I waited for the day of my expulsion. I was well aware that neither my contact at Cornell University Press nor the senior MIT professor would agree that I should allow my manuscript to be vetted by Sacrifice before its publication. The reason is obvious: it's called self-censorship.

Writing Up Ethnographic Notes

The awareness that I could be expelled at any moment had a great deal of influence on the way I wrote my notes. Some ethnographic manuals assert that the time devoted to writing up notes should be a daily task equal to the time given to participant observation, but I couldn't allow myself such a luxury.[7] My priority was to spend as much time as possible with the comrades. To reduce the time devoted to writing up my notes and increase observation time, I used three techniques:

1. Recording my voice on my cell phone while I was pretending to speak to someone else.
2. Using direct discourse even if I was writing down the dialogues a few minutes after they had occurred.
3. Using the present tense in my notes so I could use fewer words than the past tense required.

Thus I did not write, "Marcus asserts that the national leaders told him they're very afraid that, once I entered the Mussolinia militia, I could observe behaviors or listen to conversations that, if they were recounted in a book, could harm the organization."

Instead I wrote, "The national leaders want you to conduct your research in Rome because they fear they can't control you."

Many hours of recordings remained on my phone for the duration of the research, and I confess I never found the time to transcribe most of them until after my expulsion. This modus operandi didn't allow me to fully exploit the potential of my notes. In some cases, not having the time to transcribe all I had recorded on my telephone meant that I forgot to pose some questions I would have liked to ask the Sacrifice militants.

I love ethnographic manuals, but I had no choice. If I had spent many hours developing my ethnographic notes, I wouldn't have been able to devote so much time to participant observation. If I hadn't devoted so much time to participant observation, I wouldn't have been able to write my notes, because I was well aware that my presence in the militia was only temporary.

I think a concrete example is useful.

While I was typing into the computer a long interview that Cincinnatus had allowed me to record, Leonidas texted me on WhatsApp, and our chat, what with one thing and another, lasted some twenty minutes. One of his messages read: "The problem isn't fighting against the adversary in front of you. The real problem is fighting against the enemy you have inside, that is, the bourgeois culture, because we all grew up in this crappy bourgeois society."

When I had finished my chat with Leonidas, I immediately started to transcribe his texts, and while I was searching the Internet for an article on MMA fights (which I finally found),[8] Marcus, whom I had asked to put me in contact with the Carthage militia leader, phoned to tell me that the latter was expecting a call from me.

The Internet has made the work of writing up ethnographic notes much harder. On a single day I might receive up to eighty WhatsApp texts.

To carry out comparative research, and also to gather the greatest amount of information in the least possible amount of time, I lived simultaneously with two militias in two towns nearly twenty miles apart. Almost every day I had to drive along an often very busy road. The journey from Lenintown to Mussolinia could take as much as an hour. Not to mention that damned railroad crossing which, when the barrier was lowered to let trains through into central Lenintown, created a long line of automobiles and increased the length of my journey. In addition, I entered the militias at a time of year (from spring to summer) when Sacrifice was organizing numerous initiatives. The fine weather meant you could leave the militia offices, whether to hand out pasta, distribute flyers, go to bars, or, obviously, take a walk with comrades and chat.

One time I returned to my home in Lenintown at three in the morning and had to wake up again at seven, exhausted, to drive back to Mussolinia. At nine we started handing out pasta, and at one I left Mussolinia to go to the Lenintown headquarters, where Leonidas had assembled the comrades at two in the afternoon to prepare pasta packages to be handed out at four so that our initiative was coordinated with that of the Mussolinia militia.

As I had anticipated, the day of my expulsion arrived without any warning. Leonidas was as friendly as ever, and we were laughing and joking together. Five minutes later, he was looking at me as if I were his worst enemy. He had adopted an aggressive stance and a threatening tone; I thought that if I had spoken a word out of turn, he would have punched me in the face. During the ten minutes of interaction with Leonidas that ended with my expulsion, I learned a lot about the emotional forces that govern the behavior of individuals in revolutionary sects. I saw, from the perspective of the victim, the immense emotional power contained in Codreanu's principle of submission to the leader and absolute love for the militia.

What I saw in those ten minutes would be enough for a book in itself. This is what happened.

The Night of the Expulsion

While I was in the Lenintown militia offices, Marcus sent me a WhatsApp message, saying: "Next week there's going to be a big rock concert at the arena. Militants from all over Italy will be coming." I would have liked to go in the car with the Lenintown militants, but this wasn't possible because the national leaders had organized it as a two-day event, Friday and Saturday, and I wanted to attend both days.

I had enough money to stay overnight in Gaugamela, the town where the concert was being held. But the Lenintown militants couldn't afford this, and to save money, they told me, they would leave in the morning and then return the same night. Leonidas said to me, "Unfortunately I don't even have enough money to pay for my train ticket from Lenintown to Gaugamela."[9]

The first day I was in the arena for around ten hours. The evening of the next day, I saw both Leonidas and Marcus in the arena courtyard, but each was with comrades from his own militia. As I described in chapter 3, the arena consists of a covered section, containing the MMA cage and the stage where the rock bands performed, and an uncovered area.

I went up to Leonidas, who was drinking alcohol. Some comrades had told me that when Leonidas drinks, he can suddenly become aggressive.

Leonidas joked about the fact that there were only men around us and said, "No chance of a fuck here!" We laughed and joked together.

One of the national leaders who was always trying to show how much he despised me passed close by and, without even looking at me, spoke brusquely to Leonidas: "Come with me. I have to talk to you." The two conversed some twenty yards away, but it was impossible to hear what they were saying because the music was too loud. Leonidas listened in silence, then opened his eyes wide in astonishment and bent toward the national leader's mouth as if he needed to hear more clearly words he could hardly believe.

Then Leonidas stood up straight, and the expression on his face changed from astonished to thoughtful, as if he wanted to organize his thoughts after receiving an order that bewildered him. I figured that Leonidas had talked to the man for about five minutes, but I didn't look at my watch because I had my eyes fixed on his face. Adrenaline flowed through my body.

I was frightened.

In a few seconds my mind tried to work out the best strategy for putting an end to my research without getting myself beaten up. I remembered that, when the Sacrifice comrades greeted a person whom they acknowledged as physically and morally superior, they would say, "Respect!"

I said to myself, *Submit and use the word "respect."*

For me it was a matter of professional pride. I wanted to conduct that research, but I also didn't want to get beaten up. I didn't want to end up like Bill Buford, who was once punched into unconsciousness. On December 1, 2014, I gave a lecture in Lyons Hall at Boston College in which I recounted my approach stage. The hall was full, and at the end of my lecture many students said to me: "What an extraordinary story! How did you do it?" If I had appeared at Boston College with a broken nose, I'm sure the same students would have thought: *Look at that asshole! He walked into a Fascist militia and got his face smashed in. Even I could have done that!*

Probably my editor at Cornell University Press and the senior MIT professor would have thought the same thing, albeit in more elegant terms, since they were continually warning me: "Alessandro, be careful what you do. Your safety comes first! Break off the research if you find yourself in danger!"

I wanted to handle fire without burning myself; I wanted to fall without crashing.

I wanted to win.

But the most important reason of all why I didn't want to get a fist in the face was that, when I was fifteen, during a soccer match, I had taken a violent head butt. I lost consciousness, and when I got up, my face was covered in blood, some of my teeth were broken, and I could feel my nose—it's a sensation I will never forget—wobbling between my fingers like rubber. When I opened my eyes—and this was the worst thing—all I could remember was my name, and in the throes of a panic attack I obsessively repeated it for fear of forgetting it: *Alessandro Orsini, Alessandro Orsini, Alessandro Orsini* . . . The people around me asked where I lived so they could take me home, but since I had suffered a slight concussion, I couldn't remember anything. I was in despair.

My incisors were repaired almost perfectly, but even today, if I look at them closely, I can see cracks. It would take just a small thump to break them again.

I didn't want to be hit in the face by a professional boxer. I had seen some of Leonidas's matches. He was technically very good, and his punches were very powerful. Without gloves, hitting a person full in the face, Leonidas could kill someone.

He was coming toward me and I was ready to surrender. I had overcome a thousand obstacles to reach this point, and I had gathered enough ethnographic material to write ten books. It was the last round and I had to remain standing. Leonidas was stronger but I was more intelligent. We would go into the ring, and I would have to shift around him until I tired him out.

Leonidas, whom I had just been laughing and joking with, pointed his index finger in my face and, with a threatening look, said:

"You're out of the group, understand? Never come near the militia again!"

Leonidas, I have the greatest respect for you. I'll leave the militia at once. But please, can I ask you why you're throwing me out?

"You're out of the group, and that's it. Get lost."

Of course, I'll do what you want, I respect you very much. I'd just like to know if I've done something wrong so I can ask you to forgive me.

"The national leaders never authorized you to enter my militia. You told me that they had authorized it and I obeyed their orders because I'm a political soldier."

I respect you very much and I'll never approach your militia again, but I would remind you that it was Marcus who told you that the national leaders had authorized it. Shall we call Marcus?

If Leonidas had started beating me up right there at the arena, I wouldn't have had any way to defend myself or even to report him, because all around me there were only bodies covered with swastikas and Fascist symbols.

Who would have testified in my favor? Fuck, I was in the parallel world and I couldn't get out of it.

I can't begin to describe how much I missed the "crappy bourgeois society" at that moment. I thought that I would have grabbed all the crap in the world to get out of that situation, and I took a step forward in my understanding of a Fascist militia. I understood that if it protects you from violence, even a crappy society becomes desirable.

Leonidas was still lucid, although the drink had had its effect. When I realized that my response was confusing him, I stopped shifting around him and forced him to reflect. By asserting that Marcus could testify in my favor, I'd forced Leonidas to consider contradictory orders. Leonidas was supposed to obey the national leaders, but he was also supposed to obey Marcus—his direct superior. He couldn't hit me in the face without Marcus's permission.

He hesitated, and I landed the final blow: "Leonidas, I have my phone with me. I'm going to call Augustus to prove to you that I've always told the truth . . ."

Leonidas looked at me as if I had pronounced the name of God. He didn't even have Augustus's telephone number, while I, a mere member of the crappy bourgeois society, was able to phone one of the most important national leaders. While I looked up Augustus's number, Marcus approached with two other comrades from the Mussolinia militia and asked what was going on.

I told him that Leonidas had expelled me from his militia because someone had told him I hadn't been authorized to conduct my research. Marcus remained silent, with the expression of someone who doesn't comprehend what's happening.

Then he said, "I don't understand . . ."

Leonidas became agitated again and said: "I don't want to find myself in the middle of this mess because the national leaders will take it out on me. I don't want them to put me in the shithouse. You're out of my militia."

Then he said something that impressed me immensely because in all my life no one had ever promised not to stab me. "You're not to come near my militia anymore, OK? If I come across you in the street, I won't hit you, I won't swear at you, and I won't stab you. I promise that I've never stabbed anyone in all my life. I've been in fights, yes, but I promise that I've never, ever stabbed anyone in my whole life, never!" Leonidas made the typical gesture of someone swearing.

In contrast with Leonidas's agitated behavior, Marcus calmly and quietly said to me, "Come with me."

I was left alone with Marcus and the other two Mussolinia comrades, who, together with Lentulus, constituted the militia's executive committee. (Lentulus had remained behind in Mussolinia because of his work.) Emphasizing my respect for Marcus, I tried to push him into the role of Leonidas's leader. I hoped that my act of submission to his authority would put me in a favorable light and help ensure that he would defend me from any attacks.

I had to continue to submit, but in a more subtle manner, because Marcus was more intelligent than Leonidas. In a frightened voice, I said:

Marcus, do I need to worry? Is Leonidas going to beat me up?

Marcus told me that he wouldn't allow anyone to hurt me and that I could continue to associate with his militia, but first I had to clear up the situation with Augustus, who hadn't replied to two telephone calls: "At the entrance to the arena," said Marcus "there are two militants from the national executive. Let's go talk to them."

After four years, the moment had arrived to meet Terentius and Lucretia again. Lucretia spoke first, getting straight to the point:

"Why don't you want us to read your manuscript before it's published? Are you trying to hide something?"

I've already told Augustus. I'm a sociologist and I have to respect sociologists' rules. I can't let you read the manuscript because my leaders would think I'm censoring myself.

"Your leaders are in the United States and they'd never find out. Two sociologists published a book about us, but first they promised to let us read the manuscript."

I'm not a Fascist, but I also believe in honor, and I could never betray my leaders' trust.

Marcus and the other two Mussolinia comrades listened in silence. At important moments, no militant ever allowed himself to interrupt a superior. Terentius said that in the past, they had trusted two journalists who had then described Sacrifice in a way he didn't like: "Those pieces of shit!" In the end, we agreed that I would email my "leaders" to get an answer on this matter, but first I cleared up a point that was important to me:

Guys, if you've changed your mind, OK, but no one can say that I entered the militias without the permission of the national leaders, because I myself spoke to one of them, Commodus, during Harmatus's rally in Mussolinia.

At my request, Marcus confirmed that Commodus and I had talked inside the Mussolinia militia headquarters. This proved that the national leaders knew I had entered the militias. Lucretia and Terentius didn't object but said they still wanted to read the manuscript.

When I finished talking to Lucretia, I had the most important sociological experience of all. Nothing I had seen before was comparable to what I was about to witness.

The Most Important Moment

I told Marcus that I wanted to say good-bye to the Lenintown comrades and thank them for accepting me in their militia. I went over to them while they were listening to Leonidas, who stared at me with a threatening look as if he wanted to stop me from coming closer. I was violating his order not to go near his militia ever again, and I was risking a punch in the face, but it was worth it because what I saw was incredible.

I left everyone with their mouths open. I told them: "Excuse me, guys, I just want to say good-bye and thank you for having accepted me in your militia all this time. Thanks for everything."

I held out my hand, but no one shook it.

The faces of those five guys, whom I had laughed with for months, were completely expressionless. I had been observing what effects the principle of submission to the leader produces, but now my sociological perspective was much broader because I was no longer a sociologist but an enemy who represents a threat to the militia.

For an instant, there was great tension. I continued to hold my hand out, but no one moved. It was an anguishing sensation because I didn't know what to do. Then Leonidas said something that I will never forget and that I recorded on my cell phone fifteen minutes later. His tone of voice and facial expressions were those of an adult addressing a group of five-year-olds.

He said exactly this: "Guys, be polite. Come on, shake his hand."

When Leonidas saw that the comrades weren't obeying him, he used a slightly more insistent tone, but still in the gentle and affectionate manner of an adult who is urging a group of young children to do something they are frightened of doing: "I said that you can shake his hand. Come on, be polite, take his hand."

Each of them gave me his hand.

To each of them I said, "Thank you."

My Refusal

My editor and the MIT professor both advised me not to allow the manuscript to be read. Their position was very clear, and it couldn't in any way be misconstrued.

After exchanging a series of texts with Lucretia, I decided to send an email to Lucretia, Marcus, and Augustus. (I have a Ph.D. in history, and I attribute enormous importance to written documents.) After my first meeting with Camillus, I had opened a new email account that I used only for communicating with the Sacrifice militants, so as to make it easier to file the correspondence. I also did this to protect myself in case some Fascist were to accuse me of participating in Sacrifice meetings without permission or even under cover. For example, when Augustus invited me to attend the conference in honor of Venner, I sent an email to thank him, since the meeting was reserved for just a few militants.

I let Lucretia, Augustus, and Marcus know that I couldn't grant their request to read the manuscript before its publication.

This is the text of the email:

Dear Lucretia,

How are you? I hope you had a good weekend.

I refer to my latest message on Sunday to tell you that I have done everything I could. Unfortunately, I can't let you read the manuscript before it's published. I would be equally grateful if you could authorize me to continue to attend the Mussolinia militia and to allow me to interview you. If you continue to authorize me, I confirm what I already said to Augustus during our meeting at LUISS University: after I have transcribed the interviews, you can read them and, if necessary, ask me to correct them or add to what you have said. I'm completely willing to let you see all the parts of the manuscript in which you are quoted. I'm also willing to accept another request by Augustus, that is, to devote a large part of the book to the Sacrifice national leaders.

I'm sorry that other writers before me have betrayed your trust, as Terentius told me Saturday evening at the arena. I understand perfectly your reasons and your anxieties. If you do not permit me to continue associating with the Mussolinia militia, I will have the greatest understanding of your decision and I will hasten to thank the Mussolinia militants one by one for the kindness which they have always shown me. Of course I will not disturb any of them further should you refuse my request, which I would accept with the greatest respect.

I must, however, tell you, out of correctness and transparency, that should you refuse, it is probable that I will still write a book on Sacrifice, given that I have already worked on it at length over the past months, committing all my energies and my free time to totally self-financed research.

Thank you very much for the time you have given me, and I am at your disposal for any further clarification.

Alessandro Orsini

Lucretia sent me an email in which she confirmed that I was free to write a book on Sacrifice if I wanted to, but she forbade me to quote from interviews with the militants.

Sacrifice used two methods to dissuade me from writing the book.

The first was represented by Lucretia's email, in which she said she knew she couldn't forbid me to write a book about Sacrifice, but made it clear that if I did so, I would become an enemy of the entire organization.

The second was less formal. A Sacrifice militant, known as one of the most violent in all the militias, came up to me more than once while I was training in gym X and told me that if I were to publish a book on Sacrifice, my life would be ruined.

Monkeys Are More Intelligent

Nine days after being expelled from the militia, I had dinner with a woman I'll call Carla, a professional model with a degree in communication studies, with whom I had begun a relationship.

During dinner, I told her the real reason why I had spent so many months away from Rome, and I proposed that she come with me to Lenintown. Thanks to Marcus's protection, I would be able to spend a few days back in Lenintown, one of the most beautiful tourist locations in Italy.

Arriving in Lenintown, Carla told me that she didn't want to dine in a restaurant because she had recently appeared on a well-known television program, and she was afraid people would recognize and pester her. Suddenly, as we were walking toward the sea, I saw four comrades in front of us leaning against a car. Since Leonidas had ordered me not to approach any member of his militia, my body filled with emotional tension. I didn't know how to manage the situation. Up until a few days earlier, those guys had been part of my daily life, and my instinct was to greet them, but then I thought that this would anger Leonidas.

We were now in front of them, and I could see that their facial expressions were sad and dejected. The first to greet me was Camillus, who said he was waiting for Cincinnatus. Then he looked me in the eye without saying another word. I didn't say anything either, and we remained silent for a few minutes until Camillus started talking.

This was our dialogue, with Carla watching, noted on my cell phone ten minutes later:

"Did you hear?"

Hear what?

Camillus paused and smiled disconsolately.

"You really haven't heard?"

Heard what? I don't understand what you're talking about . . .

At that moment Cincinnatus arrived, and Camillus, without even greeting him, said:

"Leonidas has been arrested."

Fuck! Leonidas has been arrested?

In a voice full of sorrow and amazement, I repeated the same thing three times.

He's been arrested?

He's been arrested?

He's been arrested?

"Yes, today, at six in the morning. The cops from the special squad woke him up, handcuffed him in front of his parents, and took him to jail."

I put both hands on my head and held them there.

Fuck! I didn't know!

"The papers have already published loads of stuff online. All Lenin-town is talking about Leonidas's arrest."

And what are you going to do now? Have you got a plan? What do you think you'll do?

"We arranged to meet up here. Now we're going off in the car to discuss what we should do."

The comrades talked among themselves for about five minutes and then left in their car.

I was aghast at the news of the arrest and told Carla so. The presence of Carla was very important to me because it gave me the chance to see how the comrades appeared to a third party. Carla said to me: "I'd thought that you were a hero, that you had lived among the Fascists, in all kinds of danger, but instead these are real cretins. Have you heard the way they talk? They seem like mental retards. If I were to meet them in the street at night, instead of being frightened I would burst out laughing. These are the dangerous Sacrifice Fascists?"

Carla continued to repeat the same sentiments: "I'm shocked. I've never seen such absolute cretins. You can see quite clearly that they're social misfits who need a leader to give meaning to their lives."

I felt humiliated by Carla's words, and I tried to explain that Leonidas was a professional boxer, but Carla kept insisting that she had never seen such cretins and found it incredible that I would have wasted my time with them: "You've spent all your weekends with these mental retards? You rented an apartment in Lenintown to live with them? You must be joking!"

I forgot I was an ethnographer and, feeling offended, I said in an annoyed tone:

Sorry, but do you have to repeat the same thing like a broken record?

Carla, more determined than ever, said:

"I'm repeating the same things because I'm shocked! These are seriously retarded people! Monkeys are more intelligent than them!" Then Carla, with dozens of people around, started to jump up and down in imitation of a monkey, crying out like an orangutan, "UH UH UH!"

According to Carla, Leonidas was a guy who wanted to make a mark in society, but "since he doesn't have the qualities for being successful in the world of normal people, he's surrounded himself with a group of mental retards in order to feel he's someone."

How can you judge him if you don't even know him?

"I've never met him, but I'm sure that he's a loser who can't manage to get any gratification from life. If he attracts this type of person, he can't be anything but a loser! Now I understand why he punches girls!"

Carla thought that, with the arrest of Leonidas, the militia would certainly be disbanded:

"These guys are a group of idiots. You'll see that the group will break up. These people don't know what to do without a leader."

I told Carla that I didn't agree and that in my opinion, the militia would remain united. I asked her to let me sit down on a bench so I could record the conversation with Camillus on my phone.

Over the next few days, the militia launched a public campaign to demand that Leonidas be freed and to defend him from the Lenintown mayor, who had said, "We must thank the police for having arrested a criminal." The comrades organized a party in the militia offices to raise funds and plan a demonstration in support of Leonidas, which took place in downtown Mussolinia. My ethnographic notes continued to grow as the parallel world went to war. In the morning, when I walked across central Lenintown to have breakfast at a café, I photographed the slogans written on the walls with the anarchist symbol: "Leonidas should die in prison!" "Sacrifice = shit!"

Leonidas was in jail, but the parallel world continued to exist. It felt as if I had been expelled from the militia at the very moment when the crappy bourgeois society invaded the small world with all its troops. I agonized about missing the chance to observe everything from the inside. Even today I am still furious at having lost an opportunity I had dreamed about my whole life as a social researcher.

Why Did the Fascists Accept Me?

At the end of the book, I'm ready to answer the most frequently asked question: Why did Sacrifice allow a sociologist to live inside its militias?

Marcus agreed to do so for four reasons.

The first is that he was tired of living in a "ghetto," and this influenced his concept of the relationship between the militia and the external world and, consequently, the relationship between him and me. In contrast to Lentulus's isolationism, Marcus's political strategy was to open Sacrifice up to bourgeois society because, as he often repeated, "we're wrong to close ourselves up in a ghetto. This is what the bourgeois society wants, and we have to conquer it from the inside, like the Trojan horse."

For example, a few months before my entrance into the militia, Marcus and Lentulus had argued. The former wanted the militia to participate in the Mussolinia municipal elections; the latter was opposed to it, asserting that participation in bourgeois elections would encourage the militia's moral corruption. Marcus told me that, since he was the leader, he could have decided for the others, but in the end he gave in to protect the unity of the militia.

The second reason is that he was flattered by the fact that a university professor was interested in his militia. Marcus, who himself attended an excellent university, comes from a family that attributes great importance to education and has respect for university professors. His father has a degree and a prestigious job.

The third is that Marcus thought he had concluded an important agreement that would benefit the entire organization.

The fourth is that Marcus respected me on a personal level because, searching Google and YouTube, he discovered that I had exposed the system of rigging competitive examinations in Italian universities. Five rulings in my favor and my denunciations on television had prompted the launch of a protest movement against corruption in Italian universities. It had met for the first time at the University of Bologna on October 28, 2011, and then created a website called Per la Sociologia, managed by a group of professors from Turin, Milan, and Bologna.[10]

Journalists had described me as courageous, and on October 18, 2010, the *Corriere della Sera*, the leading Italian newspaper, had devoted an article to my public battle against a group of powerful professors who rigged public competitions in order to promote family members. This rigged examination system had forced many young Italian academics to move abroad. After finding these articles, Marcus told me, "Yours is a noble battle because young Italians should stay in Italy instead of going to enrich other countries."

Leonidas accepted me for three reasons.

First, Marcus had telephoned him to say that the national leaders had agreed to my research.

The second is that he was convinced that my book would describe him as a superhero. I never said anything to make him believe this, but his great desire to redeem himself socially, continually emerging from his in-depth interviews and from his way of relating to bourgeois society, convinced him that my book would make him famous. Leonidas always said that one day all of Lenintown would be forced to recognize his value and his intelligence. As he often remarked to me, his greatest dream was to become a member of the Lenintown municipal council: "One day, this whole town will see how much I'm worth."

The third is that Leonidas considered me a decent and loyal person, as he often said in front of the other comrades.

The national leaders accepted me for one reason alone: they thought that my research would give Sacrifice an entrée into the most prestigious political science department in Italy.

Augustus accepted because he was enthusiastic about the prospect of talking to my students and condemning bourgeois society.

LUISS University is known as the "temple of the Italian bourgeoisie." It is a private university supported by Confindustria (Italian Confederation of Industries), founded in 1974 by a group of entrepreneurs led by the Agnelli family.

Pirandello would have agreed that the arrangement was comical.

Why Did I Decide to Do This Research?

Now we come to me.

There are four reasons why I decided to carry out ethnographic research into the Fascist world. The first two are important; the last two are fundamental.

The first concerns my obsessive desire to say new things. After *Anatomy of the Red Brigades*, I was no longer able to find an interesting idea that would allow me to call into question conventional thinking about particular political phenomena. But this doesn't explain my choice of Fascists as an object of study.

The second is my great passion for ethnographic research. But this doesn't explain why I chose Sacrifice either.

The third, more fundamental reason is linked to my relationship with violence.

For six years, from the ages of nine to fifteen, I lived in a district of Naples in which violence was widespread. It left a lasting impression on me. When I was thirteen, a man was killed a few yards away from me by a bullet to the head while I was playing soccer with a group of friends. By the time I was fifteen, I had been attacked or robbed at least four times. I lost count of the times I had to defend myself, hide, or run away. I remember that, whenever I returned home after dark, there was a particularly dangerous spot along the street where drug addicts tried to rob people by threatening them with syringes. I would walk normally up to a certain point, and then, as I was approaching the dangerous stretch, I'd start running, even though no one was following me. My friends did the same—it was what we all did.

My mother had her handbag snatched twice in just a few weeks. The second time caused a panic attack because the thieves broke into her parked car, where she was sitting with my four-year-old brother Andrea, and she was afraid they wanted to kidnap him. A few months later, in July 1990, my family moved to Latina, a town of 100,000 inhabitants in the Lazio region of Italy. My father had decided to bring up his three children in a more peaceful environment.

Founded by Mussolini on June 30, 1932, under the name Littoria, Latina was known as the "most Fascist town in Italy" because of its election results and its typically Fascist architecture. Ajmone Finestra, who had fought against the Americans alongside Mussolini and Hitler, was the mayor of Latina between December 6, 1993, and May 26, 2002. His pronouncements in favor of Mussolini excited hundreds of young Fascists, who swaggered aggressively around the town.

In September 1990 I started attending the most prestigious school in Latina, developing left-wing ideas and soon becoming one of the best-known student leaders in town. My popularity was also due to the fact that in 1992 I had started working at Radio Latina One (its real name), where I produced a rock music program.

My relations with the Fascists became very tense after I was elected one of four student representatives in my high school, the Dante Alighieri school. I obtained hundreds of votes, coming in first and beating all the candidates of one of the strongest Fascist movements in Latina. After this the Fascists suggested we organize some initiatives together because their leader, who previously had been sentenced for participating in an extreme-right terrorist group, had ordered them to attract sympathizers in the most important school in the town. I despised them and wanted nothing to do with them. Today I realize that, in 1990, Fascism had been defeated only forty-five years earlier, even though it seemed like centuries to me at the time.

The situation escalated one day when, by asking the headmaster to intervene, I got a group of Fascists thrown out of my school, which they had entered surreptitiously to distribute Fascist flyers during the recreation break. (Italian law forbids outsiders from entering public schools.) They followed me home, threatened me, and assured me that they would have their revenge. I submitted a written complaint to the police, and a few days later five Fascists stopped me while I was out walking one evening with my girlfriend. One of them started slapping me and told me that if I went to the police again, they would kill me. My girlfriend yelled for help, but I was unable to react because the shock flooded my body with adrenaline, paralyzing me.

It was a great humiliation for me as the Fascist alternated slaps with insults, and while he attacked me, I retreated:

"DICKHEAD, you went to the cops?"

Slap.

"Go on, go back to the cops."

Slap.

"Do you know who you're dealing with?"

Slap.

"Answer, ASSHOLE, do you know?"

Slap.

When Leonidas told me that his militants never, ever went to the police but always defended themselves in their own way, I knew what he was talking about.

The fourth reason is that, when my family moved to Latina, I felt uprooted. I had lost all the friends I'd had in Naples and I was in a town that was new to me. I felt alone and deeply unhappy. Salvio, my new best friend, had anarchic ideas and was always laughing. He introduced me to Metallica, Iron Maiden, and the Ramones, who relieved my loneliness with their great songs. He and I were classmates during my first year at school there, but when Salvio failed his exams for the second time, he told me that he felt adrift. He changed schools and after a few months was transformed. The boy with anarchic ideas, who used to stop and joke with all the black street peddlers, entered a Fascist group. They all dressed the same way, went around together, and enjoyed hassling their left-wing contemporaries.

In brief, when I lived in Naples, I had to coexist with the problem of violence linked to petty crime. When I moved to Latina, I faced the problem of violence linked to a political culture. Although my life in Latina was infinitely easier than in Naples, I came to this conclusion: that the most effective way to fight violence is to get to know it.

ACKNOWLEDGMENTS

I wrote this entire book at the Center for International Studies of the Massachusetts Institute of Technology, where I was appointed Research Affiliate in 2011. During my frequent visits to CIS, I have had the benefit of engaging in many conversations and talks with faculty members, visiting scholars, fellows, Ph.D. candidates, and master's degree students from all over the world. I thank John Tirman, Taylor Fravel, Stephen Van Evera, Roger Petersen, Fotini Christia, Vipin Narang, Kenneth Oye, and Francis J. Gavin, as well as Barry Posen, who generously hosted me at events, seminars, meetings, and the gala dinner of the MIT Security Studies Program. I am greatly indebted to the MIT administrative staff for having always been so kind and helpful to me. I thank Serenella Sferza, Robert Murray, Phiona Lovett, Joli Divon Saraf, Michelle Nhuch, Harlene Miller, and Casey Johnson. It is thanks to these people that I spent the most beautiful days of my intellectual career at MIT. Special acknowledgments go to Spencer M. Di Scala for helping me to not forget the importance of having "historical sense," even in doing ethnographic

Acknowledgments

research. Jonathan Laurence gave me many good suggestions on many occasions. Walking and talking with him, at both the Brookings Institution and Boston College, was of great help to me. Nobody supported my research as much as Richard J. Samuels did over these years. He is the only person to whom I talked about my "ethnographic troubles" during my time embedded in Sacrifice—the only one other than Roger M. Haydon, my editor at Cornell University Press, and my father. There are no words to thank them.

212

Notes

1. The Organization of Education

1. John Lofland, David Snow, Leon Anderson, and Lyn H. Lofland, *Analyzing Social Settings: A Guide to Qualitative Observation and Analysis* (Belmont, Calif.: Wadsworth/ Thomson, 2006), 88.

2. Sudhir Venkatesh, *Gang Leader for a Day* (New York: Penguin, 2008), 18.

3. Jack D. Douglas, Paul K. Rasmussen, and Carol Ann Flanagan, *The Nude Beach* (Beverly Hills: Sage, 1977), 19.

4. Nigel Fielding, *The National Front* (London: Routledge & Kegan Paul, 1981), 11.

5. Peter L. Berger and Thomas Luckmann, *The Social Construction of Reality: A Treatise in the Sociology of Knowledge* (London: Penguin Books, 1971), 13.

2. In Praise of Suicide

1. Jack D. Douglas, *Investigative Social Research: Individual and Team Field Research* (Beverly Hills: Sage, 1976), 169.

2. Clifford Geertz, *The Interpretation of Cultures* (New York: Basic Books, 1973), 4.

3. Gary Allan Fine, *With the Boys: Little League Baseball and Preadolescent Culture* (Chicago: University of Chicago Press, 1987), 124.

4. Quotations are from Léon Degrelle, *Militia* (Padua: Edizioni di Ar, 2014), 20, 55, 57, 21, and 48.

5. Dennis Kavanagh and Christopher Riches, eds., *A Dictionary of Political Biography* (Oxford: Oxford University Press, 2015).

6. Rebecca Ann Haynes, "Reluctant Allies? Iuliu Maniu and Corneliu Zela Codreanu against King Carol II of Romania," *Slavonic and East European Review* 85, no. 1 (January 2007): 118.

7. Corneliu Z. Codreanu, *Il capo di cuib* (Padua: Edizioni di Ar, 2009), 15.

3. The Construction of the Parallel World

1. Randall Collins, *Violence: A Micro-Sociological Theory* (Princeton: Princeton University Press, 2008), 20.

2. Bronislaw Malinowski, *Argonauts of the Western Pacific: An Account of Native Enterprise and Adventure in the Archipelagoes of Melanesian New Guinea* (1922; repr., Prospect Heights, Ill.: Waveland Press, 1984), 10.

3. George Herbert Mead, *Mind, Self, and Society: From the Standpoint of a Social Behaviorist* (1934; repr., Chicago: University of Chicago Press, 1967), 142.

4. Alessandro Orsini, "A Day among the Diehard Terrorists: The Psychological Costs of Doing Ethnographic Research," *Studies in Conflict & Terrorism* 36, no. 4 (2013): 341.

5. Erving Goffman, *The Presentation of Self in Everyday Life* (Garden City, N.Y.: Doubleday Anchor, 1959), 5.

4. The War against the Far-Left Extremists

1. Max Weber, *Economia e società: Teoria delle categorie sociologiche,* vol. 1 (1922; repr., Milan: Comunità, 1999), 4.

2. Herbert Blumer, *Symbolic Interactionism: Perspective and Method* (Bologna: Il Mulino, 2008), 39.

3. Georg Simmel, *La differenziazione sociale* (1890), ed. B. Accarino (Rome: Laterza, 1982), 18.

4. John D. McCarthy and Mayer N. Zald, "Resource Mobilization and Social Movements: A Partial Theory," *American Journal of Sociology* 82, no. 6 (May 1977): 1221.

5. http://www.liberliber.it/mediateca/libri/m/malatesta/l_anarchia/pdf/malatesta_l_anarchia.pdf.

6. Psychologist Arturo Orsini's paper "Attention Is Energy" is available at http://hu-man.it/lattenzione-e-energia/.

5. Living with Contempt

1. Clifford Geertz, *The Interpretation of Cultures* (New York: Basic Books, 1973), 9.

2. Peter L. Berger and Thomas Luckmann, *The Social Construction of Reality: A Treatise in the Sociology of Knowledge* (London: Penguin Books, 1971), 45.

3. Alfred Schutz, "The Stranger: An Essay in Social Psychology," *American Journal of Sociology,* 49, no. 6 (May 1944): 499.

4. Jack D. Douglas, *Investigative Social Research: Individual and Team Field Research* (Beverly Hills: Sage, 1976), 172.

5. Kathleen M. Blee, *Inside Organized Racism: Women in the Hate Movement* (Berkeley: University of California Press, 2003), 12.

6. Piergiorgio Corbetta, *La ricerca sociale: Metodologia e tecniche. Le tecniche qualitative* (Bologna: Il Mulino, 2003), 85.

7. Alice Goffman, *On the Run: Fugitive Life in an American City* (Chicago: University of Chicago Press, 2014), 242. See also Giampietro Gobo, *Doing Ethnography* (London: Sage, 2008), 197.

8. John Lofland, David Snow, Leon Anderson, and Lyn H. Lofland, *Analyzing Social Settings: A Guide to Qualitative Observation and Analysis* (Belmont, Calif.: Wadsworth/Thomson, 2006), 88.

6. From a Fascist Perspective

1. Laud Humphreys, *Tearoom Trade: Impersonal Sex in Public Places* (New Brunswick, N.J.: Aldine Transaction, 2008), 169.
2. Bill Buford, *Among the Thugs* (London: Secker & Warburg, 1991), 306.
3. Alice Goffman, *On the Run: Fugitive Life in an American City* (Chicago: University of Chicago Press, 2014).

7. The Great Fight

1. Luigi Pirandello, *L'umorismo* (Lanciano: Rocco Carabba, 1908).
2. To be specific, the tour guide used the Italian verb *stantuffare*, which is untranslatable but which means energetically taking a woman from behind.
3. Jack D. Douglas, *Investigative Social Research: Individual and Team Field Research* (Beverly Hills: Sage, 1976), 55.

8. Soldiers Who Fight and Soldiers Who Don't

1. Arno Michaelis, *My Life after Hate* (Milwaukee: Authentic Presence Publications, 2010).
2. Arno Michaelis, "Reflections of a Former White Supremacist," *Al Jazeera*, August 28, 2015, http://www.aljazeera.com/indepth/features/2015/08/reflections-white-supremacist-150 828100415193.html.
3. Asne Seierstad, *One of Us: Anders Breivik and the Massacre in Norway* (New York: Farrar, Straus and Giroux, 2013).
4. Lou Michel and Dan Herbeck, *American Terrorist: Timothy McVeigh and the Oklahoma City Bombing* (New York: Regan Books, 2001); Martin Durham, "Preparing for Armageddon: Citizen Militias, the Patriot Movement and the Oklahoma City Bombing," *Terrorism and Political Violence* 8, no. 1 (1996): 65–79; Michael Barkun, "Religion, Militias and Oklahoma City: The Mind of Conspiratorialists," *Terrorism and Political Violence* 8, no. 1 (1996): 50–64; Brad Whitsel, "Ideological Mutation and Millennial Belief in the American Neo-Nazi Movement," *Studies in Conflict & Terrorism* 24, no. 2 (2001): 94; Pete Simi, Bryan F. Bubolz, and Ann Hardman, "Military Experience, Identity Discrepancies, and Far-Right Terrorism: An Exploratory Analysis," *Studies in Conflict & Terrorism* 36, no. 8 (2013): 654–71.
5. Thomas S. Eberle, "Exploring Another's Subjective Life-World: A Phenomenological Approach," *Journal of Contemporary Ethnography* 44, no. 5 (2015): 568.
6. Anne Honer and Ronald Hitzler, "Life-World-Analytical Ethnography: A Phenomenology-Based Research Approach," *Journal of Contemporary Ethnography* 44, no. 5 (2015): 545.
7. Max Weber, *The Theory of Social and Economic Organization*, ed. Talcott Parsons (New York: Free Press, 1968), 88.
8. Gianluca Casseri and Enrico Rulli, *La chiave del caos* (Vicenza: Il Punto d'Incontro, 2010).
9. Casseri's articles were taken down immediately after the shooting.
10. "Italy: Gunman Kills Two Senegalese Merchants," *New York Times*, December 13, 2011.

11. James Kanter, "Police Link Belgian Gunman to a Killing before Rampage," *New York Times*, December 14, 2011.

12. Interview with Alessio Sakara before his match with Brian Stann, http://www.mma mania.it/intervista-ad-alessio-sakara-prima-del-match-con-brian-stann/ .

13. Paul Cartledge, *The Spartans: The World of the Warrior-Heroes of Ancient Greece, from Utopia to Crisis and Collapse* (Woodstock, N.Y.: Overlook Press, 2003).

14. See Friedrich Nietzsche, *L'anticristo: Maledizione del cristianesimo* (Milan: Adelphi, 2003).

15. Interview with Alessio Sakara while being tattooed, https://www.youtube.com/watch?v=lJ_CJ7nt44c.

16. Alessio Legionarius Sakara Tribute, https://www.youtube.com/watch?v=vxgJjqtmico.

17. If you want to understand better what I'm talking about, click on these two links. Viewer discretion is advised: https://www.youtube.com/watch?v=pOt0Iq0OPN0 and https://www.youtube.com/watch?v=WORgObg5vW4.

18. Alessio Legionarius Sakara Tribute, https://www.youtube.com/watch?v=vxgJjqtmico.

9. My Expulsion

1. Alessandro Orsini, *Anatomy of the Red Brigades: The Religious Mind-Set of Modern Terrorists*, trans. Sarah J. Nodes (Ithaca: Cornell University Press, 2011).

2. Alessandro Orsini, "A Day among the Diehard Terrorists: The Psychological Costs of Doing Ethnographic Research," *Studies in Conflict & Terrorism* 4 (2013): 337–51.

3. The essay appears in Clifford Geertz, *The Interpretation of Cultures* (New York: Basic Books, 1973), 412.

4. Alessandro Orsini, *Il rivoluzionario benestante: Strategie cognitive per sentirsi migliori degli altri* (Soveria Mannelli: Rubbettino, 2010).

5. The councilor provided Marcus's telephone number not directly to me but to Jonathan, who then texted it to me via WhatsApp, saying that the councilor had asked him to tell me to treat Marcus with great respect.

6. Thomas S. Kuhn, *The Structure of Scientific Revolutions* (Chicago: University of Chicago Press, 1962).

7. Mario Cardano, *La ricerca qualitativa* (Bologna: Il Mulino, 2011), 133.

8. Dale C. Spencer, "Sensing Violence: An Ethnography of Mixed Martial Arts," *Ethnography* 15, no. 2 (2014): 232–54.

9. The cheapest train ticket from Gaugamela to Lenintown cost about twenty euros, around twenty-five dollars at the time.

10. http://perlasociologia.blogspot.com/p/la-storia.html.